Executive Recruiting

by David E. Perry and Mark J. Haluska

FOREWORD BY Timothy Keiningham, PhD

A Wiley Brand

Executive Recruiting For Dummies®

Published by: **John Wiley & Sons, Inc.,** 111 River Street, Hoboken, NJ 07030-5774, www.wiley.com

Copyright © 2017 by John Wiley & Sons, Inc., Hoboken, New Jersey

Published simultaneously in Canada

For general information on our other products and services, please contact our Customer Care Department within the U.S. at 877-762-2974, outside the U.S. at 317-572-3993, or fax 317-572-4002. For technical support, please visit https://hub.wiley.com/community/support/dummies.

Wiley publishes in a variety of print and electronic formats and by print-on-demand. Some material included with standard print versions of this book may not be included in e-books or in print-on-demand. If this book refers to media such as a CD or DVD that is not included in the version you purchased, you may download this material at http://booksupport.wiley.com. For more information about Wiley products, visit www.wiley.com.

Library of Congress Control Number: 2016960165

ISBN 978-1-119-15908-7 (pbk); ISBN 978-1-119-15911-7 (ebk); ISBN 978-1-119-15910-0 (ebk)

Manufactured in the United States of America

10 9 8 7 6 5 4 3 2 1

Contents at a Glance

Table of Contents

Foreword

When I first spoke with David Perry, it wasn't by choice.

David had been harassing me on LinkedIn for weeks. Finally, I gave him two minutes. I figured he'd do his spiel, I'd get bored, and then we'd be done. I get a lot of calls from recruiters, and they're typically over before they begin. Typically, they're far more focused on selling an opportunity than on truly understanding the role their client is looking to fill. I assumed that when I spoke with David, it would be more of the same.

I was wrong. Those two minutes soon turned into more than an hour.

David's approach was different. I could tell the minute he sent me the position profile, which was a detailed document that he himself had created, outlining the perfect candidate for the opportunity. The role he was recruiting for was in my wheelhouse, so he was talking to the right guy, but it was extremely rare to see it framed the way his client wanted.

David had already burned through nearly every company in the Fortune 500 without finding anyone qualified for the position — and now he was talking to me. I suggested my head of research and consulting — my second in command — for the job. I knew full well there was no chance he'd take it, and I told David just that. He must have taken that as a challenge, because within a few months — and after really getting to know the what's-in-it-for-me (WIFM) that made my head of research really tick — he'd won him over.

David's brand of raw determination shines through in *Executive Recruiting For Dummies*. This book is a game changer for anyone who hopes to attract top talent to their organization, but who doesn't necessarily want to engage an executive recruitment firm themselves or, if they do, who wants to extract maximum value from an executive recruiter. David and his co-author, Mark J. Haluska, step readers new to the world of recruiting through some of its most important elements, including why talent matters, the importance of research and of properly defining a position, and key personal characteristics that will ensure a good fit not only with the position, but also within your organization's culture.

Hiring the wrong person — especially for an executive role — is a critical mistake that at best can torch deals and at worst can sink a company. For proof, look no further than the anecdote relayed in this book about a meeting between Nike and basketball star Steph Curry, who at the time was a member of the company's stable of athletes. Curry was set to re-up with Nike, but the meeting went badly. When the Nike official displayed a PowerPoint slide featuring another athlete, things went from bad to worse. Curry went on to sign with Under Armour, resulting in a $14 billion boost to that company's valuation — all because of a (seemingly) incompetent executive at Nike.

This kind of result simply doesn't happen with David's executive searches. There's a reason why the *Wall Street Journal* nicknamed him the "Rogue Recruiter." It's because his approach is refreshingly different. He's not just concerned with ticking a box and filling a role; he's also concerned with the long-term fit of the candidate he eventually puts forward. It's why he guarantees his placements for one year after the hire date.

Even though it took David 11 attempts on LinkedIn to finally get me to agree to a call, I'm now very happy I did. Sure, he coaxed my second in command away. But he also made me realize that there are good recruiters out there — and if you read his book, you'll realize it, too.

Timothy Keiningham, PhD
New York Times Bestselling Author of *The Wallet Allocation Rule*
J. Donald Kennedy Endowed Chair in E-Commerce
The Peter J. Tobin College of Business
St. John's University

Introduction

When we told our peers in the recruiting industry that we were writing this book, they said, "You're crazy! Why would you give away your secrets?" But we felt differently. We believe anyone tasked with hiring *real* leaders should have access to a handy reference filled with expert-driven insight and information. And that's precisely what *Executive Recruiting For Dummies* is.

These days, strong leadership is more important than ever. Companies with great leaders significantly outperform their peers. At the same time, globalization, attrition, and changing demographics have led to a scarcity of executive talent. As a result, the competition for top leadership talent is fierce.

In spite of this, most recruiters attempt to draw the best talent by focusing on people who are currently looking for work — the ones posting on job boards or responding to job ads. But your goal in an executive search isn't to find the best talent currently looking for work; it's to find the best talent, period. And trust us: The best talent *isn't* looking for work. They already have a job — a *good* job.

All this is to say that you need to look at executive recruiting a little differently than the average recruiter. That's what this book is for: to help you make this important shift.

If you want to ensure your company's survival by hiring great leaders, you'll need some effective way to find them, to hire them, and to ensure they stick around. This book outlines everything you need to do to achieve this.

But that's not all. Before you can hire well, you need to take a page from the playbook of the ancient Greeks and "know thyself." That is, you must know who you are and what you want as an organization. You can't give proper guidance to an executive recruiter until you truly understand your business. This book will help you clarify your needs.

If you're ready to build a winning executive team, stocked with the best talent money alone can't buy, then *Executive Recruiting For Dummies* is for you!

About This Book

The structure of *Executive Recruiting For Dummies* is designed to help you get in and get out of the text with just the information you were looking for. Consider this book your ultimate executive recruiting reference tool. Read it in any order you want and bookmark sections you expect to return to again and again.

You'll notice several sidebars sprinkled throughout the text. (You can identify these by their gray shaded boxes.) These are simply extra tidbits that are interesting but not critical to your understanding of executive recruiting. You don't have to read them if you don't want to!

Within this book, you may note that some web addresses break across two lines of text. If you're reading this book in print and want to visit one of these web pages, simply key in the web address exactly as it's noted in the text, pretending as though the line break doesn't exist. If you're reading this as an e-book, you've got it easy — just click the web address to be taken directly to the web page.

Foolish Assumptions

As we wrote this book, we initially viewed it as a desktop and online reference for our clients. But we realized it would also serve the following types well:

>> C-level executives and search committees who want to understand how to best maximize their leadership recruitment return on investment (ROI)

>> Hiring managers responsible for building high-performance teams

>> Recruiters, both corporate and third party, whose mission is to keep up with the recruiting best practices that will enable them to deliver value to their clients and advance their careers

Icons Used in This Book

The little pictures in the margins throughout this book are designed to highlight information that's special and important for one reason or another. *Executive Recruiting For Dummies* uses the following icons:

This icon points to pieces of information you shouldn't forget.

Wherever you see this icon, you're sure to find a good idea, trick, or shortcut that can save you time and trouble.

Make sure to read the paragraphs marked with this icon; it indicates information that can help you avoid disasters.

Beyond the Book

In addition to the material in the print or e-book you're reading right now, this product also comes with some access-anywhere goodies on the web. Check out the free Cheat Sheet for info on conducting your own executive search, tools worth your time, and other handy info. To get the Cheat Sheet, simply go to www.dummies.com and type **Executive Recruiting For Dummies Cheat Sheet** in the Search box.

You can also go to www.executiverecruitingfordummies.com/downloads for templates and tools you can use in your next executive search.

Where to Go from Here

Where you start reading *Executive Recruiting For Dummies* is up to you. You can begin by perusing the table of contents and then hitting sections of interest. Or you can head to the chapter that addresses an area of executive recruiting you're currently struggling with. If, however, you're brand new to executive recruiting, we suggest you begin with Chapter 1. It provides an overview of why executive recruiting is important and how you can use it to connect with top talent and crush your competition!

1

The World of Executive Recruiting

IN THIS PART . . .

Define and make the business case for executive recruiting.

Gain an understanding of the knowledge economy and its implications on executive recruiting.

Grasp the high cost of poor hiring.

Identify core attributes of top leaders, as well as attributes that don't matter as much.

IN THIS CHAPTER

» Defining executive recruiting

» Making the business case for executive recruiting

» Understanding why top executives are in demand

» Tracking the growth of executive recruiting

Chapter **1**

3, 2, 1, Blastoff! Getting Started with Executive Recruiting

I f you ever studied the American Revolutionary War in history class, you may remember reading about Baron Friedrich Wilhelm von Steuben, a military leader recruited by General George Washington to serve as the drillmaster of the Continental Army. Incredibly, von Steuben managed to turn a ragtag collection of farmers and stable boys into an officer corps that led the Americans to victory.

"Okay," you're thinking. "But what does that have to do with executive recruiting?"

Simple. General Washington's forces faced a well-trained army of British conscripts and Hessian mercenaries. If Washington was to level the playing field, he'd need to recruit a skilled outsider who knew the enemy and what it would take to defeat them — namely, Baron von Steuben. Washington knew he couldn't achieve victory with second-rate people — and neither can you.

In today's hyper-competitive environment, business is war! If you're going to win, only the best executives can lead the charge. Locating and enlisting these executives is what executive recruiting is all about.

What Is Executive Recruiting?

Executive recruiting is the act of locating, evaluating, assessing, and attracting a top-performing executive to an organization or company. Executive recruiting applies when

>> The search for a new executive hire must remain confidential.

>> The search is for an executive who will serve on the board or sit in the C-suite.

>> The skillset needed is rare or in short supply.

>> The annual salary is $150,000 or more.

>> The position is in another country.

Most business decisions are small. A single sale, choice, or interaction doesn't add much value to a company — or damage it much if it goes wrong. Recruiting an executive, however, is a *big* business decision — one that can add tremendous value or destroy a company altogether.

Recruiting an executive — the *right* executive — is the single greatest opportunity an organization has to improve both performance and culture in one stroke. The fresh thinking brought by a skilled leader can unleash innovation, empower employees, and generate wealth for the company.

Hiring the *wrong* executive is another story altogether. A bad hire can mortally wound an organization and cause ripple effects throughout the entire economy.

REMEMBER

Recruiting an executive can make or break an organization.

Given its importance, it should come as no surprise that executive recruiting is, well, hard. Indeed, few initiatives are as demanding, disruptive, or strategically challenging as a leadership search. But when it's successful, executive recruiting is the only initiative that can move an organization or group to the next level.

Ace of Case: The Business Case for Executive Recruiting

According to a study by BTS Group and the Economist Intelligence Unit called "Cracking the Code: The Secrets of Successful Strategy Execution," companies with great leaders significantly outperform their peers. Great leadership is also a prerequisite for strong employee engagement. That's a big deal, say David MacLeod and Nita Clarke, authors of a report called "Engaging for Success: Enhancing Performance through Employee Engagement." Here's why:

» Companies with low engagement scores earn an operating income 32.7 percent lower than companies with more engaged employees.

» Companies with a highly engaged workforce experience a 19.2 percent growth in operating income over a 12-month period.

A study by the Corporate Leadership Council called "Driving Performance and Retention through Employee Engagement" revealed similar findings — most notably that companies with engaged employees grow profits as much as three times faster than competitors with a nonengaged workforce. And a 2013 report by Gallup, "State of the Global Workplace," finds that engaged workplaces

are engines of job creation around the world. Companies with highly engaged workforces outperform their peers by 147 percent in earnings per share so it should come as no surprise that the companies with the most engaged employees have excellent leadership.

The point here is that hiring the right executives can reap tremendous benefits. And yet, all too often, it's the *wrong* executive who gets hired. No one knows this better than Kevin Kelly, CEO of one of the world's best-known executive search firms. Kelly's firm studied 20,000 executive searches and discovered, as he informed the *Financial Times,* that "Forty percent of executives hired at the senior level are pushed out, fail, or quit within 18 months." This, he says, is expensive in terms of both the costs associated with hiring the individual and lost revenue. It's also, says Kelly, "damaging to morale."

Others paint an even darker picture. For example, according to one study by the Corporate Executive Board, 50 percent to 70 percent of executives "fail within the first 18 months of promotion into an executive role, either from within or coming from outside the organization." Of those, the study revealed, "about 3 percent fail spectacularly, while 50 percent quietly struggle."

In a word, "Yikes!"

A Demanding Supply Issue

In the early 1800s, our forebears witnessed the beginning of a colossal economic transformation with the onset of the Industrial Revolution. Within a single generation, old city neighborhoods and rich farmlands were cleared out to make way for the construction of steel mills, rail yards, warehouses, and office buildings. To fuel this economic boom, people migrated from the far reaches of rural America to take on jobs they would hold for the rest of their working lives.

Today, old city neighborhoods and rich farmlands are *still* cleared to make way for trade and industry. (China and India are prime examples.) But now, businesses exist in a completely different environment than they did during the Industrial Revolution. The tidal wave of economic change, pressure to increase shareholder value by the quarter rather than the year, outsourcing and right-sizing — all these trends have greatly increased the demand for top talent.

Recruiting top executives is hard. And in the years to come, it will only get harder. This is due to three key trends:

>> **Demographics:** A lower birth rate in North America combined with the aging of the Baby Boomer generation has resulted in a contraction of available executives. In other words, when an older executive retires, few younger workers are qualified to fill his shoes.

>> **Brain drain:** In the 1980s and 1990s, companies may have saved money by trimming senior management ranks. But that brain drain coupled with attrition robbed them of their ability to grow the next generation of leadership.

>> **Globalization:** Companies in first-world countries have expanded their market around the globe. At the same time, countries that were once considered third-world nations have become economic powerhouses. As a result, the global need for executive talent has been pushed beyond our capacity to produce it.

REMEMBER

Over the last three decades, demographics, attrition, and globalization have profoundly affected the labor supply — particularly for executives. The result: a scarcity of executive talent. This global shortage of leaders drives organizations to aggressively seek the best.

In this talent-hungry environment, the rules of recruiting have changed. It's no longer enough to passively collect résumés. The people who have the talent you need — who can design a top product, manage complex projects, perform marketing miracles, sell new customers, or lead your organization — are already employed, can take their pick of top opportunities, and will make a career move only if the opportunity is truly compelling.

WHERE ARE THE YOUNG UP-AND-COMERS?

We mention that a lower birth rate — at least in North America — has made it difficult to fill the shoes of older outgoing executives. But that's not the only reason. Another cause is that few companies provide young workers with the training they need to advance. In fact, according to a ten-year study of executive performance by a leadership consulting firm called Navalent:

- Seventy-six percent of respondents indicated that "the formal development processes of their organization were not, or at best minimally, helpful in preparing them for the executive role."

- Fifty-five percent of respondents indicated that "they had minimal, if any, ongoing coaching and feedback to help them refine their ability to perform in an executive role."

- Forty-five percent of respondents indicated that "they had minimal understanding of the challenges they would face in an executive role."

Although young executives have begun to assume senior and C-suite roles, according to Navalent, they lack the "experience, knowledge, relational [maturity], and emotional maturity necessary to sustain success."

Waiting around in the hopes that your ideal executive will miraculously become available precisely when you need her is foolishness. You can satisfy your requirement for people with talent, tenacity, and dogged determination only by pursuing them.

This is the impetus for executive recruiting.

Oh, Grow Up! The Growth of Executive Recruiting

Executive recruiting is a specialized branch of management consulting. The mission of an executive recruiter is to bring your opportunity to a candidate's attention and assess his fit. That means reaching out to anyone the recruiter feels fits your needs — regardless of his current "availability."

Back in the mid-1980s, when we launched our careers as executive recruiters, the profession was still in its infancy. Few people understood what it was. Honestly, we spent more time explaining to clients what an executive recruiter did and why they should use one than we did actually conducting the searches!

Since then, the profession has grown by leaps and bounds. Indeed, as the Association of Executive Search and Leadership Consultants notes in its report "2014 State of the Retained Executive Search Industry Part One: An Overview of Retained Executive Search Worldwide":

> The success of this professional service has been exponential in the past 50 years as the global economy has developed, industries have become transformed, and mobility has made executive talent available to all organizations as a key facet of competitive advantage.

According to that same report, what began as a $750 million industry in 1978 has exploded into one that pulled more than $10 billion in 2013. And projected numbers for 2016 were even higher: more than $12 billion.

Those numbers pertain to external executive recruiters — those providers hired by companies to help fill open positions. But in-house talent-acquisition teams are also on the rise. This is thanks in part to the cost of external recruiters, but also to the plethora of recruiters jettisoned by search firms during the Great Recession that began in 2007. These in-house teams have greatly lowered the cost of hiring executives under the $150,000 to $200,000 range.

Chapter **2**

Talent Show: Why Talent Matters

I n Chapter 1, we talk about how demographics, a brain drain, and globalization have led to a scarcity of talent. But that's just the half of it. Just as top talent has gotten sparse, it has also become increasingly important!

In recent years, we've entered an economic phase that's entirely new: the knowledge economy. In the knowledge economy, organizations rely on intellectual capital — knowledge — to achieve both tangible and intangible results. Indeed, companies in the knowledge economy often derive their value from intellectual capital — in other words, from the value of the knowledge possessed by their employees.

That's not all, though. As this new economy has evolved, it has also placed a premium on people's traits. According to Dov Seidman at *Harvard Business Review*, these traits include "creativity, passion, character, and collaborative spirit — their humanity, in other words." Seidman continues, "The ability to leverage these strengths will be the source of one organization's superiority over another."

In this chapter, we tell you more about the knowledge economy and how it has affected the world of executive recruiting.

Value Pack: Redefining Value in the Knowledge Economy

In 1994, Steven Spielberg, Jeffrey Katzenberg, and David Geffen formed a new Hollywood studio: DreamWorks SKG. Although each invested $33.3 million, that was nowhere near enough money to get the venture off the ground. That meant the trio would need to attract investors — *fast.*

There was just one problem. As noted by Richard Corliss in an article published by *TIME* in 1995, "DreamWorks, which plans to make movies, TV shows, records, toys and computer software, has no film studio or recording studio, no products — indeed, no pedigree but its owners' résumés."

But oh, what résumés they were! Steven Spielberg was, of course, *the* Steven Spielberg — Oscar-winning director of such film classics as *Jaws, Close Encounters of the Third Kind, Raiders of the Lost Ark, E.T. the Extra-Terrestrial, Schindler's List, Saving Private Ryan, Jurassic Park* . . . the list goes on. Then there was Jeffrey Katzenberg, who was credited with turning around Walt Disney Studios between 1984 and 1994. Films produced during his tenure included such family favorites as *The Little Mermaid, Beauty and the Beast, Aladdin,* and *The Lion King.* David Geffen was no slouch either, having launched several record labels during his career, including the eponymous Geffen Records.

DreamWorks SKG may not have had hard assets. But it did have the intangible value of its founders. Because of what these visionaries had done in the past, and because of what promise DreamWorks might hold for the future, investors from Seattle to Silicon Valley to Wall Street and beyond lined up — to the tune of $2 billion.

We're not saying hard assets are no longer relevant. But today's new knowledge economy is built more on the intangible value of people — who they are, what they know, and their ability to apply that knowledge. Instead of resources or land, *capital* today means *human capital.*

Unlike resources or land, however, human capital has control over its own worth. That is, human capital — knowledge workers — can continuously invest in their skills and training to drive up their price. In a world where practically every organization has access to a certain baseline level of technology, *people* are the difference maker. They're the value adder. As a result, the best people are highly sought after. If they choose to leave a company in the morning, they'll be hired by someone else by noon. They're in the driver's seat — and they know it.

You'll find that today's top performers have a couple things in common:

>> **They're competitive.** Like athletes, top performers are driven to improve. They want to be better and faster, to break barriers, to achieve things no one has ever achieved before.

>> **They're individualistic.** High-performing people want to be part of an elite team — but they also want to make a difference all on their own. The people you're after need to know for selfish and unselfish reasons that they'll be given the latitude to succeed both as part of a group and on an individual level.

Paradigm Shift: Understanding the New Recruiting Paradigm

Recruiting is and has always been an intensive process. But given the rise of the knowledge economy, how you compete for talent has changed.

In the old days, companies searched for talent by sending out requests for résumés. The candidates who submitted these résumés were then judged along two axes: price and performance. The process was so structured and simple, even the less-skilled members of your HR staff could handle it. And given the pace of business, there wasn't any rush. Of course, this yielded only those candidates who were actively looking for work, but that was the way it went.

Nowadays, the world moves at a speed more resembling a video game. It's zap or get zapped, in real time. And searching for talent isn't just about assessing price and performance. It's about gauging a candidate's knowledge and value and knowing what motivates them. Oh, and you aren't just focused on candidates who sent in their résumés, either. You're trying to draw candidates who aren't even looking to move. That's no easy feat!

That's not the only difference, though. Historically, companies have tried to draw top talent by offering financial rewards — large salaries and/or stock options. Google went the stock-option route, creating thousands of millionaires in the process. But these days, money is secondary. Yes, people want signing bonuses, options, salaries, and raises. But these are a given — the very least you have to offer. Once those pieces are in place, the issue of money becomes moot.

REMEMBER

Some companies — tech companies come to mind — have tried to raise the ante by providing workplace perks that range from gift baskets to beer fridges to pool tables and beyond. These perks may help to foster a collegial culture — not a bad thing — but they won't be the difference maker for a serious candidate considering a serious job.

So, what *does* motivate people? According to Daniel H. Pink, author of *Drive: The Surprising Truth about What Motivates Us* (Riverhead Books), today's knowledge workers are driven by three key things:

>> **Autonomy:** Pink describes this as "the desire to direct our own lives."

>> **Mastery:** According to Pink, this is "the urge to make progress and get better at something that matters." (The importance of mastery explains why top talent often look to work at companies that offer training.)

>> **Purpose:** This, says Pink, is the "yearning to do what we do in the service of something larger than ourselves."

REMEMBER

As work has become more knowledge based — more creative and conceptual — motivators have changed along with it.

All this is to say that if you want to draw top talent, you need to do more than dangle dollars. You need to be able to assess a candidate's real value and speak to his "why." And you'll need to do it in such a way that the candidate chooses you over the countless other opportunities he has no doubt been handed from all over the world. That's the new recruiting paradigm.

Triple Play: Three Steps for Tapping Top Talent

In this new economy, this new paradigm, any executive recruiting project boils down to three key steps:

1. Figuring out what types of knowledge and personal qualities are most important for the role

2. Figuring out how to find people with that knowledge and those qualities

3. Figuring out how to hire the person who best matches your needs

Step 1: Figure out what you're looking for

Figuring out what you're looking for — that's easy enough, right?

Maybe. But maybe not.

In today's knowledge economy, knowing what you're after — what's important — means looking beyond job titles and compensation tables. You have to be able to evaluate the *real value* of someone's contribution. To do this, you must thoroughly understand

>> What contribution you want

>> How you'll know when you find it

Especially for senior positions, companies rarely look to tick a box on a standard employee recruitment form. Instead, they're looking for something more nebulous — and more important. They're looking for someone who can deliver a quality rather than a quantity — a quality that creates value for the company.

Of course, key contributions and qualities may be difficult to identify. To help with this, Table 2-1 lists common contributions, or value requirements, and the qualities that drive them.

TABLE 2-1 **Contributions and Qualities**

Value Requirement	Corresponding Quality
Creating new intellectual wealth for the company or adding to its intellectual assets	A consuming desire to make something new — to cut a new path rather than take a heavily traveled road
Having high-energy enthusiasm for the job, regardless of the hours worked	The belief that work is a game and an integral, vibrant part of one's life
The belief that the money is not only not the most important issue, but also beside the point	An internal desire to leave a "legacy signature" on her work rather than strive for a paycheck
Enduring performance	The desire and ability to finish the race — because *not* finishing is simply inconceivable
An ability to "think around corners" to creatively problem-solve	An inner voice that says, "There's always a way to [create a technology fix/make a deal/and so on]."
The display of up-to-date professionalism at all times	The desire to grow professionally — to become the best person he can be and to invest in himself
An ever-increasing contribution	The knowledge that making an individual contribution is the key to inner pleasure
The ability to identify and develop value for your company	An instinctive grasp and ability to capitalize on real value, such as the intangible capital of brand image, staff talent, and customer relationships

As you can see, what you're looking for goes beyond skillsets and résumés. You want someone whose qualities will drive the contribution you seek. When you share a vision, you ensure a successful fit.

Step 2: Find people with the knowledge and qualities you seek

In the knowledge economy, companies leverage smart ideas to generate huge value. Not surprisingly, the people who think up those ideas are more valuable than ever before. They almost certainly already have jobs — *good* jobs — and they're not looking for new ones.

The talent you're after is busy winning. They're not surfing job boards, registering with employment agencies, or updating their LinkedIn profiles. The best of the best aren't likely to respond to — or even see — your job ads. So, how do you find someone who isn't raising her hand saying, "Here I am"? That's what this book is about.

REMEMBER

Employee surveys reveal that most people don't particularly like moving to a new organization. They'd rather change jobs within a company than leave the company altogether. This is especially true for people who believe they already work for and with the best.

Step 3: Hire the person who best matches your needs

Earlier, we talked about how, in the knowledge economy, money is a secondary driver. Sure, it's important, but when you reach a certain baseline, it's not that big of a deal. Instead, knowledge workers are driven by autonomy, mastery, and purpose.

Take companies like Facebook, Google, and Tesla. The people who work at these companies aren't driven by money; they want to change the world. That's their purpose. Or consider Google. When Larry Page and Sergey Brin founded that company to life in 1998, they didn't do it to cash in. They did it to organize the world's information and make it universally accessible and useful. (In fact, that's the company's stated mission.) And of course, there's Apple. It wasn't merely money that drove Steve Jobs to build the world's most valuable company and transform seven industries — personal computing, animated movies, music, phones, tablet computing, retail stores, and digital publishing — along the way. It was his obsession with simplicity.

Not surprisingly, top talent flock to the aforementioned companies. Indeed, these companies (and a select few others) offer tremendous cachet. People who work for them do so proudly.

Although it's true that you need to pay an appropriate wage to draw top talent, that's just the price of admission. You also have to foster a work environment that gives them what they *really* want: the freedom to lead, the ability to succeed, and the opportunity to work toward something they care about. In addition, you must conduct your executive recruiting project using only proven methods, including the following:

>> Micro-targeting the competition's executives

>> Treating each potential prospect as an individual by providing a customized approach tailored to his needs

>> Connecting with candidates on both a logical and an emotional level

>> Speaking to the candidate's values (**Hint:** It's not always about money!)

>> Delivering a value proposition — similar to an elevator pitch — that focuses on the candidate's needs, not yours

These and other methods are covered throughout this book.

Companies position themselves with top talent by making both a logical and an emotional connection.

As Skip Freeman, author of *Headhunter Hiring Secrets 2.0*, says, "Top talent is scarce — and it's likely to stay that way. That means smart organizations do everything they can to retain their key people. If you're going to persuade people to take on new opportunities, you'll need to make sure that the opportunities you're presenting are good ones . . . and woo them like they've never been wooed before!"

Chapter **3**

Rock and Role: The Role of Recruiting in Business

D o you have kids? If you do — heck, even if you don't — you've probably noticed the ubiquity of "participation awards." These are the trophies and ribbons handed out to children who play sports, take part in academic contests, or perform in music competitions, just for showing up. These days, it's not just top performers who get recognized; it's every darned kid on the team.

We get it. It's important to foster a kid's self-esteem. There's just one problem: In the real world, participating isn't cause for a celebration. Indeed, in the *real* world, participating — showing up — is the very *least* you can do. If you want to be successful in life or in work, if you want to win, you must do more than participate — much more. You must *perform*. And not just some of the time, but all of the time.

REMEMBER

To quote legendary football coach Vince Lombardi, "Winning is not a sometime thing; it's an all the time thing. You don't win once in a while; you don't do things right once in a while; you do them right all the time. Winning is a habit." (And unfortunately, as Lombardi goes on to point out, "So is losing.")

In the world of work, achieving high levels of performance in order to win is more important than ever. Why? Lots of reasons. Here are just a few:

>> **Globalization:** Nowadays, you're not just competing with organizations in your region or even in your country. You're competing with companies all over the world — most notably developing nations, where resources are often plentiful and labor is cheap. And if the recent past is any indication, it's reasonable to assume that the economies of developing nations — such as Brazil, Russia, India, China, and South Africa, often referred to as BRICS — will only continue to expand. Take China, for example. In 2006, just 20 Chinese companies made the Fortune Global 500, which ranks corporations world-wide. By 2016, that number grew to 106, including three of the top four. (In contrast, the number of American companies has fallen, from 197 in 2006 to 134 in 2016.)

>> **Demanding shareholders:** It used to be that shareholders expected results on an annual basis. Now, they think quarterly. Companies that can execute at the speed of a Bugatti will enjoy a significant advantage over ones that operate at the speed of a buggy.

>> **Advances in technology:** Changes in the technological landscape have driven an ever-faster business cycle — one in which only the highest-performing companies and employees can keep up.

>> **Disruption:** Today's businesses are disrupting yesterday's businesses, and tomorrow's will disrupt today's. Indeed, radical innovation is the force that sustains long-term economic growth, even as it destroys the economic value of established enterprises. This cycle of "creative destruction," a term coined in 1942 by Austrian economist Joseph Schumpeter, explains the rapid rise of companies like Apple, Facebook, Airbnb, Uber, and thousands of other knowledge-based businesses — as well as the precipitous plunge of companies like Kodak, Blockbuster, and Yellow Cab.

Oddly, even as business has become more competitive, requiring higher and higher levels of performance, it seems as if the culture has shifted from one that emphasizes performance to one focused on mere participation — not just for kids, but for adults, too. For proof, look no further than the tendency of most companies to distribute the same minimal raise to all employees each year, whether they deserve it or not. ("Trophies for everybody!")

That's not the only example of this troubling trend toward mediocrity, however. Here's another one: Companies spend billions of dollars on applicant tracking and talent management systems. And yet, the nation's turnover rate has remained virtually unchanged, millions of jobs go unfilled each month (while millions more remain unemployed), and when employees underperform, companies worry more about engaging them than about hiring the right people in the first place.

Somehow, these poor hiring outcomes — which are the result of poor performance within HR and which in turn drive poor performance throughout the organization — are deemed acceptable! ("Congratulations everybody! Thanks for playing!")

It's up to you to break this cycle. If your organization is going to compete — no, if it's going to *survive* — you must demand performance. And that means hiring the very best, particularly at the executive level. Doing anything less will cost you.

That'll Cost You: The High Cost of Poor Hiring

In the six months after Marissa Mayer took over as CEO of Yahoo!, the company's market value increased $17 billion. Around the same time, JCPenney, guided by new CEO Ron Johnson, saw sales decline by $4.3 billion. The way we see it, regardless of what comes next for either Mayer or Johnson, there's never been a clearer example of getting an executive hire right versus getting it wrong.

When we say hiring the wrong executive will cost you, we mean it really *will* cost you! On the low side, you're looking at the executive's compensation — say, a few hundred thousand dollars. On the high side, that number is, well, higher. Dr. Brad Smart, author of *Top Grading (How to Hire, Coach, and Keep A Players)*, has been quoted as saying, "It is painful and costly to hire the wrong person. Based on our studies the average cost of a mis-hire can be six times base salary for a sales rep, 15 times base salary for a manager, and as much as 27 times base salary for an executive." In other words, suppose you hire an executive who earns $250,000 per year, and things don't work out. According to Smart, that could be a $6,750,000 mistake!

We say it could be even worse than that. Consider this story about NBA star Stephen Curry. In 2009, the Golden State Warriors used their first draft pick to select Curry, a scrappy point guard out of Davidson College. Over the next few years, Curry would energize an organization that hadn't won a championship since 1975. In 2013, Curry, who had long been a member of Nike's stable of athletes, was due to re-sign with that company. Things quickly went off the rails, however. According to Ethan Sherwood Strauss of ESPN:

> The pitch meeting, according to Steph's father Dell, who was present, kicked off with one Nike official accidentally addressing Stephen as "Steph-on," the moniker, of course, of Steve Urkel's alter ego in *Family Matters*. "I heard some people pronounce his name wrong before," says Dell Curry. "I wasn't surprised. I was surprised that I didn't get a correction." It got worse from there. A PowerPoint slide featured Kevin Durant's name, presumably left on by accident, presumably residue from repurposed materials. "I stopped paying attention after that," Dell says. Though Dell resolved to "keep a poker face," throughout the entirety of the pitch, the decision to leave Nike was in the works.

Maybe that Nike official just had a bad day. But more likely, he was incompetent. If that was in fact the case, it seems fair to assume that Nike's HR department failed to vet him properly during the hiring process. In other words, he was the wrong hire — and this proved costly indeed. That's because Curry, instead of signing with Nike, opted for Under Armour — a move that analysts say could result in as much as a $14 billion increase in that company's value. That's *billion*, with a *B*. So to sum up: Nike (probably) made a lousy hire. That lousy hire botched the deal with Curry (who, incidentally, led his team to an NBA championship two years later). Curry went elsewhere — and now Nike's out on a potential $14 billion boost to its bottom line.

If hiring the wrong person is bad, *not* hiring the *right* person can be disastrous. Here's an example. In the summer of 2009, Brian Acton, a former engineering executive at Yahoo!, sought a new position at Facebook. Now, you would think that Facebook, a technology company that's barely a decade old but is already a global brand with a market cap of $363 billion, would employ recruiters with super-human powers — able to spot high-performing individuals from miles away, that kind of thing. But in this case, Facebook blew it. It rejected Acton. Shortly there-after, Acton partnered with another former Yahoo! engineer, Jan Koum, to develop WhatsApp, a messaging application that enables users to exchange messages on their mobile devices *without* having to pay for SMS. Five years later, Acton and Koum sold WhatsApp for a whopping $22 billion. Guess who bought it? That's right. Facebook.

Bad hires can even bring down a business. Take Enron, which claimed revenues of nearly $111 billion in 2000 only to declare bankruptcy the very next year and eventually dissolve altogether. You could easily make the case that Enron's demise was due ultimately to poor hiring. After all, it was people — including senior leaders — who engaged in the fraudulent accounting activities that ultimately brought about not only Enron's collapse, but the collapse of the company that audited it, Arthur Andersen. *Poof!* Two corporate giants — once thought of as great places to work — gone. Less than a decade later, history repeated itself when shady practices, ultimately brought about through poor hiring, destroyed such venerable firms as Lehman Brothers, Bear Sterns, AIG, and Washington Mutual.

REMEMBER

The fresh thinking of a skilled leader can have a dramatic impact on your organization's bottom line. Hire a star, and he'll unleash innovation, empower employees, and generate wealth for your company. Choose poorly, and as you've seen, you could suffer serious financial penalties — or even the destruction of your entire organization.

Hocus Focus: Putting the Focus on Hiring

Clearly, hiring the right people is critical from a business perspective — especially in leadership roles. And according to a 2014 study by the Conference Board, CEOs know this; the study cites "a clear recognition among CEOs that human capital is the engine of the enterprise." The organization's report on this study continues, "Human capital is, in essence, the thread that runs through the other top-ranked challenges — customer relationships, innovation, operational excellence, and corporate brand and reputation — and forms the basis of strategic action." After all, the report concludes, "without a talented, engaged, and properly motivated workforce, achieving progress against these challenges is impossible."

And yet, as Joel Trammell, author of *The CEO Tightrope,* said in *Forbes:* "Most CEOs spend very little time on recruiting, tacitly relegating it to a tactical fire drill instead of a core component of the company's strategic plan." This is a mistake, says Trammell, "because it encourages staffing over recruiting. Finding a person with some basic qualifications to fill a position is staffing, which doesn't require a lot of expertise. But if the business needs the best intellectual capital to be successful, and what business doesn't, CEOs must lead by building a well-managed recruiting function that is closely monitored and measured."

Companies must adopt a comprehensive approach to executive hiring and training. Otherwise, to borrow Trammell's quote from Richard Fairbank, CEO of Capital One, they'll wind up like the majority of companies, where "people spend 2 percent of their time recruiting and 75 percent of their time managing their recruiting mistakes."

Clearly, it's critical that you hire the absolute best — starting at the top. It's well known among senior leaders that greatness begets greatness — or as the saying goes, "A's hire A's and B's hire C's." You must hire the "A's."

Fitty Cent: Fitting In . . . and Fading Out

We've noticed that most people are conditioned to fit in, to get along, to not rock the boat. These days, it seems like even top executives tend to be more worried about being team players than team leaders!

Maybe that's okay at your company. Maybe your organization is so stable, so immune from disruption, that you can afford to employ people who play it safe, who go along to get along. But if it isn't, then always going the safe route — hiring people who are overly concerned with fitting in, even at the top of your org chart — will almost certainly result in your company fading out.

REMEMBER

Disruption is serious business. Even known disruptors — think Apple, Amazon, and Facebook — watch their backs. These companies know that business is global, and that whatever advantage they possess could soon be lost to a newer, nimbler, more innovative company in some far and growing corner of the Earth.

When filling an open position, don't follow the lead of the average recruiter or board of directors. Often, these types simply hire someone with the same job title and skills as the outgoing executive without first analyzing past failures or acknowledging disruptive competitors on the horizon. Not surprisingly, this approach often ends in failure.

Instead, consider that the "right" hire might be someone who is, well, a little bit different. Think about it: Many successful business leaders did not have the "right" job title or skills — Barbara Corcoran, Mark Cuban, Michael Dell, Bill Gates, and Joy Mangano come to mind.

Instead of simply accepting the org chart as presented by senior leaders, a savvy recruiter — whether she works in-house or is a third-party provider — will, in the words of Carl A. Albert, Chairman and CEO of Fairchild Venture Capital, "understand the real needs of the organization, the qualities of the right person for the position, the strengths and weaknesses of the officers not being replaced."

That's not all, however. They must also, says Albert, understand "the quality of the assets of the company, its market position, the short- and long-term goals of the organization, the goals of the board of directors, and need, if any, for a new strategy and vision for the success of the organization."

REMEMBER

Hiring the right leaders is critically important. And as we discuss in Chapters 1 and 2, thanks to a scarcity of talent, it's also really hard. It's no wonder that more and more companies seek assistance from outside experts when recruiting senior executives!

THINK DIFFERENT: STEVE JOBS

History is ripe with examples of "different" people. Some were celebrated for their success as trailblazers, while others faced humiliation — and some, like Steve Jobs, experienced both.

After co-founding Apple in 1976, Jobs found himself exiled by the company's board in 1985. Clearly, the board saw his replacement, CEO John Sculley — who had been poached from Pepsi-Cola two years earlier — as the safer choice to lead the company.

They were wrong. Under Sculley's leadership, innovation tanked, and Apple sank. In hindsight, it became clear that the board should have opted for Jobs over Sculley. Yes, Jobs would have been the more unusual choice. After all, he was more of a visionary than a businessman. But the board could have easily surrounded him with talent to shore up his shortcomings.

They didn't, though, and as a result, the company floundered for more than ten years. Indeed, it was not until Jobs returned to Apple in 1997 that the company again found its footing, thanks to the release of such innovative products as the iMac, iPod, iPhone, and iPad. Under Jobs, Apple disrupted seven different industries, from animation to music and beyond!

Who do you know in your personal network who doesn't seem to "fit in," but has gone on to achieve greatness? Would you like if that person — or someone like him — worked for you rather than for your competitor? (**Hint:** The answer is *yes.*) Next time you dismiss a candidate because of his unconventional background, take the time to look again. Like Apple, you may be rewarded for the fruits of your labor!

Chapter **4**

Key Club: Identifying Key Personal Characteristics

It used to be that machines were the center of a typical organization's universe. As a result, the role of management was to develop procedures for employees to follow in order to serve these machines. That's how they gained a competitive advantage.

These days, we live in a knowledge-based economy and society. That means a company's competitive advantage — its value and wealth — is driven by human innovation. One of the most effective ways to innovate is for two or more people to combine their existing knowledge to produce something entirely new. This is the basis of creative thinking: Mix existing pieces of knowledge and heat with discussion. There's no telling what will emerge! For proof, look no further than companies like Apple (started by Steve Jobs and Steve Wozniak), Facebook (conceived by Mark Zuckerberg and Eduardo Saverin), and Google (launched by Larry Page and Sergey Brin).

There's just one hitch: That human innovation has to happen *fast.* That's because the body of knowledge throughout the world is growing exponentially. According to Dr. Nick Bontis of McMaster University, starting in 2010, the world's cumulative codified knowledge began to double every 11 hours. To put that in context, consider that in 1975, the rate was every 7 years, and in the 1930s it was every 30 years. Essentially, any insight you may have had last evening will likely be outdated by daybreak. Or, to put another way, the shelf life of knowledge is shorter than that of a banana.

Way back in 1597, Francis Bacon said, "Knowledge is power" — and that's still true. But these days, thanks to the explosive growth of knowledge worldwide, the longevity of that power is greatly reduced. In other words, if you rest on your laurels, you won't hold onto your power for long! Your company's competitive advantage lies in its ability to identify the opportunities brought by this growing body of knowledge — and more important, its ability to exploit them. Otherwise, you can rest assured someone else will!

REMEMBER

In the Old West, there were two types of people: the quick and the dead. The same is true in business. Companies that consistently move more quickly than their competitors to identify and exploit opportunities will thrive and prosper. Those that don't will wither and die.

So, how can your company position itself to identify and exploit opportunities brought by this growing body of knowledge? The best way is to place extra emphasis on effective recruiting to ensure you put the right people in place. That means — among other things — identifying the crucial characteristics your senior leaders must possess. Another is to foster a cooperative culture — one that helps people work together to leverage their knowledge and creativity. (This has the added benefit of building your company's brand, which can in turn help you to draw top talent.) In this chapter, you learn how to do both.

Work Your Core: 28 Attributes of Successful Executives

Research shows that companies that are adept at recruiting deliver more than three times the revenue growth and twice the earnings before interest, taxes, depreciation, and amortization (EBITDA) as those that miss the mark on recruiting. To be "adept at recruiting," you must identify the right person for the job — every time. That means assessing how each candidate's specific characteristics mesh with your needs.

In our more than 50 collective years and 100,000 collective interviews in the executive search and recruiting businesses, we've observed certain specific core characteristics that *always* come into play. These attributes are far more important than a candidate's industry experience or technical skills.

We know it sounds illogical. But look at the facts: Through the ages, profiles of successful high-performance people reveal that their most important competencies had little to do with skills. Andrew Carnegie and Nelson Rockefeller are examples of that. Nor did they have to do with training or work experience, as shown by Bill Gates and Steve Jobs. Instead, they had to do with *mind-set* — in other words, their core characteristics.

Naturally, you're wondering exactly which core characteristics we're talking about. Well, wonder no more. Based on our own experience, and on input from others in the field, we've identified 28 key attributes of successful executives, broken down into five categories:

>> Character

>> Intellect

>> Business intelligence

>> Leadership

>> Emotional intelligence

Sadly, in our experience, these core attributes are fully present in less than 1 percent of the adult population. Still, if you can design your interview questions to uncover these core attributes, you'll increase your odds of hiring the right person for the job — as well as increasing the odds of your organization achieving its full potential.

TIP

Before beginning the interview process, the recruiter and head of HR should work together to construct interview questions to assess whether candidates possess these attributes.

Character

When it comes down to it, nothing — we mean *nothing* — is more important than a person's character. Your candidate could have the intellect of Albert Einstein, the business intelligence of Warren Buffett, the leadership skills of Winston Churchill, and the emotional intelligence of Oprah Winfrey. But if he lacks character, all those other qualities are moot. Candidates should have these core character-related characteristics:

>> **Integrity:** When we say *integrity*, we mean honesty, credibility, and trustworthiness. Integrity is a binary attribute. Someone either has it or she doesn't. To assess a candidate's integrity, watch for inconsistencies in her story throughout the interview process and conduct a thorough reference check.

Also scour sources like the candidate's peers, industry insiders, and, if applicable, Wall Street, investors, and even the news media for clues.

» **Persistence:** You want a candidate who is assertive and who will successfully execute programs to fruition. This person should be highly motivated — not an order taker in disguise.

» **Resiliency:** A candidate should be able to demonstrate through his words and deeds that he can take a hit — whether personally or in business — and keep moving. The last thing you need is someone who will fold early in a battle! To assess this, listen very carefully as he tells his story during the first and second interviews.

» **Mind-set:** Some people are optimists. Others are pessimists. Still others are skeptics. Whatever they are — whether they have a glass-half-empty, a glass-half-full, or an is-that-even-a-real-glass mind-set — can be beneficial, depending on the role you seek to fill.

» **Judgment:** Top leaders have a track record of sound judgment, in all sorts of situations.

» **Battle scars:** Someone who's done battle in business — and has the scars to prove it — will almost always be a better bet than someone who hasn't and doesn't. Stuff happens. It's how someone deals with it that matters. If a candidate reveals that she has never been responsible for a major disaster, then it's likely she has never had any real responsibility either. Far better to hire someone who has survived a humiliating defeat that she never wants to repeat than to take a chance on someone learning those hard lessons on your dime. Our advice? Pick the candidate who has learned to recognize the warning signs *before* you go over the cliff.

Intellect

This book may be "for dummies," but top leadership roles aren't. A keen intellect is crucial. Here's what you're looking for:

» **Intelligence:** You're not just looking for someone who's smart — you're looking for someone who is pragmatic and has good common sense. A candidate's verbal communication skills can be a good indication of this.

» **An inquisitive mind:** Earlier, we mention that the world's cumulative body of knowledge is said to double every 11 hours. That means you need senior leaders who are inquisitive enough to at least try to keep up. To assess how inquisitive a candidate is, try asking about any interests he has pursued — personally or professionally — for a decade or more.

>> **Problem-solving skills:** What is work — heck, what is *life* — if not a succession of problems to be solved? That's why anyone you place in a leadership role must possess problem-solving skills. That includes the ability to identify possible solutions that others may miss.

>> **An analytical bent:** You need leaders with solid analytical skills — someone who can consider multiple variables at once and make valid connections that elude everyone else. Even better, look for candidates who "know what they don't know," as they say. To assess this, ask the candidate to recall a time when she realized she had a gap in her knowledge, and what she did to fill that gap.

>> **Enterprising thought process:** The people who can come up with a hundred ideas to find the two highly creative — and highly strategic — schemes are the ones who can propel your company to new heights.

Business intelligence

Clearly, senior leaders should have some level of business savvy. In particular, you're looking for these qualities:

>> **An understanding of the business:** A candidate who is immersed in the guts of a business — one who has woven himself into the fabric of the industry and has developed deep and meaningful relationships with its leaders — is always a good bet. These candidates don't just have superficial knowledge; instead, they have extensive expertise, enabling them to provide superior counsel.

>> **Strategic focus:** Any candidate being considered for a leadership position must have the ability not just to capture and define a sound business strategy beyond the original product or concept, but to garner the support of stakeholders.

>> **The ability to think on their feet:** If you're looking to grow your business, then you're likely to find yourself facing novel situations and problems, with no corporate history or industry road map to guide you. You need leaders who can think on their feet.

>> **An awareness of the importance of cash:** Senior leaders must understand the critical importance of cash — particularly for an emerging company — tracking dollar and time expenditures like an entrepreneur would.

- **A tolerance for risk:** Tech guru Seth Godin says, "Safe is risky." In other words, playing it safe is a risk in and of itself. In fact, it may be the case that going the safe route is *riskier* than whatever so-called "risky" action you're trying to avoid! In today's ever-changing business landscape, you need leaders who are willing to meet stiff challenges with bold solutions.

- **Customer focus:** Senior leaders need to understand not just how markets work, but how to ensure the appropriate products and services reach your customers.

Leadership

Senior leaders are just that: leaders. If they're going to be effective, there are a few key leadership qualities they must possess:

- **Commitment:** Top candidates will have an ingrained — and unrelenting — commitment to success.

- **Passion:** Unless a candidate shows true passion for your company or industry, she simply cannot lead effectively.

- **People skills:** The best executives manage effectively, hire and fire quickly, and effectively build teams of talented people, regardless of their personalities or any quirks they may have. They also seek out talent on an ongoing basis. That way, when that perfect opportunity arises, the ideal candidate is already waiting in the wings.

- **Vision:** In the wise words of writer Jonathan Swift, "Vision is the art of seeing what is invisible to others." And how. Senior leaders must have vision — and the ability to execute on that vision — if they're to achieve greatness.

- **Initiative:** You're looking for somebody who's proactive and forward-thinking, not someone who hides behind his title and takes a reactive approach.

- **Entrepreneurialism:** Earlier, we mentioned that executives should be cash-conscious, the way entrepreneurs are. But that's not the only entrepreneurial behavior they should display. You want senior leaders who will act like they own the place — in a good way. They should have a passion for the business, display an ability to be "always on," and show vigilance to prevent small problems from blooming into crises.

- **Focus on results:** They say, "It's the journey, not the destination." We're not so sure. In business, results are the name of the game — and you need senior leaders who achieve them. That means, among other things, having the ability to recruit a quality team, enable them to work together, and drive them to perform.

Emotional intelligence

"Know thyself." That's what the ancient Greeks said. And boy, were they right. Leaders who aren't in touch with themselves will have a hard time connecting with anyone else. This is especially true today, as more millennials enter the workforce. (They may not be in your executive ranks yet, but they will be — and soon!) For best results, executives should display the following attributes:

- » **A healthy self-concept:** Executives with a healthy self-concept — in other words, a solid answer to the question "Who am I?" — are much more likely to successfully navigate any business.

- » **Strong values:** Top leaders must establish a core set of values — both at work and in life — that align with the values of the company.

- » **Empathy:** The best executives have the ability to connect with employees and customers alike.

- » **Caring:** All too many leaders view people as nothing more than fungible cogs in a machine. That's a mistake. Successful executives care about their people — and they show it.

TESTING, TESTING, 1, 2, 3

These days, emotional intelligence is more critical to an executive's success than ever before. For this reason, we've incorporated emotional quotient inventory (EQ-i) assessments into our hiring practices, and we suggest you do the same.

Which assessment tool should you use? We've used the Bar-On EQ-i Leadership Report for more than a decade. This report examines EQ-i results as they relate to leadership skills, and can be used for the general assessment of leadership strengths and weaknesses. It applies to most levels and functions of leadership, whether at the operational, management, or executive level.

Of course, you can also work with your HR department to devise behavioral interview questions to assess a candidate's attributes in these areas. But these should not serve as a replacement for the EQ-i assessment. Rather, the two assessments complement each other. For more on conducting EQ-i assessments, see Chapters 8 and 13.

Super Fly: Avoiding Superficial Evaluation Factors

Have you ever heard the term *empty suit?* It describes an executive who is incompetent. Such individuals don't know what they're doing. And yet, all too often, these empty suits wind up in positions of great power.

There's one simple explanation for this: Whoever hired the executive based his decision on superficial evaluation factors. These include characteristics like the following:

>> **Charm:** You know who was charming? Ted Bundy, that's who. And you know who wasn't? Steve Jobs. The point is, a charming personality is never an accurate predictor of success in a role. If you find yourself being swayed by a candidate's winning smile, beware.

WARNING

Whenever a client "falls in love" with a candidate, we strongly encourage the client to take a healthy step back to figure out why.

>> **Industry experience:** We're not saying industry experience is a *bad* thing. We're just saying that depending on the size of the company and its growth stage, it may not be critical. Instead of focusing on industry experience, make your decision based on a broad range of factors, including the core attributes we discuss in the previous section.

>> **Pedigree:** Yes, prestigious school credentials are a nice-to-have, especially when they come with a built-in network of high-profile executives. But they won't guarantee success. Keep the candidate's credentials in proper context, and of course, fully vet her before making an offer.

>> **"Golden boy" references:** These are references from industry leaders who have worked with the candidate, but only indirectly. In other words, although they may know the candidate, the candidate has never worked directly for or with them. If a reference can't give you specific details of a candidate's contributions, then his testimony is essentially worthless.

TIP

One easy way to rule out "golden boy" references in advance is to check the candidate's LinkedIn recommendations section. If the reference appears there, it may be legit.

The truth is, these superficial evaluation factors provide minimal insight into a candidate's abilities. The same goes for first impressions. Indeed, according to Laszlo Bock, former senior vice president of people operations at Google (he's now a senior advisor at the company) and author of *Work Rules! Insights from Inside Google to Transform How You Live and Lead,* typical interviews are a waste of time because 99.4 percent of the time is spent trying to confirm whatever impression the interviewer formed about the interviewee during the first ten seconds — an impression, by the way, that has virtually no basis in reality.

In his book, Bock goes on to review a 1998 study by Frank Schmidt and John Hunter that examines 85 years of research on how effectively different types of assessments actually predict performance. They found that

>> **Information gleaned during unstructured interviews could predict only 14 percent of an employee's performance.** A *structured interview* is one in which each candidate is asked the same series of questions, making it easier to assess and compare their answers. An *unstructured interview,* in this context, is one that is more free-flowing — although the phrase is also used to describe those moments between "official" interview sessions, such as during a coffee break, over lunch, or walking down the hallway to the next meeting, when the candidate's guard is down.

>> **Reference checks could explain 7 percent of an employee's performance.**

>> **Years of experience factored into 3 percent of an employee's performance.**

So, what was the *best* predictor of a candidate's performance? How effectively she completed a job-related task, at 29 percent. (That's why, in Chapter 14, we recommend you have your final candidate deliver a job-related presentation before you close the deal.)

Flew the Coop: Building a Cooperative Culture

Whether your new hire succeeds isn't just about his core characteristics. It's also about yours — or your company's, anyway. We're talking about the environment and culture within your organization.

Earlier, we talk about how the role of management was to develop procedures for employees to follow to serve the machines that existed at the center of the typical organization. Now, in the new knowledge-based economy, management's job is to cultivate an environment and culture that enables their people to leverage their intelligence and creativity. You achieve this by developing the following within the organization itself:

>> **Emotional intelligence (EI):** It's not just people who display EI. Organizations can, too. In organizations with high EI, employees believe in themselves. Ron Wiens, the author of *Building Organizations That Leap Tall Buildings in a Single Bound,* explains it this way: "In high EI organizations, people are aware of their emotions and are able to use them to grow their performance (i.e., they do not allow negative self-talk to tear down their belief in themselves)." It's this confidence that enables them to try new things (which in turn, drives innovation). It also reassures them that help is available if things go awry. Simply put, EI is about one's belief in one's self.

>> **Relationship intelligence (RI):** Companies with RI demonstrate caring. This doesn't just make for a happier workplace, however. It also boosts the bottom line. Simply put, caring is the basis of trust. When people trust you, they can speak openly and frankly with you. When people can speak openly and frankly with you, you can solve problems together. And when you can solve problems together, you can leverage each other's creativity and knowledge to build competitive advantage. Like James Autry — who began his career as a publishing executive and went on to write several books on a variety of topics, including leadership in a knowledge economy — once said, "I need to know that you care before I care to know what you know." All this is to say that whereas EI is about one's belief in oneself, RI is about one's belief in others.

>> **Corporate intelligence:** In winning organizations, employees demonstrate corporate intelligence. No, we don't mean they engage in corporate espionage; in this case, we mean they are savvy about the ins and outs of your business. Not only do they understand your company's goals and objectives, they *believe* in them. Indeed, they believe in them to such an extent that achieving them becomes personally meaningful. The bottom line? CI is about one's belief in the organization.

When you combine emotional intelligence, relationship intelligence, and corporate intelligence, you produce an environment where your employees are plugged in, turned on, and in tune with your organization. When you have that, it's like winning the Triple Crown of thoroughbred racing!

REMEMBER

Now more than ever, companies need leaders who can use a common mission to inspire a community of people to operate at peak levels of performance. This has deep implications for which aptitudes and qualities you recruit for, who you hire, and how you lead.

2

Planning Your Search

IN THIS PART . . .

Write your plan and share it with your client.

Assemble a solid search team, including the search committee, search chair, and external recruiter.

Identify the steps for completing an executive search.

Explore recruiting tools and resources.

Chapter **5**

Plan Do! Devising a Plan

You've no doubt heard of *The Art of War*. Heck, you may have even read it. Written by Sun Tzu during ancient times in China, this treatise is commonly viewed as *the* definitive work on military strategy and tactics — despite being nearly 2,500 years old. *The Art of War* is chock-full of wisdom on all aspects of warfare. But for us, one passage really stands out. It's on the subject of planning:

> The general who wins a battle makes many calculations in his temple before the battle is fought. The general who loses a battle makes but few calculations beforehand. Thus do many calculations lead to victory and few calculations to defeat: how much more no calculation at all! It is by attention to this point that I can foresee who is likely to win or lose.

And how.

Planning isn't just critical in warfare; it's vital in business, too. Indeed, you could make the case that planning is the most important part of running any organization, regardless of size, scope, or complexity.

Not surprisingly, planning is also key to executive recruiting — now more than ever. Why now more than ever? Simple. In recent years, the talent market has changed in ways no one ever expected for two reasons: the global financial crisis and the emerging national economies of Brazil, Russia, India, China, and South Africa, collectively referred to as BRICS. Both these developments have forced organizations of all stripes to aggressively pursue top leaders — people whose skills may mean the difference between trailing and prevailing.

At the same time, as the need for top talent has skyrocketed, the number of available leaders has not. Great leaders aren't born; they're developed over time, through education and experience. It'll take years — decades, even — to build an indigenous base of leaders in the BRICS countries. Until that happens, anyone who can design a top product, manage complex projects, perform marketing miracles, sell new customers, or lead an organization can take her pick of opportunities anywhere on the planet.

All this is to say that in this leadership-hungry environment, executive recruiting has changed. The days of passive recruiting and résumé collecting are over. Executive recruiting used to be like standing on a street corner handing out leaflets. Now, it's like looking in every company window, finding who you need, and breaking the glass to reach in and grab them.

In this hyper-competitive market, if you want to hire the best, your executive search project must be focused and your messaging crystal clear. In other words, you need a plan. That's what this chapter is all about.

REMEMBER

Of course, planning is not enough. You must also follow through. Too many people act without thinking — and too many others think without acting. You must do both. As David likes to say, "Think like a general; work like a sergeant."

Plan Up: Putting Your Plan Together

Making a project plan will help ensure you deliver your project on time and maybe even under budget by clearly outlining each process, phase, activity, and task required to complete it. The plan also details your projected time frame, including milestones, and any resources you require. Simply put, your plan — which you should commit to paper rather than simply storing it in your noggin — acts as a road map, giving the search committee and the hiring team a heads-up on what's coming and helping them stay on track.

This important document should articulate each of the following in simple language, but great detail:

>> **The expected outcome of a successful search:** This one-paragraph summary lays out the *what, when,* and *why.* That is, it defines what role is to be filled, specifies when it should be filled, and explains why it should be filled. (This last item will reflect the business outcomes called for by the organization's business plan.)

>> **Your search process:** Outline step by step what will happen during the search, from start to finish. That means doing the following:

- Identifying all processes, activities, and tasks (and the associated costs)

- Summarizing the effort needed to complete each process, activity, and task

- Modularizing sections of work to assign to others for completion

- Delineating team tasks, such as research, sourcing, and so on

- Documenting all process interdependencies

- Listing assumptions and constraints

- Identifying risks to the project (for example, supply and demand, time, geography, compensation, and so on)

- Noting success measures and key milestones based on historical averages

TIP

Chapter 7 outlines the exact steps required to complete an executive search, with subsequent chapters exploring each step in more detail.

>> **Your budget:** Establish a budget to cover *all* activities — and people — you may need to involve in the search. (This is in addition to the executive's compensation package.)

>> **Your team:** List who will be involved in the search, and what each person will contribute.

>> **Your tools and resources:** Identify what tools and resources you'll use to locate, identify, and evaluate candidates.

>> **Your timeline:** This should outline the expected duration of the search, as well as when you expect to hit various milestones toward completion.

>> **A brief executive summary:** This includes a short summary of each of the preceding plan elements.

It's not just about what's *in* your plan, however. The plan must also be

>> **Clever:** The best of the best rarely look to switch jobs. And if they do, then they have choices — lots of them. To grab their attention, it helps to get clever. For example, one client of David's sought "creative" applicants for a director of online marketing position. To intrigue top candidates, as well as root out anyone who lacked this important quality, David posted the job on LinkedIn and other job boards, instructing applicants to contact him in a "creative manner." To make things even more interesting, he omitted his contact information, forcing applicants to figure out how to get in touch. The result? David received dozens of high-quality submissions from applicants at firms ranging from AOL to *O* magazine to Disney and beyond.

>> **Results driven:** Invariably, you'll be under tremendous pressure to deliver results. To keep your hiring team and stakeholder groups on track, establish milestones and measure your progress as you go. This will also help you assess how close you are to achieving your goal.

>> **Marketing oriented:** Recruiting is the ultimate one-to-one marketing activity. Today, recruiting requires you to micro-target the competition's employees where they live (not where they work), and to treat each potential recruit as an individual. That means providing a customized response that is tailored to their needs and delivers a value proposition, like an elevator pitch. Yes, the old methods — we're talking about advertising, networking, referrals, and so on — should remain part of your plan, but they no longer suffice. By themselves, they just don't have the horsepower to attract the attention of busy executives.

>> **Affordable:** Recruiting costs money, whether you do it using in-house resources or hire it out. Unfortunately, for many companies — especially start-ups — cash is tighter than Mick Jagger's pants. In that case, you may need to take an indirect approach. Case in point: David once worked with a small company that was relatively unknown. To attract applicants for a chief technology officer position, they took an indirect approach, launching a contest that would take the winning applicant to new heights — literally. That is, they would have the opportunity to rocket to the edge of space in a Russian Foxbat fighter plane! This idea caught the media's eye, resulting in free coverage in prestigious publications like *Wired*. More important, it attracted the chief technology officer David was looking for — at a much lower cost.

>> **Realistic:** Knowing what you want to do is great. The question is: Can you do it? The plan you establish must be realistic, or it's no plan at all.

>> **Targeted:** Knowing the exact title your ideal candidate holds now, along with the candidate's exact function, gives you a specific target to pursue. So get specific. The more details, the better.

Nothing is more important to your project's success than a clear, detailed, well-articulated plan. With a plan you can organize your talent search with a laserlike focus. (Yes, you may get lucky without such a plan, but luck is unpredictable.) That's not to say your plan has to be super long, though. It should be just long enough to ensure you won't forget anything important down the line.

TIP

Clarity of purpose is both energizing and enabling. That's why you need a detailed plan.

The first time you build a project plan, expect it to take a while — maybe even as long as a week. The good news? You can reuse this detailed plan as a template for future executive recruiting projects. This will shorten the time it takes to build your plan considerably. Indeed, an experienced recruiter can develop a plan using a template in 20 minutes or so.

For an example of a detailed plan template, visit `www.executiverecruiting` `fordummies.com/downloads`.

Sharing your plan

Your plan should be clever, results driven, marketing oriented, affordable, realistic, and targeted. But there's one thing it *shouldn't* be: a secret.

After you hammer out your plan, share it with the hiring manager. Thoroughly explain exactly what is about to transpire — the complete sequence of events from start to finish. Don't just stop there, however. Also explain the underlying *why* behind each step, and what holdups you might encounter.

In our experience, people want to understand the ins and outs of the plan, not so they can execute it themselves but because they're curious and they like to learn. So humor them. Besides, educating your client is how you build trust. When you explain what's happening, how it will affect them, and how it will make their lives easier, you relieve any unease they may feel as a result of putting this important project in your hands.

Educating your clients also convinces them of your credibility — which you may need if you want them to trust you to run the program without interfering, to give you the leeway to act on their behalf, to go the extra mile at your say-so, and to remain confident in you when (not if) the project hits a snag. And, when they understand what you're doing and why, they're more likely to offer their cooperation and insight.

Don't be surprised if the first time you present a detailed plan to a new client, he or she is a bit flabbergasted by how much work is involved in the hiring process. Many hiring managers have no idea how difficult it is to fill these types of positions. That's likely because they've been misled by previous consultants, such as headhunters, who are notorious for conveying that whatever the client wants is realistic and infinitely doable — and for waltzing in out of the blue a few months later, candidate in tow.

Sure, these types of interactions may make the consultant look like a genius, but they tend to downplay the intense amount of planning and work involved, and they do nothing to demystify the hiring process or encourage the hiring manager's enthusiastic cooperation, let alone her participation. (These types of interactions may also explain why so many hiring managers seem to believe that the position they're looking to fill is the most important one you've ever worked on *in your life*, and that you have a bag of magic beans in your desk drawer that allow you to grow candidates on demand.) The good news? In our experience, when presented with a detailed plan, most executives are quick to grasp the three-dimensional-chess

CHAPTER 5 Plan Do! Devising a Plan **45**

nature of executive recruiting and the million moving pieces that comprise an executive search.

Actively engaging the hiring manager in the search improves the health of your business relationship.

Looking at a sample plan

Following is a sample plan. This is essentially an example of the short executive summary you include with your longer plan.

Needs Analysis

We will immediately dedicate time to clearly define your requirements, agree on a successful search strategy, craft a candidate road map, write a compelling position profile, and develop a confidential candidate brief.

Overview

Your upfront involvement will include a time investment of approximately two hours, as follows:

Initial requirements session:

- Discuss high-level requirements.

- Help recruit a search committee.

Next, we will produce the following and conduct a workshop:

- Develop comprehensive requirements.

- Develop sourcing strategy.

- Identify timeline and responsibilities.

- Build consensus with the hiring team.

From these meetings, we will produce the following project documents:

- Candidate road map

- Position profile

- Confidential candidate brief

Research Process

We will conduct fresh and original research on and gather competitive intelligence about your industry to find the individuals who will be impact players in your organization. As discussed:

- We will recruit from [list organizations known to be good sources of talent, as discussed with the hiring manager].

- We will *not* recruit from [list organizations that this company has agreed not to recruit from or that would result in an unwanted effect, as discussed with the hiring manager].

- We will run ads on [list where you will be running ads and why, along with the costs involved, which the hiring manager's department must bear].

- We will leverage the following social media sites: [list the social media sites you will leverage during the course of the project].

- We will research articles and publications, work company databases, and company web pages to uncover individuals who may not be obvious candidates.

Recruiting and Interviewing

We will focus on candidates with impeccable track records — proven leaders who stand out in their field. We will strategically position your opportunity to create excitement and cultivate interest. We will recruit both active and passive candidates using the confidential candidate brief created for your hire.

You and the search committee will interview viable candidates only. We will ensure that you are prepared for every interview. Throughout the process, we will provide detailed written reports on every viable candidate.

Reference Checking

We informally reference all candidates before they are presented. We will perform 360-degree references on all finalist candidates, covering leadership attributes, team-building skills, and character, as well as asking industry-specific functional questions to help build an accurate picture of the candidate's expected performance.

Offer Negotiation

We will help negotiate terms of agreement that are satisfactory to both you and your chosen candidate and present the final offer. We will also follow up with and notify all candidates who were not selected.

Onboarding and One-Year Guarantee

We will perform ongoing follow-up to ensure a smooth transition and that the new hire's performance meets your expectations.

You SLA Me! Hammering Out the Service-Level Agreement

In addition to composing a detailed project plan, outlining each step of the hiring process, you also need a service-level agreement (SLA). The SLA spells out your expectations, as well as those of your client. It also defines success for the project.

Lots of businesses rely on SLAs with their suppliers in order to run smoothly. But SLAs are common in people's personal lives as well — even yours. You likely have an SLA with your local power company to define your expectations (that your lights will turn on with the simple flick of a switch, and that the company will respond quickly in the event of a power outage) and theirs (that you'll pay your bill, preferably on time).

Defining expectations in an SLA

So what expectations should an SLA for an executive recruiting project define? To answer that, let's start what expectations it *shouldn't* define:

>> It shouldn't define an expectation that you'll complete a project in a certain amount of time.

>> It shouldn't define an expectation that you'll interview x number of candidates before making an offer.

Both these expectations are just too difficult to guarantee.

The SLA should, however, define expectations that pertain to events and transactions that *are* within your control. In other words, it's fair to say that if you do x, the client will do y within z time frame. For example:

>> If you present a candidate's résumé for feedback, you can expect an answer the same day.

>> If you call to schedule an interview, you can expect a call back within 24 hours.

>> If you require debriefing time after an interview, you'll get it the same day.

Most important, you need to explain what will happen if the client fails to follow the agreed-upon terms — namely, that it affects the schedule and may reduce your likelihood of success.

A simple SLA — even one that includes just these three points — will help to speed your project along without needlessly disrupting people's lives or stressing out your client or candidates. That being said, you can make your SLA as thorough as you like.

TIP

For an SLA template, which you can easily modify, visit www.executiverecruiting fordummies.com/downloads.

Looking at a simple SLA

An SLA doesn't need to be fancy, especially when it's being used internally. Use what follows as a guide to develop your own SLA. After both parties sign the SLA, attach it to the project plan.

How We Are Responsible to You

Complete transparency is the key to our working together efficiently and cost-effectively. Constant communication is the foundation of success. Timely and consistent dialogue throughout the search prevents any surprises. You will have all of my contact numbers to use whenever the need arises. I also suggest establishing a fixed schedule for weekly reporting to your search chair.

We will ensure that only those candidates who meet the stated requirements of the position in terms of competency, skills, and fit are referred. We will then conduct a comprehensive search as specified, until the role is filled to your satisfaction.

In exchange for the above consideration, we request you agree to the following principles:

- When you are presented with a candidate's résumé for feedback, you will provide an answer the same day.

- If we call to schedule an interview, you will ensure a return call within 24 hours.

- After each interview, you will provide feedback the same day.

Please review the attached project plan, sign it, and return it to us when you're ready to begin the project.

Chapter **6**

Team Up: Assembling Your Search Team

f you're a football fan, you know that football teams are subdivided into three main groups. First, there's the offense; the role of this group is to score points. Then, there's the defense, which works to prevent the other team from scoring. Finally, you have special teams; this includes the kicker, holder, punter, and other players with highly specialized roles.

Your executive search team is also composed of three main groups: the recruiting team, the hiring team, and the support team. In this chapter, you learn about the roles and responsibilities of everyone on your executive search team.

Who's on Your Executive Search Team?

Your search team is composed of three groups: the hiring team, the recruiting team, and the support team. So, what does each of these teams do? And who's on these teams?

Depending on certain variables — including the size of your organization and the sensitivity of the search project — some people on your executive search team might wind up wearing multiple hats.

The hiring team

Your hiring team helps you interview and assess candidates. It consists of the following people and groups:

>> **Hiring manager:** This is the person the new hire will report to. Typically, the hiring manager decides which candidate will land the job.

>> **Ultimate hiring manager:** For executive-level hires, the ultimate hiring manager is usually the CEO. For less senior roles, the ultimate hiring manager may be a vice president. On rare occasions, the board of directors could be the ultimate hiring manager. Whoever it is, the ultimate hiring manager is the one person (or group of people) who can overrule the hiring manager's decision on whom to hire.

Sometimes, the hiring manager and the ultimate hiring manager are one and the same.

>> **Search committee:** The purpose of this group is to assist the hiring manager in various phases of the search. The search committee provides for consistency in reviewing each candidate, and benefits from multiple perspectives.

>> **Search committee chair:** The search committee chair serves as a liaison between the search committee and the hiring manager and ultimate hiring manager. The ideal chair understands the needs and culture of the organization, enabling her to successfully select a qualified and talented candidate in a timely manner.

You learn more about assembling a well-functioning search committee and selecting a search committee chair later in this chapter.

The recruiting team

Your recruiting team helps you locate, identify, and recruit candidates. It consists of the following people:

>> **Internal recruiter:** This person is responsible for identifying, recruiting, and qualifying potential candidates. The internal recruiter develops *prospects* — that is, individuals identified or sourced from others — into qualified candidates who are interested in the position.

>> **Sourcer:** Sourcing is about the hunt. The sourcer is responsible for pipeline development. He identifies and engages with target talent.

>> **Researcher:** The researcher assesses the market and handles business and competitive intelligence. She produces a list of potential prospects and hands it off to either the recruiter or the sourcer.

It's not unusual for these three roles to be combined into one, handled by a single person. Or you may employ an external recruiter to handle these duties. Using an external recruiter, you increase the odds of a superior outcome in a shorter period of time. (You'll learn more about external recruiters later in this chapter.)

TIP

You may need to augment your hiring and/or recruiting team with external consultants, such as recruiters, sourcers, or researchers. (If you hire an external recruiting firm, as opposed to an independent recruiter, then you can expect it to use its own team of recruiters, sourcers, and researchers.) Either way, if you go this route, negotiate any terms and conditions, including guarantees and a hands-off clause, and get them down on paper.

The support team

Your support team helps you position the opportunity and keep track of all the details and paperwork involved in the recruiting project. It consists of the following people:

>> **Marketing lead or copywriter:** This person's job is to make you look sexy — or, barring that, to ensure your opportunity is appealing. Why is this person necessary? Because just as you screen applicants for "fit," your applicants are screening you. If you want to draw top candidates, a well-crafted job description or advertisement is a must. Bottom line? You need to grab each prospect's attention and speak succinctly to his needs.

>> **Coordinator:** The coordinator's job is to make sure all elements of the search process remain on track. He sets meetings, manages the calendars of all participants, and handles interview logistics and feedback loops. The coordinator also acts as the central repository for details on each candidate.

TIP

In our experience, the search chair's most trusted assistant makes the best coordinator. Why? Because odds are, he already has a working relationship with board members and can get to them quickly.

Search Me! Assembling a Solid Search Committee

The purpose of the search committee is to assist the hiring manager in various phases of the search:

>> Confirming the need

>> Setting the path for the recruitment and hiring process

>> Building board consensus on strategy and agenda

>> Helping to create a detailed, competency-based job description (see Chapter 10)

>> Ensuring that legal requirements for due diligence are met

>> Managing the search and selection process

>> Landing the best candidate

As you can see, there's a lot of detailed work involved — none of it trivial!

WARNING

Often, the board of directors assumes this role. But in our experience, this is a mistake. Boards of directors rarely have the experience or operational knowledge to conduct an executive search. More important, they don't have the time. Locating, courting, and winning over a great candidate isn't something you can do part-time. It involves a long-term commitment.

A better approach is to assemble a board-appointed search committee to oversee the project. This committee should include a diverse group of stakeholders. Some of these may be individual members of the board of directors. The CEO may also participate, especially if you expect you'll need help closing the deal with your top candidate. You can also include peer-level executives. (Just be sure there are no conflicting agendas. Otherwise, you may fall victim to sabotage.) When the search committee includes a variety of perspectives, it can develop a clearer view of the ideal candidate's skills, experience, and personality.

As you assemble your search committee, consider the following questions:

REMEMBER

>> Who on the board of directors has successfully conducted a CEO or executive-level search in the recent past?

If no one on the board has this experience, consider bringing in someone from the outside who does.

>> Which outside board members have successfully served as CEO in their own careers?

>> Who is best positioned to invest the appropriate time into the process?

>> Who is in the best position to evaluate and entice candidates?

The answers to these questions will help you identify possible committee members.

TIP

Keep the search committee small. Five to seven committed people is ideal. This is a small enough number to allow for animated discussions, but large enough to minimize the odds of the group being swayed by a single person.

Chair-y Picking: Selecting the Search Chair

During the first meeting of the search committee, you should appoint a chair. Who should you choose? To answer that, it helps to understand what the chair does. Here are a few of the chair's duties:

>> Building an emotional connection with the right candidate (this is crucial)

>> Working with the external recruiter to create and manage the timeline

>> Serving as the voice for the search committee

>> Driving the search process with the internal or external recruiter

>> Managing the flow of information between the search committee and the board

>> Helping the external recruiter gather data about recommended candidates from all board members and "friends" of the company

>> Evaluating and managing any internal candidates with the external recruiter

>> Checking references

>> Ensuring due diligence

>> Driving the creation, development, and presentation of the offer

>> Negotiating the offer

>> Playing "good cop" if the external recruiter needs to step aside during the negotiation phase

>> Closing the deal

REMEMBER

The search chair is often in the best position to convince the candidate there is a fit; articulate why her background, skills, opportunities, and challenges align; and explain how there is wealth to be made. This last point is critical, especially for funded ventures. Cap structures are often complex, and it's hard for newcomers to anticipate how much additional funding will be required and in how many tranches. The search chair can tell this story.

But that's not all. The search chair must also lead open discussions, promote honest communication, and gain consensus (remembering, of course, that you can't please everyone all the time). In doing so, the chair must ensure that everyone on the committee is heard, without allowing dissenters or detractors hijack the group. Above all, the chair must be extremely proactive and accessible throughout the entire search process.

The good news? While evaluating committee members to determine who would make the best chair, it will quickly become apparent who has the needed experience, as well as the time and interest to invest in the project.

TIP

We highly recommend selecting an outside board member to serve as the chair — someone who can remain detached from the internal politics of the organization.

External Affairs: Choosing an External Recruiter

An external recruiter — sometimes called a third-party recruiter, executive search professional, or headhunter — is a person or firm that helps organizations meet their recruiting needs. The external recruiter's personal network, business acumen, and methodology — along with his ability to ascertain leadership and fit — are of tremendous value in any executive search. Essentially, the external recruiter assumes the combined duties of an internal recruiter, sourcer, and researcher. Most external recruiters take full responsibility for the entire hiring project, usually working directly with the hiring manager in conjunction with HR.

According to the American Staffing Association, the United States boasts some 20,000 staffing firms, with 174,000 professional recruiters (as of this writing). That's a lot! And yet, finding a good external recruiter is no easy task. For one thing, unlike a doctor, lawyer, or any number of other professionals, there's no college degree in recruiting. Indeed, there are no educational or training prerequisites whatsoever, and virtually no licensing requirements! Nor is there an official code of conduct that governs the industry.

Still, it is possible to find a reputable recruiter. To start, decide on the following:

>> Your budget

>> Whether you want to pay a retainer or work on a contingency basis

>> Whether you want a niche recruiter or a generalist

>> Whether you want a big recruiting firm or a boutique

We walk you through each of these considerations in the following sections, as well as offer several critical questions you should ask before choosing an external recruiter.

Budgetary considerations

More often than not, the task of choosing a recruiter will fall to HR or to your purchasing or strategic sourcing department, who will be guided by senior management. And that internal department will likely look for the least-expensive option. Unfortunately, using a competitive-bid strategy to select a recruiter is about as effective as bargain-hunting for a top-notch surgeon when you need a heart transplant. You get what you pay for!

Low-fee recruiters tend to be recruiting mills. Needless to say, they don't subscribe to the notion that a true executive search professional must personally shovel tons of coal to find the perfect diamond. To make a living, these firms handle many concurrent searches, often throwing résumés at their clients as quickly as they can to see if something sticks.

It's far better to pay more for a more respectable recruiter — someone who will successfully complete your executive search as quickly and professionally as possible. Yes, retaining a top executive search firm costs about as much as a good American-made luxury sedan. But in return, you get the assurance that your search will be successful. Really, if you think about it, a high-end recruiter can *save* you money by landing the best-qualified executive in the shortest possible time.

Selecting a more respectable recruiter offers one other advantage: Because such recruiters tend to be more financially stable, they don't need to serve a large number of clients to stay afloat. That means your search will be front and center in your recruiter's mind.

The bottom line? External recruiters aren't commodities. You can't just swap out one for another and expect equal results. There's a big difference between a good recruiter and a bad one!

TIP

A good way to identify respectable recruiters is by how much repeat business they do.

Retained recruiters versus contingency recruiters

Some external recruiters are retained. Retained recruiters work exclusively on a single assignment until it's complete, and they're compensated for their expertise rather than for a successful hire. Typically, retained recruiters are paid one-third of their fee upfront. They receive the second third upon submission of a short list of candidates. The final third is due when the position is filled (regardless of whether the candidate came from them or from another source) or when the search is terminated because the desired candidate fails to materialize. Sometimes, retained recruiters develop exclusive relationships with a client company, essentially becoming their unofficial talent scout.

Other external recruiters operate on a contingency basis. Instead of charging an upfront fee, these recruiters are paid when — and only when — the client company hires one of the candidates they present. If they fail to produce a "winning" candidate, contingency recruiters are paid nothing at all, regardless of how much time they spent on the search. For this reason — and because companies often pit multiple contingency recruiters against each other to fill the same position — contingency recruiters typically conduct multiple searches at once, focusing on easy-to-fill or commodity-type positions to improve their chances of getting paid.

REMEMBER

Companies might employ multiple contingency recruiters to fill a single lower-level position, but this rarely happens at the executive level. With executive searches, confidentiality is crucial. The fewer recruiters, the better.

TIP

So, which type of recruiter should you use for your executive search? We recommend you go the retained route. Contingency recruiters just can't put in the time needed to conduct an exacting executive search. Contingency recruiters are also less likely to develop true and trusting relationships with their clients and candidates. That being said, if you aren't in any hurry to fill the position — if you have, say, 6 to 12 months — then a contingency firm might work.

CONTAINED SEARCH

In recent years, the line between retained and contingency recruiters has blurred somewhat, resulting in a new flavor of recruiting called *contained search*. With contained searches, recruiters take the same full-service approach that retained recruiters do, without the full financial commitment from the client. In this model, clients pay a one-time project initiation fee to get started. This payment funds the entire research and recruiting effort, with no hidden fees or charges added. Clients pay a second fee if and only if the search results in a hire. If your budget is tight, a contained search might be the way to go.

Niche recruiters versus generalists

Most external recruiters can be described as either niche recruiters or generalists.

Niche recruiters specialize in just one type of function or industry. For example, a niche recruiter might focus on former military personnel, financial professionals, pharmacists, restaurant managers, or computer programmers. Or she could concentrate on the pharmaceutical, automotive, construction, or retail industry. The list is endless!

Niche recruiters who focus on a particular industry are often people who used to work in that industry themselves. As a result, they know a great deal about it and have a bursting Rolodex of contacts. For example, you might see a senior semiretired HR executive set up shop to recruit HR professionals.

REMEMBER

More often than not, a recruiter who focuses on a specific industry will brand her firm accordingly. For example, if the recruiter focuses on retail, she might name her company ABC Retail Recruiting. This type of branding is smart, because it positions the recruiter as a specialist, which makes it easy for potential clients to find him.

The fact that a niche recruiter knows your industry and has loads of contacts makes her very attractive indeed — especially if you're looking to fill a position quickly. But using a niche recruiter has some serious drawbacks:

>> **Niche recruiters — reputable ones, at least — are often bound by "hands-off" agreements.** Often, recruiters have a hands-off agreement with their clients. This agreement prevents the recruiter from poaching any of the client's employees, rendering her Rolodex essentially useless. That shrinks the talent pool from which these recruiters can ethically recruit from "Olympic-size" to "kiddie."

> >> **Due to economic swings, niche recruiters may have a limited life span.**
> For example, when the real estate market crashed in 2007, thousands of niche
> recruiters who focused on real estate or construction went belly up.

Unlike a niche recruiter, a generalist may not know much about a particular industry. However, because his client base is spread across multiple industries, those hands-off agreements are less of a problem. It's not that these recruiters don't have hands-off agreements with their clients; they do. But odds are, they don't have them with every single one of your competitors.

Often, generalists hold a degree in some aspect of executive management, such as industrial relations, business administration, or finance. And chances are, they've worked in one or more industry. As a result, generalists tend to be a bit more well rounded than niche recruiters, possessing a variety of talents. Arguably, you *could* call a generalist a jack-of-all-trades, master of none. But in our experience — and we've partnered with hundreds of them over the years — generalists are master strategists and researchers, skilled at locating, assessing, and attracting talent.

TIP

So, which type of recruiter should you use — a niche recruiter or a generalist? It depends. You may want to use a niche recruiter when

> >> The need is urgent and time is tight (a matter of days or weeks).
>
> >> Deep domain experience is the critical business driver.
>
> >> The niche recruiter is not bound by hands-off restrictions with any of the companies you'd like to recruit from.

TIP

You may be better served by using a generalist when

> >> The need is less urgent and you have more time (two to four months or more).
>
> >> Deep domain experience is *not* the critical business driver.
>
> >> You want to attract executives who bring novel or innovative thinking from outside your industry.

Big firms versus boutiques

In recruiting, size matters — but not in the way you might think. Boutique search firms often have an advantage over large ones because large search firms have more clients and are bound by more hands-off agreements to prevent poaching.

The bottom line? Despite their large Rolodexes, most large search firms don't have as extensive a reach as you might think. Tools like ZoomInfo and LinkedIn have leveled the playing field, giving boutique firms access to millions of executives — and no hands-off list.

The larger the firm, the smaller the pond it fishes.

Critical questions for external recruiters

In choosing an external recruiter, there are several key questions to ponder. You can pair these with the recruiter scorecard in the next section, using them in tandem to select the best recruiter for your firm.

>> **Is the recruiter free to recruit from your direct competitors?** Some large recruiting firms are prevented from recruiting from thousands of organizations due to conflicts of interest. Find out whether the external recruiter you're considering is constrained in this way. If his hands-off list includes organizations you may want to poach from, he's probably not a good fit.

>> **Does the recruiter understand the role you need to fill?** A good external recruiter will help you refine the job description based on her market knowledge. Defining the role, responsibilities, and qualifications upfront will produce superior results.

You can tell a lot about an external recruiter by the amount of due diligence she performs to define your requirements. The more, the better!

>> **Will an experienced recruiter perform the search?** Before you sign an agreement with an external recruiting firm, meet with the recruiter or team assigned to your project and make sure you're comfortable with him. Ideally, he will be — or will be assisted by — one of the firm's principals.

>> **Does the recruiter have experience with similar recruiting projects?** Select the most expert recruiter possible. You do *not* want a recruiter who is still cutting her teeth. The risks are too high. Experience is important. Your recruiter should understand the nuances specific to sales, marketing, operations, and finance. She must also understand the differences between public-sector and private-sector companies — as well as the differences between public companies and private ones — in terms of fit pace, leadership style, accountability, and compensation.

>> **Does the recruiter have a high success rate?** Be wary of recruiters whose success rate is less than 90 percent. At the same time, be skeptical if a recruiter says he has *never* failed. A success rate of 100 percent is impossible.

(Be sure to focus on the individual's success rate, not the firm's.) Oh, and regardless of the recruiter's success rate, he should exude a 100 percent completion mentality.

» **Does the recruiter offer a performance guarantee?** Suppose the external recruiter presents one, two, or even three slates of candidates, but none is acceptable. Will the recruiter continue searching until she finds a suitable candidate, or will she walk away? Or, suppose the selected candidate doesn't work out within a predefined period — typically 30 to 90 days for lower-level executives and up to six months for more senior positions. Will the recruiter conduct a new search? Ask about these and similar guarantees upfront, and get them in writing.

» **Will the recruiter represent your company in a satisfactory manner?** Your external recruiter is an extension of your company. He represents your organization when he speaks with candidates, competitors, suppliers, and other players in the marketplace. That means he must operate in a way that enhances your company's brand — not just with the candidate you select, but also with those you reject.

» **Will the recruiter be the one who makes initial contact with prospective candidates?** Some search firms use researchers to gauge the interest of prospective candidates. The researcher then presents to the recruiter a list of interested parties. This is a bad move, however. Most executives summarily reject overtures from search firms — which means they're quickly struck from the researcher's list. As a result, the recruiter never learns of the executive, never finds out why the executive rejected the overture, and is unable to repackage the opportunity in a more enticing way. Far better to have the recruiter make initial contact, with the understanding that it may take five or six attempts to draw the executive in.

» **Does the recruiter understand what a typical search entails?** To tease this out, ask the recruiter a few questions, like how many contacts she usually makes in a search, how she sources candidates, and how long an average search typically takes. Also find out what sorts of problems she has encountered on searches like yours and how she has handled them. Just don't expect her to give away all her trade secrets. She shouldn't, and she won't.

» **Can the recruiter articulate a well-conceived search strategy?** Where you start your search and how far afield you go depends on your requirement for domain or functional expertise (or both). It's best to start domain-centric searches within the locale of your head office, expanding as needed according to geographic hubs. For functional searches, you should picture a dartboard.

The search should start at the bull's-eye, which represents the position's geographic location, and expand outward in concentric circles. For example, if you were searching for a regional VP, you'd start your search where the remote office is located and try to contain it there to ensure candidates are plugged into local markets.

» **Has the recruiter ever had profit and loss (P&L) responsibilities?** When it comes to recruiting, senior executives want to know they're being assessed by a peer who understands their concerns — in other words, someone with P&L experience. On the flip side, to feel at ease, recruiters need to see the people they're recruiting as their peers. If the recruiter is nervous about assessing a more senior person, that senior person will detect the recruiter's unease in a nanosecond. Odds are, he'll decide the recruiter is too junior to bother with — meaning you may lose a viable candidate.

» **Does the recruiter serve on any boards or committees related to your industry?** Next to robust research, access to key decision-makers will make or break your search. Having a recruiter who serves on the board of directors of an industry association or is viewed as an industry insider will work to your advantage.

» **Does the recruiter's domain expertise help you?** Suppose your company is headquartered in New York, and you're looking for a new CEO. If you want to limit your search to CEOs already in New York, then a recruiter who specializes in the New York market might be most effective. If, however, you want the best CEO period, whether that person lives in New York or not, a recruiter with a broader focus might make more sense.

» **Is the recruiter located in the same geographic area as the position?** This may or may not matter, depending on your needs. A recruiter with knowledge of the local area may be able to fill the role more quickly. But if it becomes necessary to look outside the local area, that recruiter might be at a disadvantage.

» **Can the recruiter devote adequate time to your search?** A recruiter's schedule is a by-product of his business model — that is, whether he is retained or works on a contingency basis. Contingency recruiters often work five searches for every one they complete. Moreover, to stay afloat, they must work several searches at a time. If your recruiter has taken on too many searches already, your search won't get the time and attention it deserves. If this is a concern, opt for a retained recruiter.

Recruiters who use a low-volume model will likely deliver the best results.

» **Will the recruiter work on your search until it's successfully completed?** Again, this depends on the recruiter's business model. Retained recruiters are contractually obligated to focus on your search — and your search alone — until it's complete and you're satisfied with the result. Contingency recruiters, on the other hand, will likely attempt to fill the position as quickly as they can, regardless of fit. If they're unable to do so, they may lack the incentive to finish the job. You want a recruiter who can dedicate herself to your search project until it's complete.

As you assess external recruiters, be realistic about the time and effort it will likely take to land your dream candidate.

>> **Does the recruiter conduct business in an ethical manner?** Many professional organizations require members to practice their trade in an ethical manner. Ideally, your recruiter will belong to one. If so, verify his affiliation with the organization and what standards the organization requires members to uphold.

>> **Will the recruiter approach active and passive candidates with equal fervor?** To attract the ideal candidate, your recruiter must approach passive candidates — people who are not currently seeking a new position. If she approaches only active candidates — people who *are* currently looking — you'll miss out on 80 percent to 90 percent of the candidates who are actually qualified for the role. Moreover, if you limit your search to active candidates, you may find yourself in competition with other prospective employers, limiting your odds of success. Yes, it takes more time and skill to attract someone who isn't looking for a new job. But it pays off.

>> **Can the recruiter structure executive compensation packages?** The best compensation plans are tied to performance. That means your recruiter needs to identify what drives a candidate to perform. This issue becomes more important the higher up the new hire will be.

>> **Does the recruiter have experience relocating executives?** A seasoned recruiter will discuss relocation with every candidate at first contact — and every round of interviews that follows — to head off any unanticipated issues during the close. Better to deal with these issues from the start than at the last minute.

>> **Is the recruiter willing to meet with all relevant stakeholders?** Your recruiter should be willing to spend as much time as necessary with relevant stakeholders to wrap his head around the position, marketplace, and culture. For positions at the C-suite level and all VPs, that includes meeting with external board members. The idea is to arm the recruiter to the teeth with corporate knowledge so he can serve as an effective emissary.

>> **Can you see the recruiter becoming a true partner?** A true partner is someone who is a peer and acts accordingly. She looks out for your best interests, ensuring a full search is necessary before undertaking one and offering alternatives if needed. A true partner also showcases her candidates, warts and all — never altering a candidate's résumé to fit your search. And she'll never raid your company for other clients or exhibit other unethical behavior. Finally, true partners will help you with jobs big or small — or if not, she'll refer you to someone who will.

>> **Is the recruiter objective?** Your recruiter should be able to openly and honestly discuss the strengths and weaknesses of every candidate he brings to the table against the backdrop of your requirements. He should also be able to offer objective advice — even if it means leaving a candidate at the altar and starting fresh due to issues that arise during interviews or the checking of references. Oh, and if a recruiter thinks your expectations are out of line with reality — for example, maybe your compensation package is inadequate — he should say so.

>> **Does your recruiter have a sensible process for checking references?** A top-notch recruiter won't let you make an unconditional offer without thoroughly vetting the candidate first. She'll also encourage you to personally redo at least one of the reference checks she has completed to check for accuracy and consistency. Finally, she'll help design the reference questions to ensure the extraction of meaningful information.

>> **Will the recruiter provide you with highly detailed supplemental candidate information, such as a confidential candidate brief?** A confidential candidate brief is a highly detailed document that contains each question asked of the candidate, the candidate's response, and any supplemental notes from the recruiter. (For more on confidential candidate briefs, see Chapter 10.) If a recruiter fails to produce this type of documentation — or to perform other due diligence — he's nothing more than a body shop. We advise you to walk away.

The recruiter scorecard

As mentioned, you can use the recruiter scorecard (see Table 6-1) to assess prospective recruiters. Answer each question by choosing yes, no, or maybe. Each *yes* counts for 5 points. Each *no* is worth 0 points. And for each *maybe*, add 2½ points.

TABLE 6-1 **The Recruiter Scorecard**

Question	Yes	No	Maybe
Is the recruiter free to recruit from your direct competitors?			
Does the recruiter understand the role you need to fill?			
Will an experienced recruiter perform the search?			
Does the recruiter have experience with similar recruiting projects?			
Does the recruiter have a high success rate?			
Does the recruiter offer a performance guarantee?			
Will the recruiter represent your company in a satisfactory manner?			
Will the recruiter be the one who makes initial contact with prospective candidates?			
Does the recruiter understand what a typical search entails?			
Can the recruiter articulate a well-conceived search strategy?			
Has the recruiter ever had profit and loss (P&L) responsibilities?			
Does the recruiter's domain expertise help you?			
Is the recruiter located in the same geographic area as the position?			
Can the recruiter devote adequate time to your search?			
Will the recruiter work on your search until it is successfully completed?			
Does the recruiter conduct business in an ethical manner?			
Will the recruiter approach active and passive candidates with equal fervor?			
Can the recruiter structure executive compensation packages?			
Does the recruiter have experience relocating executives?			
Is the recruiter willing to meet with all relevant stakeholders?			
Can you see the recruiter becoming a true partner?			
Is the recruiter objective?			
Does your recruiter have a sensible process for checking references?			
Will the recruiter provide you with highly detailed supplemental candidate information, such as a confidential candidate brief?			
Subtotals			
Total Score			

To tally the scorecard, add up your points.

>> **80 to 120 points:** You should seriously consider partnering with this recruiter.

>> **60 to 79 points:** This recruiter *may* be okay, but it wouldn't hurt to interview a few others to see if you can find someone better.

>> **59 points or less:** Don't hire this recruiter.

TEN WAYS TO BUILD RAPPORT WITH AN EXTERNAL RECRUITER

Here are ten easy ways to build rapport with an external recruiter:

- **Convey to the recruiter your expectations and how you like to operate.** The best recruiters are flexible and will work to match to your style.

- **Treat the recruiter as you would a trusted partner or your best staff.** Openly communicate your company's situation, needs, problems, and objectives.

- **Listen to the recruiter with an open mind.** Her advice can save you a lot of time and trouble! *Remember:* Executive search is as much an art as it is a science. If your recruiter has a gut feeling about something, you'd be wise to pay heed to it.

- **Allow the recruiter to evaluate candidates you've identified internally just as he would the candidates he has found through his own sources.**

- **Discuss your selection biases and those of your recruiter.** For example, what David calls "political animals" drive him nuts, but he knows to ignore this bias.

- **Be inquisitive.** Ask the recruiter about her strategy, status, problems, market feedback, selections, and so on.

- **Touch base regularly — every week or so — to monitor the recruiter's progress and share any shifts in specifications or priorities.** If the search runs into a strong headwind, up the frequency of these communications to twice a week. You have a right to know what's going on with the search!

- **Be open and candid about any problems that arise during the search, but don't finger-point.** Instead, foster a problem-solving environment.

- **Be accessible.** Exchange home and cell numbers so you can be reached easily. It's the simplest way to demonstrate your commitment to the search's success.

- **Introduce the recruiter to your administrative assistant.** Your assistant can keep the recruiter in the know about your availability or lack thereof — for example, when you'll be in board meetings or on vacation.

No recruiter on Earth will earn a perfect score. That doesn't mean he can't meet your needs.

A WORD ON FAILURE

If a search fails, there may be a perfectly good reason — and more often than not, the client is to blame because she mistakenly believes there is an infinite supply of eminently qualified candidates whom she hasn't yet met. If the recruiter *is* to blame for a failed search, however, it's probably because he didn't work from a detailed list of requirements or he misread the corporate culture. Either way, a failed search may cost you more than just money and time. Indeed, the opportunity cost incurred because the right executive is not in position may be many times larger. You're best off taking time to interview and scrutinize your recruiter upfront, even if doing so delays the start of the project a few days.

IN THIS CHAPTER

» **Performing a needs analysis**

» **Generating the necessary documentation**

» **Researching the market**

» **Sourcing and recruiting candidates**

» **Interviewing the short list and checking references**

» **Making an offer**

» **Onboarding the new hire**

» **Hosting a kickoff meeting**

» **Troubleshooting the hiring project**

Chapter **7**

Dividing to Conquer: Parceling Out Your Process

Chapter 5 is all about the importance of devising and documenting a plan for your executive search project. This plan includes a summary of the expected outcome of a successful search, the project's budget, who's on the hiring team, the tools and resources you'll use, and an executive summary. It also lays out your search process, briefly outlining each phase. To review, these phases are as follows:

1. Performing a needs analysis

2. Generating the necessary documentation for the search

3. Researching the marketplace to pinpoint who to hire

4. Sourcing candidates

5. Actively recruiting and screening prospects

6. Interviewing and assessing candidates

7. Checking the background of each person you want to hire

8. Creating and presenting a formal offer of employment

9. Onboarding the new hire

This chapter discusses each of these phases in more depth, outlining the steps involved. It's meant to serve as an overview, to show you how all the pieces of an executive search project fit together. You find out even more about each phase throughout the rest of this book. (Look for cross-references throughout this chapter.)

TIP

Think of each phase in the process as a module — an entity all its own. This offers two advantages:

>> It makes it easier to modify or update a single phase.

>> If you've assembled a hiring team, you can easily distribute chunks of the hiring project to members of that team as needed. (If you're handling the hiring project all on your own, just complete each phase in order.)

The process we outline here is somewhat detailed. It may even feel a bit like over-kill. But we like to define every step to make sure nothing falls through the cracks. That way, we don't skip something that turns out to be a deal-breaker.

Analyze This: Performing a Needs Analysis

After you've laid out your basic plan and assembled your team (discussed in Chapter 5 and Chapter 6, respectively), job one is to perform a needs analysis. That means confirming the need for the new hire and consulting with the hiring manager to identify the precise requirements for the job.

Confirming the need

Why does the position exist? What is its strategic impact? Does it contribute to revenue or efficiency, or support roles that do? Answering these questions will help you serve the hiring manager.

If there are no clear answers to these questions, the hiring team should think long and hard about whether the position is truly needed.

Defining the requirements

With the need confirmed, it's time to outline the requirements. That means inter-viewing the hiring manager to clearly define the role, as well as to

>> **Assess the confidentiality factor.** Gauge the need for secrecy, whether for competitive or legal reasons.

>> **Assess the urgency.** Yes, time is always a factor. But there's a big difference urgency-wise among filling a hole left by a key departure, recruiting a replace-ment for a planned succession, and creating a new role altogether.

>> **Gauge the difficulty level.** How hard will it be to attract the correct candi-date? One factor will be how specialized the position is. Another factor: how much time you have to make the hire. You may have months, or mere days, depending on the circumstances. Finally, how much time can you personally devote to either overseeing the project or completing it yourself? Recognize any restrictions that may affect the project and plan accordingly.

>> **Identify compensation factors:** Now's the time to talk about the total compensation package earmarked for the role.

For even more insight into the role's requirements, review the corporate business plan to identify the role's key performance indicators (KPIs).

What's Up, Doc? Generating the Necessary Documentation

Having analyzed the need, you're ready to generate all the documents required during the course of this search:

>> **Search committee charter:** This document outlines all the roles and responsibilities of the search committee.

>> **Job description:** Developing a clear and concise statement of qualifications — in other words, a job description — is critical. (See Chapter 10 for more information.)

>> **Job order:** This document clearly identifies what the position is and what type of person should fill it. (See Chapter 10 for more information.)

>> **Position profile:** You use this external marketing document to pique the interest of potential candidates. (See Chapter 10 for more information.)

>> **Confidential candidate brief (CCB):** Thanks to the CCB (covered in detail in Chapter 10), you can abstain from asking potential candidates to submit an updated résumé. The CCB not only speeds up the search process, but also reduces the likelihood that top prospects — people who already have a job they like and rate updating their résumés somewhere between having dental surgery and contracting food poisoning — will dismiss the opportunity out of hand.

>> **Interview guide:** This guide contains all the questions you need to ask during the interview process. (See Chapter 10 for more information.)

>> **Advertising copy:** Now's the time to generate any advertising and promotional copy for the position. And not just any copy — strong, appealing, error-free copy! (See Chapter 10 for more information.)

>> **Recruiting scripts:** You use various recruiting scripts to engage and qualify prospective candidates. Chapter 13 outlines a script similar to one that David has successfully employed for more years than he'd care to admit.

>> **Reference check questions:** You'll pose these questions to the candidates' references — both their *direct references* (that is, those given to you by the candidates themselves) and their *indirect references* (sources you uncover). For a thorough list of reference check questions, see Chapter 15.

>> **Rejection letter:** Like that guy in *Highlander* said, "There can be only one" — one hire, that is. That means during the course of your search, you'll reject dozens or even hundreds of candidates — including some really good ones. To ensure you don't burn those bridges, develop a rejection letter that is direct but respectful. That way, if it turns out one of these stellar candidates is right for a role in the future, you'll feel comfortable approaching her again.

Research Engine: Researching the Market

When you research the market, you identify two main things:

>> **Who to look for:** What functional position, title, and span of control does the ideal candidate hold?

>> **What to look for:** What skills, competencies, experiences, and accomplishments does the ideal candidate have?

Researching the market also involves deciding where to look for top candidates. For best results, start with the same industry as the hiring organization. That way, the new hire can contribute to the organization's bottom line sooner rather than later. You should also consider the following:

>> **Company size:** Maybe you want someone from a large Fortune 500 company. Or maybe you're after someone from a small start-up. Either way, it helps to have some idea what size organization to target for prospective candidates.

>> **Market position:** Would you prefer to hire someone who works for a leader in the industry, a challenger, or a laggard?

REMEMBER

Why would you hire someone who works for a laggard? Simple. He's the one working to turn his organization around by using disruptive tactics to gain market share. That's a good thing — and it would be an even better thing if he were on your side. Our advice, and we're speaking from experience, is to look carefully at the industry's "losers." They may be hiding some real gems.

>> **Culture:** Are you looking for a new hire from a company with an open culture (Google comes to mind), one that's more command-and-control (think Apple under Steve Jobs), or something in between?

>> **Brand maturity:** Does the ideal candidate currently work for an established brand, or for one that's young, hip, and up-and-coming?

>> **Geography:** What's the scope of your search — local, regional, national, international, or galactic? (Just kidding about the galactic thing.)

>> **Competitors:** Are you hoping to hire someone who currently works for a competitor? This can yield business intelligence, as well as access to new contacts. (Note that recruiting from direct competitors may be a nonstarter if there are noncompete agreements in place.)

>> **Associations:** Scouting professional associates is a great way to find candidates with functional and industry expertise.

>> **Suppliers:** People who work for your suppliers likely have a good sense of your industry as a whole. That makes them potential candidates for your position.

>> **Vendors:** Someone who sells your service or product line may be a good fit.

>> **Affiliates:** It could be that an affiliate currently employs your ideal hire.

Finally, you need to determine what tools to use in your search. Here are just a few options:

>> **Databases:** There are loads of databases — some free and some paid — you can use to develop your initial list of prospects.

>> **Websites:** Don't overlook websites devoted to your industry or to the function you're hiring for.

>> **Publications:** Specialized periodicals, newsletters, and journals can contain a treasure-trove of top prospects. Don't just look for articles *about* top people; look for articles *by* them, too.

>> **Conferences:** Check lists of conference attendees — particularly speakers — for possible hires.

TIP

For more on researching the market, see Chapter 11. For tools to help speed you along, read Chapter 8.

Source Code: Sourcing Candidates

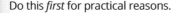

Sourcing (identifying) candidates is the focus of this phase. Your tactics will differ depending on whether you're dealing with active candidates or passive ones. (More on these two types of candidates in Chapter 13.)

Your sourcing activities for active candidates may include

TIP

>> **Identifying internal candidates:** You want to give due consideration to internal candidates because you want them to feel appreciated and to stick around. Most important, you want them to understand what they need to do to qualify for the top job the next time around.

Do this *first* for practical reasons.

>> **Advertising:** Work with your marketing department to place job ads on your company intranet, on online job boards, and in print publications. You learn how to write solid ads in Chapter 10.

>> **Engaging third-party contingent recruiters:** Many of them are specialists in their field, and they may help you complete your search more quickly.

To source passive candidates, you'll rely primarily on referrals from your network and from the search committee. You'll also draw up your own list of prospects based on research you conduct.

TIP

For more details on sourcing candidates, see Chapter 12.

Recruit Pursuit: Recruiting Candidates

Your efforts during the sourcing phase should result in the identification of several potential candidates. During the recruiting phase, you'll do the following:

1. **Pare down your list of prospects.**

2. **Choose a benchmark candidate and put her through the hiring paces.**

3. **Process all remaining candidates.**

TIP

For more on recruiting candidates, see Chapter 13.

The Big Short: Interviewing Your Short List

You've built a list. You've pared it down. All that remains is a select few finalists — no more than ten, tops. During this phase, you'll interview each of these remaining candidates to whittle down that list even further. When you're finished with this phase, you'll have identified your top candidate.

The interview phase involves five separate in-person, face-to-face interviews:

» **First face-to-face interview:** This interview isn't so different from the follow-up phone call you made during the recruiting phase (except it's not on the phone, obviously). Your main goal here is to get the candidate's story (again). You'll also fact-check his story to make sure everything checks out, and try to pin down your general impression of the candidate. Participants in this interview, which will likely last around two hours, include the candidate (duh), internal recruiter, external recruiter (if applicable), and optionally, a scribe, for taking notes.

» **Search chair interview:** During this interview, the internal or external recruiter, search chair, and, optionally, a scribe, meet with the candidate to further assess her suitability for the role. This interview typically lasts between two and three hours.

» **Hiring manager interview:** This interview is similar to the search chair interview, except that it also involves the hiring manager, who may also be the ultimate hiring authority. The point of this interview, which also lasts between two and three hours, is to assess whether the hiring authority likes the candidate and can work with him.

» **Search committee interview:** Candidates who make it this far meet with the internal recruiter or external recruiter, search chair, and search committee. This interview isn't so much meet-and-greet; it's do-or-die. As part of this fourth interview, the group convenes for a casual lunch, which helps to foster an emotional connection between the candidate and the search chair and committee — especially important if the job requires that the candidate relocate.

>> **Candidate presentation interview:** To call this an *interview* is somewhat inaccurate. It's better described as a meeting during which your top candidate delivers a presentation — for example, of the candidate's 30-60-90 plan. The idea here is not so much to assess the content of the presentation, but to gauge how she prepared for it. This will give you a pretty good sense of her general *modus operandi*.

TIP

For more on the interview process, see Chapter 14.

Point of Reference: Checking References

After a painstaking search process, you've found your ideal candidate. "Quick!" you're thinking. "Hire her!"

Whoa, Nellie.

Before you extend a formal offer to the candidate, you absolutely positively must check her references. That means soliciting the views of both direct and indirect references.

TIP

If time is of the essence, and you're confident the candidate isn't secretly incompetent or a master criminal in disguise, it's technically okay to deliver your initial offer to her. But don't finalize the deal until the reference check is complete.

Direct references are the people your candidate has submitted as references. These usually include her manager, peers, subordinates, or perhaps even clients. Indirect references are people you've identified who may be able to provide an unbiased assessment of the candidate — say, sources in the candidate's industry or contacts at firms that compete with the candidate's company. You should also conduct a criminal background check — you can outsource this — to make sure the candidate isn't hiding any skeletons in her closet.

TIP

Checking references is covered in more detail in Chapter 15.

Sound Off: Making an Offer

In this phase, you close the deal by extending an offer (contingent on references). This isn't a verbal thing; it's an actual on-paper offer letter.

Don't be surprised if, after you float this offer by him, the candidate wants to negotiate. Odds are, he'll ask for a few changes. Maybe these changes pertain to his compensation. Maybe they have to do with the role and responsibilities. Or maybe they relate to his personal situation — for example, he needs you to help his spouse find a job or assist him in finding accommodations for an aging parent. Whatever the changes, be ready to deal. Be prepared, too, to deal with a counteroffer. If this person is as great as you think he is, odds are, his current company feels the same way and will do everything in its power to retain him.

Eventually, you'll get everything hashed out. (We hope.) When you do, it's time to extend your final offer, and afterward, the employment agreement, and for your new hire to sign them both.

TIP

You can read more on closing the deal in Chapter 16.

All Aboard: Onboarding the New Hire

You're *so close* to the finish line now. There's just one thing left to do: Onboard the new hire.

No, it's not the recruiter's job to train the executive in her new role. But it is the recruiter's job to ensure the company is happy with its new hire (and vice versa). That means scheduling touch points with the new hire on her first day, first week, first month, and every month thereafter for a full year. It also means conducting quarterly calls or meetings with the search chair to discuss the role, responsibilities, and fit from his perspective. You'll conduct these quarterly conversations for at least one year. (We do them for two years.)

TIP

A PROCESS CHEAT SHEET

An executive recruiting project has a thousand moving pieces — and that means things don't always proceed as planned. Trust us: You'll need to expect the unexpected. It happens all the time. To free yourself up to tackle these surprises, it's smart to maintain a checklist to keep track of the parts of the project you *do* expect. You can find an example at www.executiverecruitingfordummies.com/downloads. (Note that this example also includes coverage of developing an action plan and assembling your team, covered in Chapter 5 and Chapter 6, respectively.)

TIP

If you go the meeting route with the search chair, hold the first one off-site (and maybe subsequent ones, too). This is to ensure privacy in case you need to discuss sensitive issues. It's also so you can focus on the conversation without being interrupted by office staff.

TIP

Read more about on onboarding in Chapter 16.

Get Your Kicks: Hosting a Kickoff Meeting

To parcel out all the pieces of your hiring project, it helps to host a kickoff meeting with everyone involved — the hiring manager, search chair, search committee, and staff. This meeting will help you to align your people, processes, and project from the very start.

TIP

If people join in by teleconference, mute their line so they can't speak and you don't hear what may be going on in the background.

Start the meeting by introducing yourself. Then stick to a strict agenda. This will allow for a productive and professional meeting for everyone involved. Discuss the following topics, in order:

>> **Executive summary (3 minutes):** The executive summary is a high-level overview of the problem faced by the client, the proposed solution to the problem, and the plan for implementing that solution. Essentially, it answers these three questions:

- Why are we recruiting this executive?

- What's the desired end result?

- How does this executive contribute to meeting the organization's business plan?

>> **The goal of the search (2 minutes):** During this part of the kickoff meeting, offer a detailed description of the goal of the search. This will help to manage everyone's expectations for the project.

>> **The project's scope and deliverables (5 minutes):** This is where you discuss exactly what the project covers, and how what is covered will be delivered. This is important because a big part of a successful kickoff meeting is managing client expectations (and the expectations of everyone else involved).

>> **Project members and their roles (5 minutes):** Who's doing what? That's what you talk about here. Lay out each part of the process, the person in

charge, and her goals. If the project work involves collaboration, you should also mention what will be needed from the client for each part of the process.

TIP

If you, the recruiter, are part of a team, have each person on that team participate in the meeting. That way, everyone will gain a complete understanding of the client's expectations. Plus, if the client has any questions, having each member of your team present will increase your chances of providing the answers you seek.

>> **Key performance metrics and success factors (3 minutes):** How will you assess the various people involved in the project? We're not just talking about the recruitment staff — we're also taking about the hiring manager, search committee, and search chair. Be as specific as possible here, drawing from any meetings you've already had with the hiring manager and what's detailed in the service-level agreement (SLA).

>> **Communication plans (5 minutes):** When time is of the essence, as it is in an executive search, communication is key. During this part of the meeting, share your communication plans — including why communication is important and who will be leading communication efforts.

List all the meetings that will be conducted throughout the project life cycle, including:

- Weekly status meetings

- Project plan status updates with search chair

- Search committee updates

- Task and activity planning sessions

Mention what collaboration and communication tools will be used and how the participants can receive training on them if need be.

Finally, explain the timeline for receiving feedback from the client, as outlined in the SLA. While you're at it, explain why this feedback is so important — first and foremost because you need it so you can provide updates to candidates in a timely manner.

At the start of the meeting, inform everyone that you've allotted time for questions at the end. Ask that they hold all questions until that time — and stick to that. Also, let them know how to reach you if they have further questions after the call or later down the line.

To be mindful of everyone's time, limit the meeting to no more than 30 minutes.

REMEMBER

This is your meeting. You should be the only one speaking until the very end, when you take questions. You need to show people that you're in charge from the get-go and that you mean to run this project with tight reins.

Here Comes Trouble: Troubleshooting Your Hiring Project

No matter how carefully you approach them, your hiring efforts may still go off the rails. Fear not. This section identifies common problems, possible causes, and suggested solutions.

When your search hasn't yielded enough qualified candidates

Often, you'll hear the hiring authority complain that she hasn't seen enough quality candidates. If the person in charge of the search is an internal recruiter or works in HR, there are several possible causes and solutions to this problem:

>> **Online job postings aren't well targeted.** Try using a job-posting service that specifically caters to the type of position you're trying to fill. LinkedIn is a good choice. So is ExecuNet, which caters to executives only. Or use a search engine to find relevant associations that post jobs on their websites. (Search for the name of the function or industry and the word *association.*) Some sites even post jobs for free.

>> **The recruiter depends too heavily on Internet job postings, job fairs, and internal referrals.** Launch a referral program (or improve your existing one) for employees who talk up your company to their friends, family members, colleagues, and other contacts.

Also, use resources like LinkedIn to research potential candidates. Then contact them using the site's InMail service. Or, cold-call them. (If you go that route, it's not a bad idea to contract with a skilled cold caller.)

>> **The recruiter relies too heavily on the company's applicant tracking system (ATS).** There are two problems with applicant tracking systems:

- Applicants — even really good ones — rarely know what keywords to use when they post their résumés.

- Most — and when we say "most," we mean "nearly all" — résumés you receive through an ATS for a particular position will be wildly off-target.

Identifying qualified candidates using an ATS is a little like finding your silver Toyota Corolla in an airport parking lot. It's not easy, and could take a while. If you don't have the time and resources to do it in house, consider contracting that function out on an as-needed basis.

>> **There's a disconnect between the hiring authority and the internal recruiter.** This one's easy: The hiring authority and recruiter simply must

make time early in the process to identify the exact needs required for the new hire.

>> **The internal recruiter is buried under other work.** Sadly, many HR departments must do more and more with less and less. If that's the situation here, then your only real option is to contract with an external recruiter — either a contingency recruiter or a retained recruiter — to complete the search. This person can be hired to work on site or off, and if you keep him busy, the rate will be quite reasonable.

>> **The job postings are boring — more like a to-do list than a description of an exciting job opportunity.** Conduct an Internet search for "boring job postings." We promise, you'll find ample suggestions for writing attention-grabbing job postings! To tide you over, we'll just say to avoid generating the typical cattle-call ads that agencies use to cull résumés. You know the ones — they're boring, and provide no detail whatsoever. (For an example of a good ad as well as a bad one, see Chapter 10.)

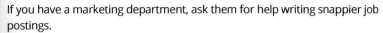
If you have a marketing department, ask them for help writing snappier job postings.

>> **There just aren't many quality candidates in the area.** If the position has a base below $150,000, and efforts to fill it using internal recruiters have proved fruitless, there are contingency recruiters who will gladly try to help you. When you go that route, be sure to ask whether they're bound by a "hands-off" list. If so, it may scuttle your ability to attract top passive candidates.

What if you're working with a contingency recruiter? Here are a few possible causes and suggested solutions for a lack of qualified candidates:

>> **The contingency recruiter doesn't have access to the hiring authority, so she has to work from secondhand information.** The hiring manager needs to meet directly with the contingency recruiter and HR to review the requirements. Be sure to allow enough time for the contingency recruiter to ask as many questions as necessary.

>> **HR isn't returning the contingency recruiter's calls.** This is a common grievance — one that often results in the contingency recruiter moving on to some other assignment with a more responsive client. The best way to address this is for the hiring authority to ask both HR and the contingency recruiter for a regular status report. This will reveal whether these two parties truly are working together.

>> **The hiring authority isn't not returning the contingency recruiter's calls because he has no time to provide updates, set up interviews, debrief after interviews, and so on.** If the hiring authority has no time to connect with the contingency recruiter during normal business hours, he can call the

recruiter in the evening or during the weekend. Almost all contingency recruiters will accept calls during these off hours.

>> **The contingency recruiter is bound by a hands-off list.** Sometimes, whoever contracts the contingency recruiter fails to ask if she's bound by a hands-off list. If she is, employees of any organization on that list are off-limits. In that case, you may need to contract with one or two more contingency search firms. Just be sure to verify that they *aren't* bound by such a list!

>> **The contingency recruiter accepted too low a fee.** If you're paying the contingency recruiter less than some other client is, you can reasonably assume he'll prioritize the needs of that other client over yours. With the exception of high-volume recruiting assignments, contingency recruiting rates are around 20 percent to 25 percent. This normally includes a guarantee period of between 30 to 90 days or even up to one year. If you're paying less than this, you're not your recruiter's priority — and you shouldn't be.

>> **There just aren't many quality candidates in the area.** If a general contingency recruiter comes up short, find one who specializes in recruiting the function in question and has successfully recruited candidates and relocated them to your area. Or, opt for a retained recruiter.

If you're working with a retained recruiter, there are a couple explanations for a dearth of qualified candidates:

>> **There's a disconnect between the hiring authority and the retained recruiter.** You fix this the same way you fix a disconnect between the hiring authority and an internal recruiter: by making time early on for the retained recruiter and hiring authority to meet to identify the exact needs required for the new hire.

>> **The retained recruiter is bound by a hands-off list.** Like contingency recruiters, some retained recruiters are bound by hands-off lists. If the person who secured the retained recruiter failed to inquire about this, and the recruiter *is* bound by such a list, then you may find yourself unable to recruit top talent. If you find yourself in this predicament, consult with your legal team to negotiate your way out of the contract and select a new search firm. (Again, be sure to verify that the new firm *isn't* bound by such a list!)

Finally, regardless of who's conducting the search — HR, an internal recruiter, a contingency recruiter, or a retained recruiter — a lack of acceptable candidates may be due to multiple hiring authorities being involved in the project, each with a different idea about the ideal candidate. If this is the situation you're in, don't proceed with the search until all hiring authorities reach consensus regarding the candidate's must-haves.

When your hiring process takes too long

If your hiring process takes too long, odds are your top candidate will no longer be available by the time you're ready to make an offer — which is bad. Whether HR, an internal recruiter, a contingency recruiter, or a retained recruiter is running the show, reasons for this problem (and suggested solutions) may include the following:

>> **Top talent isn't inclined to wait months for an offer.** Streamline your interview process to make it more efficient and less time-consuming. Ask yourself which steps are absolutely necessary and which aren't.

>> **Too many people are involved in the hiring process.** Keep your search committee small. Involve only those people who absolutely must be part of the hiring process.

>> **Background checks take too long.** Unless you're conducting some Jason Bourne–style background check, like for the FBI or CIA, it should take no longer than a few days (or even a few hours). If background checks consistently take longer, your vendor may be at fault. In that case, find a new vendor. If the fault lies with your HR department, fix the problem behind the holdup. Regardless of the cause for the delay, don't leave the candidate hanging. Inform him of the delay.

If you've contracted with an external recruiter — contingency or retained — the problem may simply be a lack of communication. If the hiring authority or HR fails to provide the external recruiter with status updates in a timely manner, candidates who are still in play may lose interest due to a lack of communication. In other words, by the time these candidates *do* hear from you, they've checked out. To fix this, make sure the hiring authority or HR updates the external recruiter on at least a weekly basis. (It may work best to ask the recruiter to start this exchange each week. That way, it won't fall through the cracks.) Then have the recruiter pass those updates along to any candidates under consideration.

When good candidates drop out after the first interview

No matter who's doing the hiring — someone from inside the company or an external recruiter — there are two main reasons a good candidate might drop out after just her first interview:

>> **The candidate was treated poorly during the interview.** Maybe she was kept waiting. Maybe someone treated her rudely. Whatever the reason, to prevent this problem in the future, treat *all* candidates as you would an important client.

>> **Someone asked illegal interview questions.** If the candidate claims she was asked an illegal question, the company's most senior HR executive must work through the chain of command to identify who asked the question and ensure it doesn't happen again. What if the guilty party is a super-senior executive? In that case, the HR executive should consult with the company's legal counsel. Lawyers are paid to advise top executives on dangerous hiring practices.

When good candidates refuse the offer

It's your worst nightmare made real: You step your top candidate through countless interviews over a period of several weeks or even months, and at the end of the process you make him an offer. And then? *He turns you down.* Here are a few reasons why:

>> **You low-balled him.** Some companies think they can hire A players for less than their true market value. Those companies are wrong. If you have the funds, offer your top candidate what he's *really* worth. If you don't have the funds, see if you can sweeten the deal with some perks — a flexible schedule, work-from-home opportunities, or what have you. If that doesn't do the trick, you may have to accept that you can't land an A player and start scouting the B and C teams.

>> **He accepted a counteroffer from his current employer.** There are lots of ways to prevent candidates from accepting a counteroffer — but the best one is to ask the candidate throughout the interview process whether he'd be open to accepting a counteroffer from his current employer, and if so, what he would take. Hopefully the answer will be no, but if it's yes, you can craft your offer accordingly. (For more on handling counteroffers, see Chapter 16.)

If you search online for "prevent candidates from accepting a counteroffer," you'll get more than a million hits. Our advice? If you're an internal recruiter, search that phrase and see what comes up. Or hire an external recruiter who already knows how to handle counteroffers and put her in charge.

>> **You didn't "sell" the opportunity.** The hiring process is a two-way street. It's not just about the candidate selling you on him; it's about you selling him on you. The best "salesperson" in this scenario is the hiring authority. Either way, that person should share with the candidate what excites her about the company, why it's rewarding to work there, and what's in it for people who excel.

Chapter **8**

Don't Be a Tool: Exploring the Tools of the Trade

R iddle us this: How do executive recruiters continue to enjoy such success in the face of near constant attempts to use technology to commoditize them, the way technology has commoditized stock brokers, travel agents, and countless other professionals?

We have two explanations. The first is *kaizen.* Japanese for "change for better," *kaizen* is a Japanese business philosophy that centers on continuous improvement. During our careers as executive recruiters, we've continuously worked to improve. We recognize what works and do more of it, and we recognize what *doesn't* work and stop doing it. As we like to say, "If something works, adopt it; if not, a-drop it."

The second explanation is one we've borrowed from an Italian economist named Vilfredo Pareto (1848–1923). Pareto observed that 20 percent of the Italian people owned 80 percent of the country's wealth. But what he found even more fascinating than this discovery — called the *Pareto principle* or, more commonly, the *80-20 rule* — was that it seemed to apply to more than just wealth. Indeed, for a great many events, roughly 80 percent of the effects come from 20 percent of the causes. Think about it: Twenty percent of any sales force produces 80 percent of sales. Twenty percent of customers cause 80 percent of problems. Twenty percent of your carpeting gets 80 percent of your foot traffic.

The same is true of executive recruiting. Twenty percent of what you do in executive recruiting causes 80 percent of the results. If you want to recruit the best people faster, you have to focus like a laser beam on that key 20 percent of actions. That's what we do, and it explains why we haven't gone the way of the gas station attendant who filled you up, washed your windshield, and checked your tires before sending you on your way.

In this chapter, we fill you in on tools you can use to get the most out of your efforts.

Daily Digest: Our Everyday Tools

For us, there are some tools we use just once in a while. But there are some tools we use every day. Some are websites geared toward connecting with professionals. Others are project management tools. Some are for performing assessments. And some are to facilitate communication.

Tools for connecting with professionals

When it comes to connecting with professionals, we lean heavily on three popular tools:

>> **ZoomInfo:** ZoomInfo (www.zoominfo.com) is a cloud-based summarization search engine. Not a day goes by that we don't use this tool to "zoom in" on senior executives, managers, and high-end individual contributors who may not be listed elsewhere, including on social networking sites. (As of September 2016, David has logged more than 4,200 sessions on the site!) ZoomInfo uses a summarization engine to track summaries of more than 140 million people from 12 million companies. These summaries include work history, education, and other key info, all compiled from multiple sources across the web. It's no surprise that ZoomInfo is a staple in the toolbox of most direct marketers — and what is recruiting if not direct marketing?

TIP

For tips and tricks on using ZoomInfo, watch the "Recruit Like a Shark" webinar, delivered by David along with ZoomInfo's Will Frattini. It's available here: https://youtu.be/A_EqTo-ntUk.

>> **LinkedIn:** Unless you've been living under a rock, you've probably heard of LinkedIn (www.linkedin.com). Originally designed as a social network for business professionals, the site has morphed into the largest online recruitment resource in the world. As the leading network for business professionals, it has become a vast repository of information about passive candidates.

Any executive on LinkedIn can be found on ZoomInfo, but the opposite is *not* true. For this reason, we always lead with ZoomInfo. LinkedIn does, however, have tools that are specifically built for recruiting active job hunters and researching passive job hunters. You learn more about these tools in Chapter 12.

>> **ExecuNet:** ExecuNet (www.execunet.com) is a little like LinkedIn, in that it's a professional networking site. But it's different from LinkedIn in that it's a closed, private network. That is, to be allowed on the network, you must meet a threshold of experience and tenure. Once accepted, most members stick around even after they find a job because of the camaraderie and because they know it's a good place to start recruiting for their own teams. David has used ExecuNet since the late 1980s.

Project-management tools

An executive search is a complicated project. To stay on top of things, we use both of the following tools:

>> **OpusPro:** OpusPro (www.opuspro.co), which is cloud-based workflow management software that works how you work. That's because it was built by a former executive recruiter specifically for executive recruiting. When you use OpusPro, everyone involved in the project — including the client, if you so desire — will know at a glance what he needs to do and when he needs to do it. Trust us: OpusPro will save you a ton of time managing people and projects!

>> **Invenias:** We use Invenias (www.invenias.com), a SaaS-based applicant-tracking program, in conjunction with OpusPro. That is, OpusPro is the frame-work, and Invenias is the candidate management tool. Using Invenias, you can direct-source ZoomInfo, LinkedIn, Facebook, Twitter, BoardEx, and the other services you subscribe to and create both your short list and your long list. It's also possible to track your activities on projects, parse and organize résumés and profiles, and create detailed reports for clients. You can use Invenias with Outlook, online, or through apps built for your smartphone or tablet.

Assessment tools

An important step in any executive search is assessing the candidate's personality for the purposes of establishing fit. To achieve this, we use two main tools:

>> **Great People Inside:** We use Great People Inside (www.greatpeopleinside.com), a cloud-based assessment platform, on every project to assess appli-cants before a formal interview. It offers numerous predefined assessment

and survey tools, which you can use as is. In addition, you can use it to build an assessment that fits your needs to a T. That's where the tool really excels!

>> **Bar-On EQ-i:** David has used the Bar-On EQ-i Leadership Report from Multi-Health Services (MHS) for more than a decade. This report examines EQ-i results as they relate to leadership skills. You can use the report for the general assessment of leadership strengths and weaknesses to assist in leadership selection, placement, and development decisions. It applies to most leadership functions, at the executive, management, or operational levels. To learn more, visit www.mhs.com/product.aspx?gr=io&prod=eqi&id=resources.

Communication tools

Obviously, communication is critical during any executive search. But not just any communication — *confidential* communication. For that, we stick with the following:

>> **WhatsApp:** Instead of communicating using regular text messages, which can be intercepted, we use WhatsApp (www.whatsapp.com). A fully secure texting service, WhatsApp enables you to keep communications private and confidential. That's no easy feat when you're recruiting a top executive! Most have executive assistants who intercept and answer their corporate — and sometimes even their private — emails. Corporate emails can also be intercepted and read by corporate IT departments.

REMEMBER

When we're courting and recruiting an executive, we take no chances. As soon as we make initial contact and establish trust, we urge them to switch to WhatsApp to communicate with us. (And it's great for international travel, too.)

>> **Skype:** Skype (www.skype.com) allows users to communicate via voice (using a microphone), video (using a webcam), or instant message (IM). If you need to interview a candidate who is located elsewhere, Skype is an excellent tool. Skype-to-Skype calls are free. Or you can use Skype to place calls to landline phones or to mobile phones (via a traditional telephone network) for a fee.

>> **Starbucks:** "Is there a Starbucks nearby where you'd be comfortable meeting me?" We swear, we ask that question dozens of times every week. Why Starbucks? It's convenient and reliable, and people trust it. The Starbucks app (www.starbucks.ca/coffeehouse/mobile-apps) makes it easy to find nearby locations and even order drinks ahead of time. That way, you don't have to waste time standing in line — you can focus all your attention on the candidate.

Recruitment Rock Stars: Following Top Thought Leaders

Tons of people claim to be experts in executive recruiting — but of course they're not. Really, there are only a few worth following (apart from us, obviously). Here, we've collected a list of top people:

>> **Peter Clayton:** Peter is the award-winning founder, producer, and host of *Total Picture Radio* (www.totalpictureradio.com), the first podcast focused on HR, recruiting, leadership, innovation, and career management. Clayton also covers important conferences and events in HR, recruiting, leadership, and innovation, and serves on the Awareness and Branding Committee for the Candidate Experience (CandE) Awards Council.

>> **Jim Durbin:** Think of Jim Durbin as the recruiting industry's Seth Godin. Nicknamed the "social media headhunter," his core competency is working with digital natives in marketing and technology. He understands how employees react to change, giving him the ability to strategize and execute sound hiring decisions across multiple industries. For more on Jim Durbin, visit www.socialmediaheadhunter.com.

>> **Michael Keleman and Jerry Albright:** Michael and Jerry co-host *The Recruiting Animal* (www.blogtalkradio.com/animal), a weekly podcast on recruiting. This podcast is not for the faint of heart. These guys aren't afraid to call bull during their discussion, and they tend to raise a ruckus when guests try to duck a question. But they're spot on, and the after-show discussion — often involving hundreds of recruiters around the world — is chock-full of insight.

>> **Peter Leffkowitz:** If you're looking to transform a corporate talent acquisition division into a highly productive internal SWAT team of recruiters, then Peter is your guy. Since 1986, he has developed and guided the largest training and consulting company in the staffing industry: Morgan Consulting Group. To find out how to receive training from Peter, visit www.morgancg.com.

>> **Janette Levey Frisch:** A labor lawyer, Janette pens an informative blog called The EmpLAWyerologist (www.theemplawyerologist.com) to help you stay ahead of changes to employment law — and out of court. She's not just an expert on the law when it comes to recruiting, however. Her candid advice can significantly minimize your chances of facing lawsuits, government audits, and worker disputes.

>> **Gary Stauble:** Seasoned executive recruiters frequently consult with Gary to increase their production. He is a time management and productivity strategist for entrepreneurs and recruiting professionals "who want to work smart

and live large." His company, The Recruiting Lab (www.therecruitinglab.com), provides training, tools, and support to help solo recruiters create a reliable foundation for their business.

>> **John Sumser:** A true industry insider and thought leader, John hosts a popular podcast, HR Tech Weekly, accessible from HR Examiner (www.hrexaminer.com). For John, people are the story — the leaders who transform HR into a thriving business contributor. His scope of observation spans technology and behavior, and his 25 years in the space is unrivaled.

>> **Rayanne Thorn:** A branding and marketing executive in the HR and recruiting technology space, Rayanne Thorn hosts HR Latte (www.blogtalkradio.com/hrlatte), a quick-hit podcast centered on business, HR, and recruiting. Thorn interviews industry innovators and experts who take recruiting and HR to the next level, covering such diverse topics as new tech, data and analytics, mobile and social comms, unconscious bias, bullying in the workplace, leadership, and so much more. For more on Rayanne, visit www.intrepid.media/author/rayanne.

Even More Recruiter Tools

So far, we've hooked you up with the tools and resources we use the most. But these are just the tip of the iceberg. In this section, we list a dizzying number of additional resources to help you with your executive search.

Leading social networks

Due to the high level and sensitive nature of our work, we tend not to advertise job openings on social media. That's not to say, however, that we don't use social media to garner leads, communicate with candidates for our current search, and scout leads for future ones. And we're not alone. According to iCIMS, an applicant tracking software company, three-fourths of the companies surveyed use social media to find talent — and that number is only going to grow.

REMEMBER

Whether you're a corporate recruiter or a third-party provider, the sooner you jump on the social media recruiting bandwagon, the sooner you'll be able find the talent you're looking for — now and in the future.

General purpose social media sites

The following general purpose social media sites can be used in your executive search:

TIP

>> **BlackPlanet:** BlackPlanet (www.blackplanet.com), the largest social network targeted at African Americans, features job-related groups and forums. It also includes a job-posting section that works in conjunction with Monster. These tools, along with the site's searchable member-profile section, can be a big help if you're recruiting for a company that has made diversity hiring a top priority.

>> **Classmates:** Classmates (www.classmates.com) enables users to connect with high-school friends. This cohort might prove useful for filling job postings.

Alumni networks — be they for high schools, colleges or universities, or places of employment — are another good source for prospects.

>> **Facebook:** Why would you *not* put Facebook (www.facebook.com) in your recruiting arsenal? With more than 1.7 billion members, it's hands-down *the* largest social network on Earth. Surprisingly, although a multitude of recruiters look for candidates primarily on LinkedIn, the candidates they so actively seek are on Facebook — as evidenced by the results of the 2016 Job Seeker Nation Study, which reports that 67 percent of social media job seekers use that site.

>> **GitHub:** If you're looking to hire skilled software developers and engineers — always in demand — then check out GitHub (www.github.com). Its membership boasts up-and-coming as well as established talent in these areas.

>> **Google+:** Google's social community, Google+ (http://plus.google.com), boasts more than 300 million members. It offers instant messaging as well as a popular videoconferencing feature called Hangouts. Oddly, compared to platforms like LinkedIn, Twitter, and Facebook, Google+ is sometimes viewed as the redheaded stepchild of the social media world. But the truth is, Google+ attracts a lot of tech-savvy types. That, plus the fact that it's associated with Google — which not only boasts the world's largest search engine but also unmatched email and blogging tools — makes Google+ fertile hunting grounds.

>> **LiveJournal:** On LiveJournal (www.livejournal.com), users can maintain blogs, journals, or diaries. Several prominent public figures use this service, especially in Russia, where it partners with an online newspaper. It's offered in 32 languages.

>> **Meetup:** Meetup (www.meetup.com) connects people with similar interests — personal or professional. It also facilitates meetings offline. In terms of recruiting, it can be helpful. For example, you might search for meetups that center around a particular industry topic in a specific geographic area, and then visit the page for that meetup to see who plans to attend. You can then use sites like LinkedIn to research those attendees, essentially prescreening potential prospects. Or use Meetup to organize and host your own recruiting events.

>> **Plurk:** Plurk (www.plurk.com) is a social networking and micro-blogging service that enables users to post links or short messages (up to 210 text characters). Most of Plurk's traffic comes from Taiwan.

>> **Reddit:** Members of Reddit (www.reddit.com) — there are more than 100 million in all — submit content. Then other members vote to rank these submissions. Content is organized by areas of interest, called *subreddits*. Reddit is a little bit more complex than, say, Facebook or Twitter. But with a little practice, it can be well worth your time. That's because Reddit offers a wealth of talent. It has job boards, where you can post listings in almost every city in the United States. Reddit also provides a forum for job seekers to post their résumés in order to obtain feedback. If a job seeker who posts a résumé appears to have the qualifications you're looking for, simply send her a private message to request more information and start a dialogue about the job you're recruiting for.

>> **StumbleUpon:** StumbleUpon (www.stumbleupon.com) StumbleUpon is a social network that enables users to uncover personalized content. It's a way for people to discover and recommend content to others. You can even rate the content. On StumbleUpon, you'll find experts in everything from aquiculture to zoology.

>> **Twitter:** Twitter (www.twitter.com) is a little like Facebook. Users post things to share them with others. The difference: Twitter posts, called *tweets,* are limited to 140 characters, and anyone can see them (unless the user's account is private). Twitter users can also send private messages, called direct messages (DMs) to other users on the site. As far as recruiting goes, you can use hashtags and tweet chats to connect with a huge pool of candidates. An estimated 55 percent of Twitter users follow companies on this site, 34 percent have applied to tweeted job postings, and 33 percent use Twitter to communicate with companies and recruiters.

>> **Tumblr:** Tumblr (www.tumblr.com) is a micro-blogging social network with more than 200 million members. Tumblr users post blogs that others can follow, making it a good way to announce new products or promotions.

>> **YouTube:** YouTube (www.youtube.com) is a social network that enables users to upload, view, and share videos. Available worldwide, it's one of the most accessed sites on the web. People don't just post videos on YouTube for entertainment purposes, however. Companies, universities, and the military have successfully used YouTube as a recruitment tool. You can follow their lead and create a YouTube channel of your own. Videos can be far more engaging than text, enabling you to attract the attention of top candidates who may not have given your opportunity a second glance otherwise.

Professional networks

Although LinkedIn is by far the largest professional network, it's hardly the only one out there. Here are a few others:

>> **Care2:** Care2 (www.care2.com) connects activists from around the world with individuals, organizations, and businesses making an impact.

>> **Ryze:** Professionals use Ryze (www.ryze.com) to expand their business networks by connecting with industry professionals and like-minded individuals. They can also share practical advice, tips, and resources.

>> **Solaborate:** A portmanteau of *social* and *collaborate*, Solaborate (www.solaborate.com) enables technology professionals and companies to connect, collaborate, discover opportunities, and create an ecosystem around products and services.

>> **Viadeo:** Viadeo (www.viadeo.com) is a social network for business people, mostly in Europe. It's offered in seven languages and has more than 50 million members.

Social communication tools

WhatsApp and Skype aren't the only communication tools out there. Here are a few others:

>> **LINE:** LINE (www.line.me) is a social network that enables its 200 million active users to exchange texts, images, audio files, and videos. Although it's available worldwide, its largest user base is in Japan.

>> **Telegram:** Telegram (www.telegramchat.com) is an instant messaging social network focused on privacy and multiplatform availability. The site, which has more than 50 million active users, is available in eight languages. People use the site to send encrypted and self-destructing messages with photos and videos.

- **Viber:** Using Viber (www.viber.com), you can make phone calls or send text messages to other Viber users free of charge. You can also call or text non-Viber users, although that costs money.

- **WeChat:** WeChat (www.wechat.com) is a mobile app that enables you to connect with other members — half a billion in all — by voice or text.

Recruiter associations

No matter what your chosen field, you have to keep up with news and trends. There are lots of ways to do this — networking, reading trade and professional journals, and so on. But joining a professional association is a great way to draw on lots of resources at once. We list several here:

- **Alliance of Medical Recruiters (AMR):** www.medrecruitersalliance.com

- **Association of Executive Search and Leadership Consultants (AESC):** www.aesc.org

- **American Staffing Association (ASA):** www.americanstaffing.net

- **Colorado Talent Recruitment Network (CTRN):** www.ctrn.org

- **Electronic Recruiters Exchange (ERE):** www.eremedia.com/ere

- **Illinois Search & Staffing Association (ISSA):** www.issaworks.com

- **Massachusetts Association of Personnel Services (MAPS):** www.mapsweb.org

- **Missouri & Kansas Search and Staffing Association (MKSSA):** www.mkssa.com

- **National Association of Executive Recruiters (NAER):** www.naer.org

- **National Association of Legal Search Consultants (NALSC):** www.nalsc.org

- **National Association of Personnel Services (NAPS):** www.naps360.org

- **National Association of Physician Recruiters (NAPR):** www.napr.org

- **National Insurance Recruiters Association (NIRA):** www.insurancerecruiters.com

- **New Jersey Staffing Alliance (NJSA):** www.njsa.com

- **Northwest Recruiters Association (NWRA):** http://nwrecruit.wildapricot.org

- **Ohio Staffing & Search Association (OSSA):** www.ohiostaffing.net

>> **RecruitersCafe:** www.recruiterscafe.com

>> **Recruiters Connection:** www.recruitersconnection.com

>> **Recruiters Online Network (RON):** www.recruitersonline.com

>> **Society for Human Resource Management (SHRM):** www.shrm.org

>> **Top Echelon:** www.topechelon.com

Mobile recruiting apps

According to Glassdoor, as of 2014, nine out of every ten job seekers used mobile apps in their job searches. That means you need to use these apps, too. Here are a few to get you started:

>> **CareerBuilder for Employers:** With this iPhone app, you can access candidates anywhere, any time through your existing CareerBuilder account. Get the app here: http://itunes.apple.com/us/app/careerbuilder-for-employers/id440693834.

>> **InstaJob:** This app, available for iPhone and Android devices, enables you to create appealing visual job ads right from your smartphone. Get the app here: www.careercloud.com/instajob.

>> **PeekYou:** Use this iPhone app to browse through social media links, photos galleries, web content, and more. Get the app here: http://itunes.apple.com/us/app/peekyou/id352084860.

>> **Search for People:** This iPhone app enables you to search for people in multiple social networks — including Facebook, Google+, and LinkedIn — all at once, with no registration or authentication required. Get the app here: http://itunes.apple.com/us/app/search-for-people/id532606286.

>> **SmartRecruiters:** The SmartRecruiters talent acquisition platform enables you to market, collaborate on, and manage your search. This mobile version of the tool allows you to do it on the go. Get the app here: www.smartrecruiters.com/recruiting-software/collaborative-hiring/mobile-hiring-app.

>> **Talent Xray:** This app, for both iPhone and Android devices, enables you to source candidates on LinkedIn, Twitter, and Google+ without limitations — and without logging in to those platforms. Get the app here: www.careercloud.com/talent-xray.

Miscellaneous recruiter resources

Not every recruiting resource fits into a neat category. We've gathered those here:

>> **Active Hire** (www.activehire.com/post-jobs): This is a free job-posting website.

>> **Aevy** (www.aevy.com): This tool enables you to search for, find, and get in touch with people. There is a free version, as well as a fee-based one.

>> **All Star Jobs** (www.allstarjobs.com): Employers, recruiters, and employment agencies can post jobs here. There's a free job-posting function, as well as a fee-based one.

>> **AngelList** (www.angel.co/recruiting): This free recruiting website specializes in finding talent for start-ups.

>> **BlueSteps** (www.bluesteps.com): This website, maintained by the Association of Executive Search and Leadership Consultants (AESC), offers career services for senior executives, providing them with continuous exposure to search firms that are members of the AESC.

>> **Boolean Black Belt Sourcing and Recruiting** (www.booleanblackbelt. com/free-sourcing-recruiting-tools-guides-resources): This site offers a treasure-trove of posts and how-to guides on a variety of sourcing and recruiting topics and technologies.

>> **Buffer** (www.buffer.com): Buffer is a social media management tool.

>> **Connectifier** (www.connectifier.com): This site maintains a database of more than 400 million candidates (and growing), which recruiters can leverage to locate exceptional job candidates. It also offers a web browser plug-in that appears whenever you view a profile on social media to display additional information such as email addresses.

>> **Email Hunter** (www.emailhunter.co): Use this tool to hunt down email addresses.

>> **Followerwonk** (www.moz.com/followerwonk/bio): This tool enables you to dig deeper into Twitter analytics — who your followers are, where they are located, where they tweet, and so on. You can also use this tool to find and connect with new influencers within your niche and access visual socializations to compare your social graph to others.

>> **FullContact for Gmail** (www.fullcontact.com/gmail): This free add-on for Google Chrome displays social profiles and job titles for the sender of each message in your Gmail inbox.

» **HubSpot** (www.hubspot.com): A free customer relationship management (CRM) tool. Simply enter a prospect's email address, and let HubSpot take over. Using HubSpot, you can design a more targeted marketing program to reach prospective clients.

» **Indeed** (www.indeed.com): This site is search engine for job listings and résumés worldwide.

» **LinkedIn: Cool (Free) Tools for Recruiting** (www.linkedin.com/groups/3104747/profile): This LinkedIn group for professional or in-house recruiters houses tools for Boolean searches, data mining tools, social media widgets, email address finders, phone number finders, resources for finding employer vacancies, resources for finding both active and passive candidates, and more.

» **MailTester** (www.mailtester.co): Want to make sure the email you have for a contact still works? Run it through this free email testing site.

» **Microsoft Outlook Social Connector** (http://support.office.com/en-us/article/Turn-on-the-Outlook-Social-Connector-255447e8-82cd-48e7-9b79-1dd8721a2907): This Microsoft Outlook feature aggregates business and personal updates from all your contacts across Outlook, Facebook, LinkedIn, and Windows Live in a centralized location.

» **Pluck** (www.pluckhq.com): It used to be that finding a needle in a haystack came down to which sourcer knew more than the others. Now, finding contact information for elusive professionals who might never appear in a résumé database is as easy as enlisting a few bots on Pluck.

» **Recruit'em** (www.recruitin.net): Recruiters employ this free and easy-to-use tool to find people on LinkedIn, Google+, and other sites.

» **Recruiting Tools** (www.recruitingtools.com): This website offers access to loads of free recruiting tools and articles.

» **Recruitment Geek LinkedIn X-ray Search Tool** (www.recruitmentgeek.com/tools/linkedin): Use this free search tool to search profiles on LinkedIn. Essentially, it conducts a Google search with the relevant Boolean operators built in.

» **ResumeGrabber** (www.egrabber.com/resumegrabber.html): This résumé-sourcing software includes search scripts developed by leading industry experts for sourcing résumés through Google, Yahoo!, Bing, and other search engines.

» **Salary Inspector** (http://chrome.google.com/webstore/detail/salary-inspector/ohdgikkchafapofonnddadalgedibpca): A Google Chrome extension, Salary Inspector enables you to view estimated salaries based on job title and location when you view LinkedIn profiles.

» **The Search Authority: Tools** (`http://thesearchauthority.weebly.com/tools.html`)**:** This page contains a list of useful search tools and resources.

» **Tip Sheet: Boolean Search Stings** (`www.mcgill.ca/caps/files/caps/gcs2014_linkedinbooleansearchtips.pdf`)**:** This document lists several handy tips for conducting Boolean searches on LinkedIn.

» **TweetDeck** (`http://tweetdeck.twitter.com`)**:** TweetDeck displays your Twitter stream, notifications, messages, and activity feed in column form, all on one screen, making it easy to tweet like a pro.

» **ZipRecruiter** (`www.ziprecruiter.com`)**:** This online service enables employers to post open positions to more than 50 job boards in one stroke, and allows employees to search its large database of job postings.

3
Doing the Pre-Search Prep Work

Chapter **9**

Resign of the Times: Reacting to a Resignation

t's Monday morning. You're two sips into your tall Americano, recalling the events of the preceding weekend with longing. You have, to quote *Office Space*, a mild "case of the Mondays."

One of your top executives walks into your office. You like this person. Really, she does such a great job. What would you do without her? You smile and greet her warmly. And then — *wham* — out of nowhere, she resigns. Suddenly, your mild case of the Mondays feels more like a terminal diagnosis.

The resignation of a trusted and valued executive can be incredibly disruptive. Fortunately, however, it's not a death sentence for your organization. There are steps you can take to maintain positive relations with the outgoing employee and to find her replacement in a timely manner. That's what this chapter is all about.

Lizard Warning: Getting Control of Your Lizard Brain

Given how serious the resignation of a key executive is, it's no surprise that the person who *receives* the resignation often experiences what can only be described as a fight-or-flight response. If this happens to you, don't feel bad — it happens to pretty much everyone in this situation.

The fight-or-flight response is helpful if you're facing a saber-toothed tiger. In that scenario, it's a *good* thing when your amygdala — the primitive part of your brain that's often referred to as your *lizard brain* — sets off a reaction that floods your cells with adrenaline, sharpens your sight, intensifies your awareness, increases your respiration rate, and decreases your perception of pain.

This primitive, automatic, in-born, lizard-brain response is less useful, however, if you're not actually in physical danger. In fact, when faced with the resignation of a top executive, the fight-or-flight response might just make things worse. That's because it could cause you to say or do something that will make it impossible to

>> **Understand why the person wants to leave.** This could help you prevent the departure of other key executives in the future. (**Hint:** It probably has to do with his manager. Most people don't quit companies; they quit bosses.)

>> **Maintain a strong relationship with the executive after he leaves.** This could come in handy in the future.

>> **Leave the door open for later.** If things don't work out at his new job, you may want to hire the executive back.

You must not give way to your lizard brain! Instead, you must quickly gain control of the situation. That means planning ahead to avoid any major missteps and make a counter-offer. We know, that's easier said than done. (In the immortal words of former world heavyweight champion Mike Tyson, "Everybody has a plan until they get punched in the mouth.") But do it you must.

What not to do

Before we get into what to do when a key player resigns, let's talk about what *not* to do:

>> **Don't hand the executive a box, march her to her office, demand that she empty her desk, and escort her to the parking lot.** You might think this is required for security reasons, but it's not. If the executive were going to steal something or sabotage the organization, you can bet she would've already done it.

>> **Don't tell her how disappointed you are in her for leaving.**

>> **Don't try to make her feel guilty about leaving.**

TIP

Your organization almost certainly has some sort of protocol for dealing with the resignation of a senior executive, including a succession plan. Prepare yourself for such an event by committing this protocol to memory *before* someone resigns.

Reprogramming the simulator

If you're a *Star Trek* fan, you may remember the Kobayashi Maru. This was a simulation-based training exercise for cadets at the fictional Starfleet Academy to gauge how they would respond when faced with a no-win situation. *Star Trek II: The Wrath of Khan* reveals that Captain James T. Kirk, played by the inestimable William Shatner, famously reprogrammed the simulator while he was a student at the academy to allow for a "win" scenario.

TIP

You may hear the phrase *Kobayashi Maru* used to describe a no-win situation or a situation in which finding a solution means redefining the problem (and perhaps testing one's character along the way).

Well, just like a Starfleet cadet, you may feel like you're facing a no-win situation all your own. "Do nothing," you're thinking, "and I lose a valuable employee. React poorly, and I not only lose a valuable employee, but I drive him into someone else's open arms." See? No-win. But in fact, there's a way to "reprogram the Kobayashi Maru," so to speak. That's by taking a third approach: asking the executive, "Is there anything I can do to change your mind?"

Most likely, the answer will be no. In that case, here's what you do:

1. **Stand up, shake his hand, and congratulate him.**

2. **Ask if he has thought about how to make the transition as smooth as possible.**

3. **Ask if he has someone in mind to replace him.**

4. **Invite him to sit down and tell you all about what he'll be doing in his next role.**

By respecting his decision, by not doing what he expected, you elevate yourself in his eyes and lay the groundwork for hiring him back later. In other words, you've reprogrammed the simulator to win.

Overriding your lizard brain to "reprogram the simulator" — in other words, remaining calm, rational, and friendly — offers a few key advantages:

>> The outgoing executive will retain positive feelings about you and your organization, which increases the chances he'll come back if he finds out the grass isn't so green at his new job.

TIP

This happens more often than you'd think. In fact, David's services have been secured several times to rehire former employees shortly after they've departed. You want your best employees to know you're *always* open to discussing your return.

>> The outgoing executive may have good ideas for ensuring a smooth transition and about who should replace him.

>> The executive could be able to provide you with intelligence that could help you prevent other executives from leaving.

>> You may be able to persuade the executive to stick around a little longer than the typical two weeks. This buys you time to consider your next move.

Next Steps: Key Decisions after a Resignation

When a key person resigns, it's time to make some key decisions, like the following:

>> Do you really need to replace the executive?

>> Can you use the succession plan to select a replacement?

>> What level of competency is required?

Do we really need a replacement?

First, decide whether you really need someone in the vacated role as it's currently structured. In assessing this, ask the following questions:

>> **Could you distribute the role's responsibilities to others on your senior staff?** For example, if your chief security officer decides to pursue a new opportunity elsewhere, could you split her responsibilities among your director of information security and chief information officer?

>> **Could you break the role into several pieces and distribute them among several directors who might not be ready to assume the larger role but would relish the learning opportunity?**

>> **Could the work be done by a more junior employee?**

REMEMBER

Just because an executive leaves the company does not mean you have to replace her right away — or ever.

If the answer to any of these questions is *yes*, you need not go to the trouble of an executive search. If the answer is *no*, you need to proceed.

Can you use the succession plan?

Your next step is to request a copy of the succession plan. This plan should outline who inside the organization is currently qualified (or nearly qualified) to assume the executive's role. If you have a succession plan, it covers the position in question, and it has earmarked an employee who is fully qualified and ready for placement, then promote that person.

WARNING

If your company consists of more than 20 people, you must have a succession plan in place. If you don't, you need one — pronto. Either hire someone to develop and update your succession plan on a semiannual basis or outsource the job to a qualified consultant.

DEVELOPING A LEADERSHIP PIPELINE

As part of a succession plan, smart companies maintain a leadership pipeline. As explained by Jack Zenger at *Forbes,* a "leadership pipeline is used to create a more systematic, visible system of identifying candidates for succession, combined with the processes for their development." Pipeline development is a crucial component of any successful succession plan, and gives you a big jump if you have to replace an outgoing executive.

Firms that must rely on external recruitment during a transition in leadership will find smaller and smaller pools of qualified, talented executives — and increased competition to hire those same executives. This puts these firms at risk. Developing a leadership pipeline offers an important safety net. Organizations that invest in developing a leadership pipeline are better positioned to thrive in the face of change.

The best of all possible worlds is to have a strong pool of internal talent, which you can benchmark against a strong pool of external candidates. This enables you to select the right person at the right time.

With talented leaders retiring at an ever-increasing rate, companies that don't prioritize succession planning will find themselves at a distinct competitive disadvantage!

What level of competency is required?

Finally, decide what level of competency you need for the job. Generally, you have three choices:

> >> **A rock star:** This is someone who will put the business on the map and help you crush your competitors.
>
> >> **A steady Eddie:** By this, we mean an experienced person who has not yet hit his prime.
>
> >> **A warm body:** This could be anyone with some modicum of related experience, but who isn't too pricey.

It may seem like we're down on the last two options, the steady Eddie and the warm body. Nothing could be further from the truth. Seriously, why pay extra for a rock star if you don't need one? Nevertheless, you do need to decide from the start whether you want the best of the best (a rock star) or the best of the rest.

Suppose you decide to go the rock-star route. To quote Jeff Boss, former Navy Seal and author of *Navigating Chaos: How to Find Certainty in Uncertain Situations,* "The challenge with rock stars isn't in identifying them — they stick out like a pair of you-know-whats on a bull. The problem falls in keeping them engaged, curious enough to continue their exemplary performance, and coaching others to rise to similar occasions." Salty language aside, we completely agree. But we would add a second difficulty associated with rock stars: hiring them in the first place.

Above and beyond the typical process outlined throughout this book, hiring a rock star requires:

> >> **Attention:** Pretty much everybody wants to hire rock stars — but the ones that actually *do?* They manage it because they put their senior people on the task. Courting a rock star can't fall to an internal recruiter or even your HR manager. Instead, a senior executive or retained recruiter should do the wooing.
>
> >> **Money:** We're not gonna lie — rock stars are expensive. That being said, money is *not* a factor beyond what they say they want or need. With rock stars, it's never just about money.
>
> >> **Clarity:** To land a rock star, you must be able to answer her "What's in it for me?" even more clearly than she can — and with complete sincerity, too.
>
> >> **Trust:** You must foster your relationship with a rock star, building his trust, well in advance of a sudden opening. He needs to know you — and know you have his best interests at heart.

TIP

For *real* rock stars — we're talking the Mick Jaggers, Patti Smiths, and Bonos of your industry — you don't have to wait for an opening or a resignation. You can create roles for rock stars based on the contributions you believe they can make.

ACQUI-HIRES AND LIFT-OUTS

What if you receive multiple resignations from the same team at once, or a resignation provides you with an opportunity to assemble a new team? In that case, you have two options:

- **Acqui-hire:** An acqui-hire is when a big company buys a smaller company — usually an early-stage start-up — not to take over that business, but rather for the express purpose of acquiring its employees. This strategy was extremely popular in Silicon Valley — Yahoo! was a particularly big proponent — but it has fallen out of favor in recent years due to spotty performance.

- **Lift-out:** In this scenario, you "lift out" a group or team at another organization in its entirety. This approach can be quite effective. Indeed, research shows that great performers who move with their team become successful in the new company more quickly than those who move alone or are assembled as part of a new group. That's because the team already works as a unit. They don't need to get acquainted or iron out group dynamics. In a lift-out that is well planned and well executed, you'll see a boost to your company's bottom line almost immediately. A lift-out is not for the faint of heart, however. It's one of the most aggressive moves you can make. Invariably, you'll want to contract this out to a professional.

Several years ago, a senior technology executive at one of David's clients jumped ship for a competitor, just as David's client was preparing to take his own company in a new direction. Rather than engaging in years of legal wrangling over the defection (which might have proved fruitless, given that the competitor was much larger than David's client), David's client took the opportunity to "lift out" his competitor's vice presidents of sales and marketing.

Of course, just as you can lift out a team from another company, another company can lift out a team from you. If that happens, quick action is required. You'll need to

- Map out a legal strategy for how to respond with clients, suppliers, and so on.

- Collect, preserve, and analyze evidence related to the lift-out.

- Develop a factual narrative.

- Differentiate legal issues from business issues.

(continued)

(continued)

Even better, prepare for the possibility of a lift-out by doing the following:

- Periodically reviewing the contractual obligations that have been placed on employees

- Diversifying risk by spreading responsibilities to multiple employees

- Establishing a contingency plan to deal with a lift-out

- Identifying and protecting trade secrets and confidential information

- Constantly monitoring employees who access confidential information to reduce the chances of a lift-out and limiting who can access client lists or IP assets

IN THIS CHAPTER

» **Identifying your client**

» **Writing the job order**

» **Detailing the job description**

» **Composing the position profile**

» **Writing job ads**

» **Collecting a confidential candidate brief**

» **Creating an interview guide**

Chapter **10**

Documentation Station: Generating the Necessary Documentation

Y ou're under the gun. You have to hire a key executive — and you have to do it *yesterday*. Naturally, it's tempting to grab the job description of the executive who just left and go, go, go!

Trust us: That's a bad move. In today's hyper-competitive world, conditions change fast. It's far better to start each search from scratch. In our combined 50 years of experience, every project that went smoothly from beginning to end, was quick and efficient, and resulted in the right hire started with one thing: a clear picture of exactly who we were looking for. When you understand exactly what type of person you need to hire from the outset, it ups the odds you'll know him when you see him. Failing to follow this advice may cause you to waste time, hire the wrong person, or worse, reject the right one.

REMEMBER

Successful organizations devote much more time to creating this clear picture of the position — and who best to put in it — than on executing the search.

To focus that picture, you must carefully and methodically think through the requirements of that open position and document these needs. That means taking the following steps (each of which requires, on average, two full days of work):

1. Writing the job order

2. Creating the job description

3. Crafting the position profile

4. Writing a confidential candidate brief

5. Developing the interview guide

In this chapter, you find out how to complete all these tasks to generate the necessary documentation. You also find out how to compose winning job ads. With this documentation in hand, you'll be able to convince your client to take your search seriously.

REMEMBER

Capturing the real need on paper (and, of course, getting agreement from the search chair and search committee) will help ensure you hire the right person — someone who will complement the executive team and remain successful in the job for years to come.

First Things First: Who Is Your Client?

Under most circumstances, your client is the ultimate hiring authority, best defined as the person the new hire will report to. For example, if the position you seek to fill is a VP position that will report to the president, the president is your client. If it's a CEO position, your client is the chairman of the board.

Before you embark on the search, you'll want to hammer out a few issues with your client:

>> **Turnaround:** If you send search-related materials to the client — résumés, memos, and so on — how quickly will he turn them around? If you can, push for same-day turnaround. Anything more than 24 hours won't fly. A great candidate is hard to find — and you don't want someone else to snap her up while you're waiting for your client to weigh in on her.

>> **Scheduling:** If you land a hot prospect, you'll need the client to interview that person. Find out ahead of time the best days and times to schedule interviews with the client.

>> **Speed:** Of particular interest here is how many interviews the client typically conducts before he's comfortable making a decision. You'll want to know upfront in case you need him to speed things up. (More on this in Chapter 14.)

>> **Process:** What is the client's go-to interviewing process? For example, does he interview first and then introduce the potential hire to his team, board, or peers? Or is it the other way around?

>> **Technology:** Find out whether your client is willing to use technological solutions, like Skype, to move the hiring process along. If you're hunting, say, a senior sales executive — a road warrior who is always on the move — this can be a real timesaver. Ditto if you intend to recruit out of state. When you don't have to worry about the logistics of interviewing in person, this type of technology enables you to broaden your search.

>> **Confidentiality:** Is the opening public knowledge? Or does it need to be held in strict confidence?

Also, ask the client what attracted *him* to the company. His answer will help you

>> Assess how effectively he'll be able to sell any leading candidates on the role.

>> Consider whether you want to emphasize that aspect of the firm in the job description and position profile (assuming, of course, that the thing that attracted the client is still a "thing").

TIP

Speaking of things, here's one more thing — and pay attention, because this thing is super important: Ask your client what the consequences would be if the position were to go unfilled. It seems like such an innocuous question, but it isn't. Asking this question enables you to gauge the client's sense of urgency. Perhaps more important, it reminds your client of the ramifications of failure — specifically, of *his* failure to do what's needed to help you hire the right person. The bottom line? Asking this question is a great way to ensure the client's cooperation and commitment to providing swift feedback and following through on any promises he makes. See the nearby sidebar, "The implication quadrant," for more on this key question.

THE IMPLICATION QUADRANT

We're not the ones who came up with the idea of asking this one key question. A recruiter named Scott Love is. Love is famous in recruiter circles for developing a little thing he calls the *implication quadrant.* The implication quadrant (shown below) helps you convey to your client the risk of leaving a problem unsolved, as well as the value of your working together to hire the right person. Love says that the implication quadrant helps you "get to the point where there is an emotional context between the opening and how it affects [the client] personally and emotionally." Love continues, "You are not selling to companies. You are selling to people, and people make buying decisions based on emotion." That's a sound observation from one of the best in the business!

	Positive	Negative
Professional	What good things will result in the office if you place your candidate?	What bad things will happen in the office if the position goes unfilled or if the wrong candidate is hired?
Personal	How will that affect your client personally?	How will that affect your client personally?

Illustration courtesy of Scott Love

Order Up: Writing the Job Order

A *job order* is a written record of an employer's need to fill a vacant position with a qualified worker. You write a job order at the outset of the search to clearly iden-tify what the position is and what type of person should fill it. It's an internal document, which you'll use to compose the job description and other recruiting materials.

The job order contains the following information:

>> General information about the job and company

>> What the position entails

>> Compensation information

>> Why the job is open

>> Desired educational background of the new hire

>> Desired professional experience of the new hire

>> Desired management style and personal characteristics of the new hire

>> The company's pattern of growth

>> How quickly the new hire should get up to speed

>> Keys to success in this position

Like we said, you should start each search from scratch — and that includes writing the job order. This may seem counterintuitive. Wouldn't it be faster to just adapt the old job order for that position? In a word, no. We've learned from hard experience that building each job order from the ground up is the quickest, most efficient, and most reliable method to find the right person to fill the position.

So, how do you write a job order? It's all about asking questions. But not just any questions — the *right* questions. And you must direct these questions to the right person: your client, the ultimate hiring authority.

REMEMBER

Yes, the ultimate hiring authority is a busy person. And yes, you'll take up a lot of her time asking these questions. But don't feel weird about it. It's way better to take up her time before the search than to take up even more later because you failed to get all the information you needed!

WARNING

BE ON THE LOOKOUT FOR PERSONAL BIASES

During this session, you may uncover several personal biases that could cloud your client's judgment during the interview phase. For example, no one is likely to ever say, "I don't like fat people." However, you'll often hear people say that high-energy types, active people, or people who played sports in college seem to fit in best. These statements might or might not be true. Either way, you need to be on guard for biases on the part of the client that may prevent you from hiring the best person for the job.

Speaking of personal biases, a client's personal bias may get your client — *and you* — in trouble with the Equal Employment Opportunity Commission (EEOC) if a disgruntled candidate decides to file a grievance. It would also do you (not to mention your bank account and company reputation) well to remember that very senior hiring authorities often have a tendency to be ignorant of or unconcerned with EEOC requirements with regard to candidate profiling and illegal interview questions. Consider yourself warned!

By asking these questions, you can ensure that you don't enter the search with false assumptions, and that you identify important changes to the role since the last time the position was filled (assuming it's not a new position). And in case you're wondering, these are the same questions any reputable search firm would ask!

In the following sections, we walk you through the questions you should ask.

REMEMBER

Whatever the answer, you want to actively — yet quietly — listen. Write everything down. Then explore the context of each answer. This is not a cross examination — you're merely seeking clarity on the client's thoughts.

What is the job title?

What's the title for the position? That might be an easy question to answer — or it might not. Odds are, you're filling an existing position — in which case you may be able to simply reuse the same title. But before you decide to go that route, do some research. Ascertain whether that title is in fact an accurate description of the role, and assess whether it sizzles enough to grab the attention of the candidates you want to attract. If you're filling a new position, start by picking a descriptive title as a placeholder, with the understanding that it will change as you gather more information about the position.

TIP

Early in your talks with the ultimate hiring authority, ask whether the title is set in stone or if you can rename if it's a deal breaker for the desired candidate. Asking about this early on makes it easier to bring it up again later — even if the initial answer is no.

Where is the job located?

Will the new hire work from the head office? From a satellite office? Or could she work from wherever? For some organizations and positions, "from a satellite office" or "wherever" are perfectly legitimate answers. For others, top executives really should work from the head office — and live in that same community rather than flying in on Monday and back out again on Friday. For example, community-based organizations likely expect top executives to be out and about in the community on weekends, rubbing elbows with stakeholders.

Who will the new hire report to?

Don't just find out the boss's name. Get his full title, as well as the name and title of *his* boss. While you're at it, find any information you can about the boss online — for example, on a personal website, on social media, or on LinkedIn or Glassdoor. (More on Glassdoor later.) Also inquire about his normal work hours and discuss under what circumstances it would be appropriate for you to call him at midnight on a Sunday. Finally, include details about the boss's assistant, including the assistant's name; his corporate and private email addresses; his direct-dial work phone number, cellphone number, and home phone number; and his secure fax number. (Yes, most companies still use fax machines to securely send sensitive documents.)

TIP

Now is also the time to document all relevant reporting relationships. If there are dotted-line, or indirect, reporting relationships, identify them now. You need to understand whose opinion *really* matters and whose input takes priority. But be warned: This is, and must remain, an internal document. You'll use it to answer any related questions, but you should not distribute it to prospects or outside recruiters or executive search professionals. How your company is structured may tell competitors a little *too* much.

What does the position entail?

So, what, exactly, does the position entail? In other words, what do you want the new hire to *do?* That's what you need to find out next.

First, ask your client to identify the position's core competencies, key responsibilities, job duties, and functional tasks. Then create a list of these, ranking them from most important to least important. Later, when you write the job description and position profile, you'll decide whether the less-important of these make the cut, if they'll be considered "nice to haves," or if they'll get dropped altogether.

Then ask your client to detail the biggest challenge(s) for this position in as much detail as possible. As you did with the key responsibilities, job duties, and functional tasks, rank these challenges from most important to least important. (Again, you might mention these in the job description and position profile.)

Now you're ready to discuss day-to-day job info, such as the following:

>> How many employees will the candidate be responsible for now?

>> Who are these employees?

>> Will the candidate be directly responsible for these employees? Or indirectly responsible?

>> How many employees might the candidate be responsible for in the future?

>> Who will the candidate interact with on a daily basis? These might include other executives (don't just look at the org chart; map the indirect chain of command, too), customers, partners, suppliers, board members, or other stakeholders (politicians, members of the press, and so on).

>> How much time will the candidate spend with each group? The answer might be in hours, days, weeks, or years — whatever makes the most sense in the client's organization and for this search.

What kind of compensation are we talking?

Obviously, you'll need to include in the job order some info about compensation. Specifically, you'll need to ask your client about the following:

>> **What is the expected first-year compensation?** This includes the base salary range (the ideal starting salary and the absolute most she's willing to pay for a top candidate), expected annual bonuses, and stock options.

>> **What are the benefits and when do they go into effect?** These include medical benefits, time off, retirement, and fringe benefits.

>> **What is the position's growth potential?** Do you expect the position to expand in terms of responsibility and compensation over the next 12 to 24 months?

Why is the position open?

Why does the client need to fill this position? Is it due to a pending expansion? Or is it because the incumbent quit, retired, or was terminated? Either way, you'll want to include this information in the job order.

If it's the latter — that is, the incumbent quit, retired, or was terminated — you should specify whether there will be an overlap period so the outgoing executive can train the incoming one. You should also identify whether the incoming exec should have skills that differ from (or are stronger than) the outgoing one's. If so, which ones?

What type of educational background is required?

Maybe the new hire should have a degree with a specific specialty. For example, an engineer might need a degree with a specialization in electrical, civil, mechanical, aeronautical, or one of a host of other areas. Or maybe the position requires someone with a specific kind of certification. If so, find out if that certification must be issued by a particular educational or training institute. (For example, the PMP designation for project management professionals is a designation issued by a specific granting body.) Also find out if the certification must be recognized globally. Finally, detail any additional training that may be vital to the role.

REMEMBER

Be as specific as possible here. That way, you don't wind up recruiting the wrong person.

What type of experience are you looking for?

Obviously, you need to know what type of work experience — what industry and at what level — the ideal candidate will have. And you'll need to know how much experience candidates need in order to be considered. But that's not all: You should also be able to say *why*. You must thoroughly understand the nuances of experience so that you can qualify people into your process without wasting their time (and yours).

In addition, you should ask your client the following questions:

>> **Are you willing to consider candidates from other industries or with other positions?** If so, which industries and which positions?

>> **What type of track record would a successful candidate have?** You should be able to quantify in absolute terms what the candidate has accomplished with other companies that would make him ideal for this role.

>> **What companies would you like to see in the candidate's background?** Some companies are known for hiring or producing the type of talent you're looking for. For example, someone who graduated from General Electric's University Development Center or Disney University might make a strong contender.

>> **Are there any companies that you would *not* like to see in the candidate's background?** It's easy to recruit candidates from certain companies — only because those companies are so badly run. But beware: If you hire from this pool of candidates, the result may be that he infects your staff with the bad practices of his old firm.

>> **Are there any certifications the candidate must carry?** Maybe PMP, MSCE, or CPL certification is a must, or maybe a certain certification would be a "nice to have."

In addressing these questions, it helps to consider the backgrounds of the previous two executives who held the open position. If those executives were strong employees, you'll want to try to pinpoint what it was about them — their experience, their education, or their approach — your client would like to replicate.

Conversely, if they were lousy employees, you'll want your client to identify which of those aspects to avoid. Ask the following questions:

>> What company, industry, and country did they come from?

>> How long did they work here?

>> Why did they stay?

>> Why were they successful here?

>> Why did they leave?

>> Where did they go?

TIP

To gather this information, your client's firm should conduct exit interviews with outgoing employees. The insight they'll gain from these interviews will prove invaluable!

What type of management style would you prefer?

What is the ideal candidate's management style? Or, put another way, what style will work best with the people she'll be managing? Think about how effective the person who *used* to have this role was as a manager (assuming there was such a person) and decide whether you should find someone with a similar style — or not.

In addition to management styles, you should also consider leadership styles. What type of leader is needed for the role? Autocratic, democratic, participative, *laissez faire,* or something else entirely? The same goes for decision-making styles. Do you need a consensus builder? Or someone with a more aggressive decision-making style?

REMEMBER

In our view, *true* leadership is situational. Sometimes the leader should use an autocratic approach; other times, she can be more democratic. But in the end, it doesn't matter what we think. What matters here is what your client thinks!

TIP

The terms *autocratic, democratic, participatory,* and *laissez-faire* may mean different things to different people. For this reason, it's wise to spend some time defining these terms upfront. Consider giving everyone involved a glossary of terms at the outset to ensure you're all on the same page.

Also at issue is the ideal candidate's communication style. Do you need an analytical communicator — someone who likes hard data and real numbers? Or an intuitive communicator — someone who avoids getting bogged down in details and looks at the big picture? Maybe you need a functional communicator — someone who focuses on plans, timelines, and processes. Or maybe a personal communicator — someone who values emotional language and connection — is more what you're looking for.

REMEMBER

Different roles might call for different communication styles, but pretty much any role will require that the candidate have good communication skills. According to *Forbes,* candidates should "speak up, use strong and clear language, communicate with passion and energy, and display positive body language by standing tall, making eye contact, offering a firm handshake and using an authoritative tone of voice."

What personality type would be the best fit?

It's important to pin down what type of person will be the best fit. Do you need someone who is outgoing and gregarious? Someone who is contained and soft spoken? Someone formal, or someone more laid back? As you ponder this, think about the firm's culture, and what type of personality the incumbent executive (if there was one) had.

The issue of "fit" is tricky. It's the most subjective part of assessing any new hire — and the most oft-cited reason for a new hire's termination. Identifying what types of people thrive in your organization upfront can help you avoid the costly and time-consuming mistake of hiring someone who just won't work well with your team.

REMEMBER

If what the person does is more important than how he does it, his personality type may not be as important as his skill set. Like in *Star Wars.* Yoda was hardly gregarious or outgoing (although he did have a good sense of humor). And yet he was the perfect teacher for Luke Skywalker.

How important is executive presence?

Does the position require someone with executive presence? That is, does it need someone who has, in the words of *Forbes,* "the ability to project gravitas — confidence, poise under pressure, and decisiveness"? Are "speaking skills, assertiveness and the ability to read an audience or situation" required? And does the candidate need to look the part?

What is the pattern of growth or decline for the company, division, and/or group during the last two years?

Carefully plot this on an x- and y-axis. This will be one of the first things a prospect wants to know (if she doesn't already). Oh, and if the pattern of growth has been negative, it's a great opportunity for someone to turn things around. You'll use this information to shape your pitch to potential candidates. You'll also use it to narrow the field of prospects. For example, if your company is in high-growth mode, and you're looking for a chief financial officer, you'll probably want to avoid finance people who are accustomed to an austerity approach to management — in other words, saying no to every request for capital to grow. Or maybe that's precisely who you *do* want to target, to give them a chance to start saying yes. (Live a little, right?) Either way, you need to know.

TIP

You might include the pattern of growth as a visual in the position profile you create to entice prospects. (More on the position profile later in this chapter.)

How quickly does the client expect the new hire to make a contribution and what results does the client expect?

Clearly define what outcomes the client expects of the new hire with regard to getting up to speed. Prospective candidates will want to know upfront. In fact, odds are, these candidates won't proceed unless these expectations are clear and, in their assessment, reasonable.

What is the key to success for this position?

This question encourages your client to reflect on what has worked best for this role in the past. Maybe the answer is experience. Maybe it's personality. Maybe it's management style. Or maybe it's some combination of these (or other) factors.

Detail Work: Detailing the Job Description

You've written the job order. What's next? Using the info you amassed in the job order to craft the job description, that's what. A *job description* is a list of a job's general tasks, functions, and responsibilities. It may also indicate who the person who takes the job will report to, any qualifications or skills needed to perform the job, and a salary range.

Yes, we know. That sounds a lot like a job order. But these really are two different things. A *job order* is used primarily by the recruiter — whether an internal corporate recruiter or a third-party recruiter (generally referred to as a *headhunter, executive recruiter,* or *executive search professional*) — to gather, analyze, and synthesize a job's specific requirements. In contrast, the *job description* is a document used within the company itself to define its needs.

Sometimes, the recruiter writes the job description, using the job description as its basis. Other times, a job description may already exist. In that case, the recruiter checks the existing job description against the job order to make sure they match up.

Crafting a job description is a three-step process:

1. Performing a SWOT analysis

2. Writing a draft job description using the SWOT analysis and job order as your guides

3. Soliciting input from key stakeholders to finalize the description

Performing a SWOT analysis

What, pray tell, is a SWOT analysis? Simply put, it's a way to assess an organization's strengths and weaknesses (the internal factors that affect your business), as well as opportunities and threats (the external factors that play a role in your success or failure), and to compare them to those of their competitors. (In this context, *competitors* might mean direct competitors, indirect competitors, suppliers, and so on. After all, every organization competes for talent at the executive level!)

>> **Strengths:** Strengths are the things that make an organization better than its competitors. Examples of strengths include popular products or services, an established customer base, a golden reputation in the marketplace, strong management, qualified employees, ownership of patents and trademarks, or anything else that sets the company apart from the competition.

Strengths should always be gauged against those of a competitor. Something you do just to keep up with the competition is not a strength. It's a necessity.

REMEMBER

>> **Weaknesses:** These are the areas in which a company does not perform well, making it vulnerable to aggressive competitors or negative market forces. Weaknesses might include poor management, employee problems, high turnover, lack of marketing and sales expertise, lack of capital, bad location, poor products or services, a damaged reputation, and so on. These conditions make it more difficult to attract the right candidates, so it's imperative to identify them now.

>> **Opportunities:** Opportunities are things that could make your business stronger, more enduring, or more profitable — for example, the emergence of new markets or the expansion of old ones; possible mergers, acquisitions, or strategic alliances; a competitor going out of business or leaving the marketplace; or the availability of a desired employee.

>> **Threats:** Threats are the things that could adversely affect a business. Threats might include changing marketplace conditions, rising company debt, cash-flow problems, the entrance of a strong competitor in the market, competitors with lower prices, possible laws or taxes that may negatively affect the company's profits, or strategic partners going out of business.

Performing a SWOT analysis will reveal how the organization rates within its industry. This information can then be used to identify the ways in which the position you seek to fill is superior (or not) to similar roles in competing companies, and how best to structure the job description and position profile to attract the talent you need. It'll also help you anticipate any concerns that prospective candidates may have about the organization, and to negotiate from a position of knowledge when you find the person you want to hire.

REMEMBER

Ultimately, the purpose of a SWOT analysis is to help companies build on their strengths, minimize or correct their weaknesses, leverage opportunities, and formulate a plan to deal with potential threats.

Performing a SWOT analysis is no small task. Usually, it's done in conjunction with the search chair and maybe the search committee. (If the role you're filling is of the super-senior variety, you might want to do it with the board instead.) The good news? There's a chance that other departments will have already done a lot of the heavy lifting for you. Marketing and sales often conduct SWOT analyses to ensure they understand how the company is perceived in the market. And odds are, the finance group has a business analyst on staff who can help you out, too.

How do you perform a SWOT analysis? To start, grab a piece of paper and draw one vertical line and one horizontal line on it to divide it into four quadrants or squares. In the top-left square, write *Strengths.* In the top-right square, right *Weaknesses.* In the bottom-left square, write *Opportunities.* Finally, write *Threats* in the remaining square.

Next, detail the company's strengths, weaknesses, opportunities, and threats in the appropriate squares. There will be obvious ones, of course — like, "The company is the market leader for product *x*." But you'll also want to try to uncover SWOTs that are a bit less apparent. See Figure 10-1 for guidance.

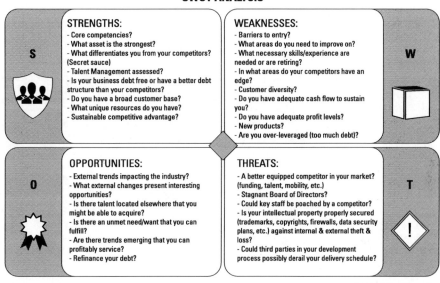

SWOT ANALYSIS

STRENGTHS:
- Core competencies?
- What asset is the strongest?
- What differentiates you from your competitors? (Secret sauce)
- Talent Management assessed?
- Is your business debt free or have a better debt structure than your competitors?
- Do you have a broad customer base?
- What unique resources do you have?
- Sustainable competitive advantage?

WEAKNESSES:
- Barriers to entry?
- What areas do you need to improve on?
- What necessary skills/experience are needed or are retiring?
- In what areas do your competitors have an edge?
- Customer diversity?
- Do you have adequate cash flow to sustain you?
- Do you have adequate profit levels?
- New products?
- Are you over-leveraged (too much debt)?

OPPORTUNITIES:
- External trends impacting the industry?
- What external changes present interesting opportunities?
- Is there talent located elsewhere that you might be able to acquire?
- Is there an unmet need/want that you can fulfill?
- Are there trends emerging that you can profitably service?
- Refinance your debt?

THREATS:
- A better equipped competitor in your market? (funding, talent, mobility, etc.)
- Stagnant Board of Directors?
- Could key staff be poached by a competitor?
- Is your intellectual property properly secured (trademarks, copyrights, firewalls, data security plans, etc.) against internal & external theft & loss?
- Could third parties in your development process possibly derail your delivery schedule?

FIGURE 10-1: Performing a SWOT analysis.

© John Wiley & Sons, Inc.

TIP

To assess the organization's weaknesses, it helps to do a little sniffing around to find out what its employees say about it. Good places to start include Glassdoor (www.glassdoor.com), PayScale (www.payscale.com), Vault (www.vault.com), The Muse (www.themuse.com), Comparably (www.comparably.com), and Blind (http://us.teamblind.com). You can also try Google and the Better Business Bureau if the organization is large enough.

Finally, here are some general questions to spark discussion:

>> What about each of the company's main competitors stands out?

>> What does the organization offer that its competitors do not?

>> What doesn't the organization offer that its competitors do?

>> What is the company's rank or position in the industry? What about its competitors?

>> How long has the organization been in operation? What about its competitors?

>> How is compensation — salary, bonuses, options, equity — determined at the company and at its competitors?

>> Are the organization's benefits better than, comparable to, or worse than those offered by its competitors?

>> Are the organization's advancement opportunities better than, comparable to, or worse than its competitors?

>> What is the organization's forecasted growth? What about its competitors?

>> Is the company in expansion mode? What about its competitors?

>> How is the company's core operation trending? What about its competitors?

>> How valuable is the company's credibility? What about its competitors?

>> What was the company's revenue percentage increase or decrease for the previous year? What about its competitors?

After you have filled in all four squares, you can use this information to devise strategies to leverage your strengths, minimize your weaknesses, and reduce your vulnerabilities and potential threats to recruit exactly the right person.

TIP

Prospective candidates will also want to know which departments in the company are strong and which are weak.

Drafting the job description

With the job order and SWOT analysis complete, you're ready to write the first draft of the job description. And by you, we mean *you*. You're the one who talked to the ultimate hiring authority to hammer out the job order, and you're the one who conducted the SWOT analysis. That means you're the one who understands the details and nuances of the position and, therefore, the best person to craft the draft.

The job description should include the following information:

>> Job title

>> Who the position will report to, as well as the organizational reporting structure

>> A brief summary of the position, including whether it's a new job or an existing one

>> The specific functional requirements of the job

>> Required education and experience

TIP

It doesn't hurt to also pinpoint specific accomplishments by a candidate that would make him the perfect fit. You might not include this information in the job description, but you'll use it to write the position profile (discussed later in this chapter).

In addition, regardless of what type of executive you're looking to recruit, you must include the following information in the job description. (As you read some of these, you'll probably be all, "Whoa, *déjà vu.*" That's because a lot of them match up with the details of the job order.)

>> **Responsibilities:** What responsibilities does this role entail? To answer this, look to the company's business plan to identify what results the company wants the new hire to produce. Does it want the new hire to build the business? Turn it around? Flip it? Modernize it? Stabilize it? Does the role require a person to carry on with the established foundation or start from scratch? Look at the role in light of the organization's past, present, and future needs. Then reconstruct the role from the ground up to reflect what the organization needs today.

>> **Activities:** Lay out the specific activities involved. While you're at it, detail where there is overlap with other executive functions and decide who owns the end result, and identify the contact points with those other positions.

>> **Leadership style:** What leadership style does the position call for now? What will it call for three to five years from now?

>> **Authority:** Draw the org chart to identify the touch points throughout the company and flush out relevant connections. For example, in some organizations, the COO handles HR; in others, HR falls under the CFO; and in still others, HR is autonomous, reporting directly to the CEO or president. These are the types of organizational relationships you want to document here. Also delineate any informal networks. This is especially important in family-run businesses, where family members may have influence over upper management beyond what their position might normally call for.

>> **Performance requirements:** Establish observable and measurable performance requirements. That way, prospective candidates will know what's expected of them from a performance standpoint. Establishing these requirements from the get-go also ensures that the new hire will know where she stands as soon as she comes onboard.

>> **Skills:** Here's where you list the skills needed to do the job — both hard skills and soft skills (see the nearby sidebar). Also note whether the current team's skills mix is appropriate, and how the new hire might affect other roles or bolster weaknesses in other areas of your management team. Be sure to account for any specific skills unique to the industry in question. Finally, include a projection of which skills may be required two or three years down the pike, but don't make that your focus. About 80 percent of this section's content should focus on the organization's present-day needs.

REMEMBER

Successful recruiting requires an understanding of exactly where the company is in its evolution from start-up to multinational, how fast it's changing, and what the current and future skills gaps look like.

>> **Experience:** Specify whether (and how much) candidates must possess experience in the company's industry and whether (and how much) they should have experience in a comparable role elsewhere. Also, delineate what experiences are an absolute must versus nice to have. Finally, indicate which requirements are flexible and which are not.

>> **Personal qualities:** What personal qualities are required for the role? In assessing this, consider the company's environment and culture and the personal styles that tend to work best. Do you want more of the same? Or are you looking for someone who will run counter to the established company culture — perhaps to act as a change agent of sorts? Also, consider what personal qualities will mesh best with the new hire's superiors, peers, and subordinates.

>> **Compensation:** Here's where you specify all elements of the compensation package — including how much (if at all) the company is willing to stretch in the event the perfect candidate comes along. (You'll probably want to gather some objective market data to come up with this number.) In addition to base salary, list whatever else company employees receive and value. On a related note, specify whether the company is willing to pay relocation costs (assuming relocation is absolutely necessary). For a complete list of compensation issues, consult this book's website at www.executiverecruitingfordummies.com/downloads.

WARNING

Many job descriptions are worded so loosely, they're essentially useless. This ambiguity will cause the best candidates to self-select right out of your hiring process. As you write the job description, it's absolutely essential that you use specific and clear language. The bottom line? When a prospective candidate reads a job description, he should be able to say with no hesitation whether he is — or is not — qualified for the job.

Comparing apples to apples

You may be wondering why we had you perform that SWOT analysis earlier. Here's the answer: You'll use it to evaluate how the opportunity you've laid out in the job description stacks up to similar opportunities in other companies. For example, if you've written a job description for a VP of operations, you'll want to get a sense of which aspects of that position will be more (or less) attractive to candidates with equivalent positions in other companies.

Finding wiggle room

Now is the time to decide if there's some flexibility in hiring based on the strengths of your best candidates. For example, you might decide to be flexible about how many years of experience you require. Or maybe there's some wiggle room when it comes to salary, perks, or terms of employment (for example, fixed term, at will, or salaried employee versus consultant).

Here are two other areas that might allow some flexibility:

>> **Education:** Do you *really* need a P.Eng.? Or would a civil engineer with ten years of experience running billion-dollar, multi-stakeholder programs suffice? You may find that some education requirements may unnecessarily restrict your potential talent pool.

>> **Location:** Can the job be done remotely some (or all) of the time? This is especially relevant with VP of sales roles, where customers may not live in the same area as the company's headquarters.

You might rank these in order of importance. Ask yourself what's more important: salary or experience? Experience or education? Your answers to these questions will help you if you find someone who would be a great candidate except for that one factor. If you decide that one factor isn't as important as the others, that person may still be in the running!

Soliciting input

When your draft of the job description is complete, you're ready to solicit input. But from who?

Obviously, you need input from your client, the ultimate hiring manager. But that's not all. You'll also want feedback from the search chair and search committee, as well as from any future peers of the new hire. If the assignment is for the CEO, CFO, or president of a company, odds are you'll also want to involve the board of directors, as well as any senior leaders who will directly interact with the incoming exec.

WARNING

Seek input and feedback only from people who matter. If you involve too many people, you run the risk of developing a spec that sort of meets everyone's needs, but fails to get at the meat of the role.

In our experience, the best way to solicit input is by assembling this team of people and reviewing the draft job description together. This is an effective treatment for the dreaded (and sometimes fatal) Hurry Up and Wait syndrome. Choose an impartial board member, tap the search chair (if that person has time), or hire an outside facilitator to lead the discussion. This person should root out dissenters, acknowledge their concerns, and gain agreement (not to be confused with compromise) on the final job description.

TIP

Yeah, we know. Assembling a group of executives is harder than herding hamsters. For help, hit up the hiring authority's assistant. She has the weight of the hiring manager behind her — not to mention access to everyone's calendars.

One more thing: Be ready to rein in your "advisors" if they continuously hold up irrelevant examples of what other companies are doing and insist that you do the same. For example, just because companies like Google, Uber, Alibaba, and Airbnb talk about, say, growth hacking doesn't mean you should. No matter how sexy it might sound, if it's inappropriate for your industry, you'll just wind up looking silly — and unless you're a clown school, that's going to turn off prospective candidates. Organizations require different mixes of skills and experiences, and that's what this discussion needs to focus on.

By the end of the discussion, everyone involved must be in agreement as to the contents of the job description. If there is even a hint of disagreement, it will be immediately flagged by intuitive candidates, and may derail your entire hiring initiative.

REMEMBER

It's the search chair's job to get agreement on the final document.

Styling and Profiling: Composing the Position Profile

The job description explains what the position entails and what type of person would be a good fit. It's about what *you* need.

No offense, but it's not all about you and your needs. You also have to consider what your potential candidates might want. Why? Because unlike other types of capital — natural capital, manufactured capital, financial capital, and social capital — human capital in a free society has a say in whether you use it. That is, no matter how attractive a candidate may be to you, if you want to employ her, she can — and often will — say no.

That's where the position profile comes in.

In effect, the position profile is a marketing tool. It's like a corporate brochure. The mission of the position profile is to catch the eye of top candidates. Think of it this way: If your job description is a humble silver sedan, then your position profile is a flashy red Ferrari.

The position profile answers one key question: What's in it for me? When you provide prospective candidates with the information they need to answer this question, you're guaranteed greater success in attracting your ideal hire. In fact, we've seen position profiles foster a swell of interest in jobs that were less appealing than a bran muffin.

Creating a position profile demonstrates to potential candidates that your organization is serious; that your executive team has taken the time to paint a full, accurate picture of the ideal candidate; and most important, that you're not just winging it.

So, how long should the position profile be? And what should it contain? The position profile should be brief — five to seven pages. Any longer, and you'll lose your audience. As for what it should contain, here's a rundown:

>> **Cover page and opening statement:** The cover page should feature the company's logo and the job title, along with an attention-grabbing graphic that conveys the essence of the company or the role.

The opening statement's job is to tout your company as a great place to work. To that end, it contains five to seven paragraphs that describe the company, including its vision, mission, and products or services. It also provides pertinent stats, such as the number of employees, annual sales, industry accolades, and whatnot, and notes the position of the company within its industry.

Above all else, the opening statement kindles curiosity. This is a tall order — which is why we suggest you seek the help of a marketing professional for this part of the position profile.

WARNING

You might be tempted to include links to more information on the overview page. Don't. All that does is distract the prospective hire. If you want to provide that type of info in the position profile, do it on the last page.

>> **Position description and job details:** The position description is a tightly worded — yet compelling — overview of the position, including its title, major responsibilities, and desired outcomes. This piece of prose should pique the prospect's curiosity and provide enough info to qualify (or disqualify) him from consideration straight off.

The job details offer more depth as to the roles, responsibilities, and objectives. As you write this piece, keep the job description handy. You'll want to refer to it often to fill in these details. If you want, the job details can include a list of the future hire's peers and an org chart for his department or division. Or, you can keep this info private until you're down to your final selection.

TIP

To make the position profile easier to read, use bullet points in the job details section (and anywhere else that makes sense). People automatically assume the first line they read is the most significant, so put the most noteworthy point at the top and list the rest in order of importance — especially if it contains more than five bullets.

>> **Specialized knowledge, skills, and abilities:** Here's where you list any qualifications that are absolutely mandatory, along with those that are merely preferred. This list should include specific skills, years of experience, certifications, licenses, education level, and technical proficiencies.

WARNING

The laundry list of skills often present in job postings on job boards are designed to cast a wide net — which is exactly what you *don't* want here. These catch-all descriptions do more harm than good.

>> **The ideal candidate:** This section, which may run a full page, cites the qualifications and core competencies required for the role. It should also note the desired personality traits and soft skills — think communication, work ethic, attitude, and values. Finally, it should list any accomplishments the ideal candidate will have achieved. These should be consistent with what you might expect from someone who's held a similar role at a competitor.

TIP

When citing accomplishments that pertain to growth, skip the dollar signs and go with percentages. For example, suppose someone oversaw a $5 million increase in sales. If the organization had only $2 million to begin with, that would be a big deal. But if it was a multi-billion-dollar company, then not so much. Conveying growth as percentages more accurately conveys the importance of the accomplishment.

The depiction of the ideal candidate should be a bit of a stretch — something the ideal candidate would view as the next step in her career. Ultimately, the purpose of this section is to show the prospective candidate why she is qualified (or not) — and, for the eminently qualified, to see herself in the role.

>> **Next steps:** This section is for prospective hires who'd like to learn more about how to proceed. It contains detailed contact information, including a dedicated phone number and email address, as well as the best times to get hold of you or the recruiter responsible.

One thing the section should *not* contain: a call for a résumé. Why? Simple. For most executives, the idea of updating their résumés is about as enticing as a root canal. In fact, they hate it *so* much that if they have to do it, they'll probably skip contacting you altogether — especially if they're happily employed elsewhere. Remove this blockage by inviting them to engage in a friendly conversation *without* supplying a résumé first.

>> **Frequently asked questions:** You can use the frequently asked questions section — which is optional — to anticipate what questions a prospective hire might have about the position and organization and answer them. (Don't go too crazy — four or five questions and answers will do.) For example, you might include compensation information here. You can also use this section to provide links to the company website, newsletter, annual report, or whatever else you think might pique a candidate's interest.

As you've seen, the position profile should use clear language and be neither too descriptive nor too vague. But there's something else: a good position profile should reflect the company's character and brand. That means employing a vocabulary and writing style that matches your company's culture. For example, if your business is a start-up with a very distinct ethos, you want to communicate that ethos through the words you use, the feeling your writing evokes, and the visual appearance of the profile. If that means straying from the norm, so be it. In the end, your goal is to attract people who are right for the position *and* the company.

TIP

If your organization has a successful and widely read blog, consider using a similar style of writing in the position profile.

Ad It Up: Writing a Solid Job Ad

Back in Chapter 7, we mention that one way to source candidates is to place job ads on your company intranet, on online job boards, and in print publications. But if that ad is lousy, it could do your search more harm than good. A–players respond to challenges — the opportunity to have an impact — not the typical laundry lists of "desired skills and responsibilities," which appear all too frequently in job ads.

Following are two examples of job ads — one bad one, and one that makes the grade.

Bad job ad

Here's an example of a bad job ad:

Executive Vice President, Engineering

We are a new electronics start-up. Looking for engineers with experience in electrical power systems, aircraft design, drone flight engineering, active control, systems integration, and machine learning.

Job Type: Full-time

Required Education: Master's

Required Experience: 5 years engineering

This ad — well, it stinks. It contains nothing even remotely enticing. Opening statements like "We are a new electronics start-up" only undermine the ad — start-ups are by definition "new." There's barely any detail — certainly not enough for anyone to rule himself in or out. Bottom line? This ad typifies the generic cattle calls that agencies use to cull résumés from the Internet, and that executives are loath to respond because they're so used to there *not* being a real job behind it. Will it garner a big response? Yes. But not by anyone who is actually qualified. Instead, it will attract hundreds or perhaps even thousands of people who *think* they might be qualified and have nothing to lose. This is a recruiter's worst nightmare: receiving thousands of responses from unqualified people.

Attention-grabbing ad

Here's an example of a great ad. It describes the role with precision, and would be of interest only to those who are qualified. That's exactly what you want when you run an ad: responses from only those people who meet the requirements exactly.

Vice President Engineering

Job Description

Vice President, Engineering (Electronics)
Location: Los Angeles, CA, or San Francisco, CA
Complete relocation package.

All inquiries will be held in the strictest of confidence. Our client is an award-winning organization with a rich history of providing technically advanced instrumentation to municipal and industrial markets.

In business for 40 years, this company has experienced years of steady growth and has gained a stellar reputation in its industry. This organization is a worldwide leader for the industrial and environmental markets. Its primary market is in the environmental arena. Customers include municipalities, industry, and government environmental groups.

The main industrial markets are in heavy industry, including pulp and paper, chemicals, mining, textile, steel, petroleum, and food-processing industries. In 2014, our client joined forces with another global leader in engineered solutions whose energy measurement products are distributed internationally and widely used in hydronic heating and cooling systems.

This is a unique opportunity in that the successful candidate will be personally mentored by the founder for the purpose of eventually taking over the reins of the organization upon his retirement. We are now conducting immediate interviews, and that's where you come in.

Attractions and Successes

- The company is an employer of choice as it has almost no employee turnover and high employee loyalty.

- This organization's products use cutting-edge technology.

- The company has experienced years of steady growth and there is now enormous opportunity for substantial growth.

- Our client has a strong reputation for quality products and exceptional service.

- They are agile. The company creates all products in-house, and is fast-moving, flexible, and robust — capable of rapid response to opportunities.

- The organization has strong reseller and distribution-channel relationships.

- The culture at our client's company is driven based on success factors. It is a positive culture that understands the potential and opportunity in front of them, and is ready to embrace change.

The Position

You will play a key role in new product-development efforts as well as implementing improvements to existing products, the conceptualizing and day-to-day management of simultaneous projects, delivering manufacturable designs to agreed specifications within time and budget constraints, while fostering innovative solutions to customer needs.

You will use your background in product development to lead product-engineering efforts, which include product design, hardware and software product management, supplier interactions, and product verification and validation activities. You will build on the company's excellent reputation for exceptional product quality by capturing the essence of the company history and culture to apply industry trends and business savvy going forward.

You must have a history of strong leadership, deep practical engineering knowledge, and a proven track record for timely project delivery, project management, cost control, and customer satisfaction. In essence, you will

- Oversee and be actively involved with the R&D, Engineering, and Product Development teams to ensure the company's products and service remain cutting edge

- Lead, participate in, or support the following product development activities:
  - Concept, planning, design, and execution stages of major new products or product enhancements
  - Risk assessment
  - Prototyping and testing concept designs and initial engineering builds
  - Pilot production
  - Design reviews
  - Design verification board: hardware/software testing, product validation, and usability testing
- Provide product leadership during pre-production, including strategic planning for product development activities, to create technology for existing and expanded markets/offerings
- Provide leadership for the engineering team
- Plan and coordinate the long-term objectives and standards of performance for the department
- Lead new product-development projects from concept through production launch
- Lead productivity efforts and implement improvements to existing products
- Collaborate with cross-functional teams to research and understand consumer and customer wants/needs, benchmark competitive products, and develop innovative products that are cost-effective and meet those wants/needs
- Develop and optimize product costs to maximize value and competitiveness
- Lead manufacturing trials, testing, measurements, and related documentation from initial trials through production qualification
- Evaluate results using statistical analysis and propose/lead changes to product design, tooling, and/or process
- Conduct engineering evaluation and tests to validate the robustness and proper performance of new products
- Evaluate product non-conformances and recommend design modifications
- Research design options and perform experiments to determine potential design feasibility

- Identify, integrate, and refine technologies and products that can be used to create and enhance the company's products to satisfy requirements

- Apply technical principles and concepts to product designs

- Provide technical support for solving product quality problems as needed

- Work on special projects as assigned, such as competitive analysis and productivity projects in collaboration with the VP, Sales, and Marketing

- Be a student of current industry trends, ensuring that the company maintains and expands its technology leadership position

Specialized Knowledge, Skills, or Abilities

- Work well in a cross-functional environment

- Make quick, reasoned engineering decisions and drive processes to conclusion

- Reduce broad requirements into a structured engineering solution

- Conceptualize and think strategically

- Develop strategies for enhancing communication, problem solving, teamwork, and innovation across functions

- Work with others to develop integrated strategies for improving engineering processes and operational efficiencies

- Understand customer requirements and translate them into solutions

- Focus on and manage key initiatives that balance both short- and long-term objectives

- Communicate effectively with senior management and customers (written and verbal)

- Manage the engineering division's operating and capital budgets

Our Ideal Candidate

Our client is seeking a "business leader" who will bring knowledge and creativity to the position, has practical business sense, and can provide the discipline to drive results, as this role is designated to succeed the founder, who has retired. You're an impact player. You're a leader who is comfortable playing a central role in helping the business translate its requirements into practical solutions to address the market. Obviously, you're good under pressure. You can formulate workable strategies, establish priorities, and then lead the team to deliver against them. You're a problem solver capable of running autonomously with a demonstrated ability to get the job done and work with others.

Qualifications and Core Competencies

- A university degree in electrical engineering

- Strong business acumen and applied experience in the instrumentation or technology environment

- 10+ years of industry engineering experience

- Experience in developing and supporting products through their entire life cycle

- The desire to drive accountability across project teams and functional team members

- Competence in electronic hardware and software design

- The ability to manage diverse projects of varying complexities simultaneously

- The ability to focus on efficiency of production, as well as establish production reporting procedures

- A proven record of creativity and a sense of passion for product design

- The ability to apply technical principles and concepts to product designs

- Experience with industrial and municipal markets an asset

- Experience in ultrasonic technologies an asset

Your Personality Characteristics

You're a strong leader who can act as a catalyst for continuous improvement with a dedicated group of employees. You are unusually adept at building partnerships within the organization and can nurture relationships with outside service providers. In summary, you:

- Are in it for the long haul

- Have a high level of integrity

- Are more engineer than manager or an exceptional engineer with management capability (you have a strong hands-on engineering attitude)

- Want to be in a smaller environment that values and encourages employees who accept challenges

- Have a high degree of mechanical aptitude (hands-on)

- Are product development/engineering focused

- Are accountable, with a strong "owner's" mentality

- Are trustworthy, passionate, and decisive

- Are profit and loss savvy, with business maturity

- Are service oriented and customer focused

- Appreciate the culture and history of the company

- Are entrepreneurial

- Have a professional demeanor

- Energize people to achieve personal and organizational success

- Are an independent thinker, willing to take risks

- Foster collaborative working environments where people actively share information, rely on each other's expertise, deliver on commitments, and trust in each other

- Are a creative problem solver who fixes problems, not just identifies them

Next Steps

Let's talk. Managing Partner David Perry is leading the search with Mark Haluska. All inquiries and discussions are strictly confidential until you decide you're interested in the opportunity. And you need not have a current résumé prepared to have a preliminary discussion with us. To get started, please contact David Perry (613-236-6995 or dperry@perrymartel.com) or Mark Haluska (724-495-2733 or haluska@comcast.net). For more information on Perry-Martel International, Inc., please visit our website at www.perrymartel.com at your convenience.

No Résumé? No Worries! Collecting a Confidential Candidate Brief

David talking here. Early in my career as a headhunter, I became the go-to guy when an executive search hit a dead end. I was the "closer," so to speak. I had a knack for convincing prospects who had showed exactly zero interest in a position — who were perfectly happy where they were — to at least speak with me about it, and maybe even interview for it. (One client called this "resurrecting the dead.")

Even so, I was plagued by one problem: As we say earlier, most executives would rather get a root canal than update their résumés. Why? Because updating one's résumé is painful, and takes forever to do. Nevertheless, at some point, I really *needed* their résumés — or at least, I needed the information their résumés would contain. So, what to do?

Enter my co-author, Mark. I met Mark back in 1999, on an electronic bulletin board for recruiters. Mark had created a brilliant tool he called the confidential candidate brief — CCB for short.

To generate a CCB, Mark created a form geared specifically toward the position in question. This form contained a series of hot-button questions, designed to tease out information about the prospect. After his first phone call with the prospect — assuming it went well — Mark would email the form to the prospect. Instead of updating her résumé, the prospect could simply fill out the form — a process that usually took no more than 20 minutes of her time — and email it back. Mark would then evaluate the information she provided — essentially a résumé custom built for the position — to determine whether the prospect might be a good fit for the position. (Of course, all of this happened confidentially.) Problem solved!

REMEMBER

In many cases, the CCB reveals *more* than a résumé. How do we know? Because more than once, we've had a prospect submit her résumé; be immediately rejected; resubmit her résumé, but this time with a CCB; and be considered — and sometimes even hired — for the position.

You, too, can use a CCB to quickly and unobtrusively obtain an accurate picture of a prospect's qualifications. Indeed, the CCB essentially acts as the first interview — only better. With the CCB, the prospect can take her time to answer your questions thoughtfully and with as much detail and color as she chooses. This will give you significant insight into her character. The CCB also enables prospects to screen themselves into (or out of) the search, basically doing all the grunt work for you! As an added bonus, the process of generating the CCB leaves the prospect with the impression that the organization knows exactly what it's looking for to fill the position and, perhaps more important, is considerate of her time.

REMEMBER

If the prospect isn't a good fit or decides not to proceed, at the very least, thanks to the CCB, you'll have left her with a great impression — which means she'll certainly take your calls in the future!

Building the form for a confidential candidate brief

The CCB form contains four main sections:

>> **Contact information:** Here, ask for the prospect's personal email address and his phone numbers (his direct line at work, his cellphone number, and his home phone number). Also ask what the best time to contact him during the day is.

>> **Current employment:** In this section, ask for the candidate's current title and the dates of employment at his current organization. If he's left that position, ask why.

>> **Position-related questions:** This is it — the meat of the CCB. This section features several questions designed to determine whether the prospect is a good fit for the role. The questions should derive from the information in the position profile. They should be easy to read, conversational, and presented in order of importance. They can be behavioral in nature — that is, they can ask the candidate to describe a time in the past when he displayed certain behaviors. (Think: "Tell me about a time when. . . .") Or, they might be situational, in which case the interviewer presents a problem or situation and asks the candidate how he would handle it. (Think: "What would you do if. . . .")

WARNING

It's best to omit questions pertaining to personal interests. Ditto questions designed to gauge "fit." These will be addressed later, in a face-to-face interview.

>> **Questions of a legal nature:** Here's where you dot your *i*s and cross your *t*s, legally speaking. Specifically, you want to cover the following:

- The status of any noncompete agreements in effect

- The status of any nondisclosure agreements in effect

- Whether he has the legal right to work in the country where the position is located

- The status of any other current employment negotiations

- Permission to keep his file in your database, with a guarantee of privacy

- Permission to share his information with the search committee

WARNING

The CCB form should be 100 percent fluff-free. Otherwise, you'll find that most executives — whose time is at a premium — will simply dismiss the exercise.

A sample confidential candidate brief for a CFO

To help you wrap your head around the whole CCB thing, we've provided a sample CCB form — in this case, for a CFO. Why a CFO? Because every company has one, and most CFO roles are pretty much the same regardless of company size, whether it's public or private, and irrespective of industry. Compared to, say, the CEO role, or the VP of sales or marketing, there's not much variation among CFO positions.

Full Name:		Today's Date:
Cell Phone:	Direct Line:	Home Phone:
Personal Email Address:		
When is the best time to contact you? (Please include your time zone.)		
Are you currently employed? Yes ☐ No ☐		
Current/last job title:	Dates employed:	
Current/last employer's company name:		
If you are currently unemployed, please explain the circumstances that led to this status. ☐ Not applicable (I am still employed as of this date)		
You left your last position because:		
Are you willing to relocate to the New York City area? ☐ Yes ☐ No		
Optional Comments:		
This position will require you to raise a minimum of $70M to $100M (USD) in funding from various sources. Have you ever raised a substantial amount of funding? ☐ Yes ☐ No		
If yes, at what company?		
What was the funding goal?	How much were you able to raise?	
How long did it take you to raise this amount?		
Who were the funding sources?		
What did you personally do to gain buy-in from those funding sources?		
Have you worked for a company that quickly scaled to build a distribution network? Yes ☐ No ☐		
If yes, what was your job title and what role did you play in the growth?		
The founder wants ABC Corp. to grow to a billion-dollar company within 3 to 4 years. How would you go about making the founder's vision a reality?		
What is it about ABC Corp. that excites you about this opportunity?		

How would your superiors, peers, and subordinates describe your leadership style?
What is the key to a successful budget?
Working in a start-up situation, what has been your most significant accomplishment? How did it benefit your employer's bottom line? Quantify and qualify this information.
What factors do you take into account when developing a company's overall financial strategy? What framework, information, and advisors do you use to make the right recommendations?
How do you manage multiple direct reports whose individual tasks relate to varied areas of finance and administration?
What day-to-day approaches and overall strategies do you use to keep your team motivated, productive, and aligned with the company's needs?
How do you oversee the quality of the day-to-day accounting when you're operating at a high level? In what ways do you personally check quality or get involved in the process?
What do you do to keep turnover low? What is the net result?
Are you bound by non-disclosure agreements? Yes ☐ No ☐
Do you work under an unexpired employment agreement? Yes ☐ No ☐
Are you legally authorized to work in USA on a full-time basis? Yes ☐ No ☐
Are you currently in discussions with any other employers regarding a possible new employment opportunity? Yes ☐ No ☐
Optional comments:
Do we have permission to store your information on our privately owned secure database? Yes ☐ No ☐
May we provide our client with the information contained in this form? Yes ☐ No ☐

Reviewing a confidential candidate brief

When the prospect returns the CCB form, you'll want to review his answers. Here's what you want to find out:

» Are the candidate's answers relevant?

» Are they concise?

» Did the candidate spell-check his answers?

» Can the candidate communicate effectively in writing?

» How thoughtful were the candidate's answers?

» Do the candidate's answers make it seem like he was in a hurry to plow through the form, giving the questions little thought?

» Does it seem like the candidate cut and pasted his answers from another document? Or does it seem like he really tried to answer *your* questions?

» Did the candidate provide proprietary information that should have remained confidential?

WARNING

If a candidate shares proprietary information, it's a huge red flag. In fact, it's so bad, it should automatically disqualify the candidate from consideration. After all, what's to stop him from sharing *your* proprietary information in the future?

The answers to these questions will give you a good idea of whether to proceed with this candidate. (We talk more about interpreting the CCB and how it fits in your interview process in Chapter 13.)

Guidance System: Creating a Detailed Interview Guide

Nine times out of ten, you need the candidate way more than the candidate needs you. After all, she probably already has a job — and one she likes. So you don't want to blow it by conducting poor interviews. That's why you write an interview guide: to usher you through the interview stage. Prospects form impressions of the company with each interaction — especially interviews. One misstep could sour a prospect on the opportunity. For example, no senior executive would tolerate a generic "Tell me about yourself" during an interview. Candidates expect you to have done your homework and to know everything about them before the interview. That's why the interview guide is so important!

When interviewing senior executives, there should be no off-the-cuff questions!

So, what is an interview guide? Simple. It's a document that contains several questions that relate to the competencies required for the role. You'll use the job order and job description to write these questions, many of which will be unique to the role. Candidates' answers to these questions will reveal their qualifications, traits, characteristics, and behavioral tendencies, improving your ability to identify and hire the right executive for the role. The interview guide should be so thorough that an inexperienced interviewer would be able to pass as a pro *and* be able to assess the answers provided by the interviewee.

The interview guide is an internal document. It is not for public consumption. Only those involved in the interview process — the ultimate hiring manager, search chair, search committee, and recruiters (internal and external) — should have access to this document. The candidate should not have access to this document, however.

You must create a unique interview guide for each specific position. Although some questions will be more generic, designed to assess leadership style and management skills, others will be specific to the role being filled.

Contents of the interview guide

Often, the interview process occurs in several stages. That means you'll need specific questions for each stage. These include the following:

- >> Basic qualifying questions to gauge the candidate's skill and experience at a macro level, to be asked by phone (see Chapter 12)
- >> Questions to tease out the confidential candidate brief
- >> Recruiter screening questions
- >> Initial face-to-face questions
- >> Search chair questions
- >> Ultimate hiring authority questions
- >> Search committee questions

As you might expect, interview questions tend to get deeper, more specific, more personal, and more pointed the farther along you are in the interview process. Some will be behavioral, while others will be situational. During the final stages of the process, these questions will help you cull the truly excellent candidates from the merely great ones. By the end of the process, the final candidate may have answered as many as 50 specific questions, which in turn generate dozens of follow-ups.

Each successive step in the interview process will prompt new questions.

Sample questions

While it's true that each interview guide will be unique, there are some standard questions that apply whether you're hiring someone in engineering, sales, marketing, finance, operations, administration, or what have you. These questions primarily pertain to past performance, as well as leadership and management style:

>> To what key factors do you attribute your career success to date?

>> What do you consider to be some of your most outstanding qualities?

>> What is your greatest strength or asset?

>> In what areas have others been particularly complimentary about your abilities? Why?

>> During past performance reviews, what have your superiors consistently cited as your major assets? Why?

>> From a performance standpoint, what do you consider to be your best attributes?

>> If I were to speak with two or three of your peers, in what areas would they describe you as particularly effective?

>> Regarding this position, in what areas do you feel you would be a particularly strong performer? Why?

>> Describe your three greatest strengths and tell me how you used them to bring about improvements in your job.

>> What two or three major accomplishments best demonstrate your key strengths?

Interview guides can take days to compose. The intricate weaving of questions is best left to an experienced recruiter or HR professional.

KNOW THE LAW!

Many senior executives are not super hip to what may or may not be asked in an interview — which is bad. To ensure you're in compliance with current laws, it's wise to run the questions in your interview guide by legal — but remember, you're not asking for permission to ask what is needed. Rather, you're asking if the questions you want to ask are legal.

That being said, to quote employment and HR attorney Janette Levey-Frisch, "Do not be tempted to have HR actually fashion your interview questions. If you do, you are likely to receive a series of questions that very closely follow a prepared job description." The problem with this? According to Levey-Frisch, "Rarely if ever do questions based on a job description allow for one to weight the essential skills, behaviors, and cultural fit necessary for success."

One more thing: Sometimes, executives *do* know which questions are off limits, so they try to cover themselves by having the recruiter (that's you) ask them. Don't fall for this trap. If you do, both you and the client will be considered liable.

Chapter **11**

Research Party: Conducting Candidate Research

Y ou've taken the job order from the hiring manager. You've nailed down a precise and accurate job description. You've composed an enticing position profile that highlights the job's potential for your target audience. And you've crafted an impressive confidential candidate brief (CCB) — one that will intrigue candidates and help them engage in a dialogue about the role, without having to write a résumé. In other words, you know what the ideal candidate *looks like.* Now all you need to do is find out where that ideal candidate *is.* That's what this chapter is all about.

Hope Is Not a Strategy: The Importance of Candidate Research

Suppose you wanted to take a dream vacation. You wouldn't just walk into a busy airport, amble up to the counter, and say, "I want to go on my dream vacation. Could I have a ticket please?" If you did, you'd likely wind up with nothing more than a baffled stare from the ticket agent (and maybe a cavity search by the TSA). No, instead, you would think about what kind of trip you wanted to take — a beach trip, a mountain vacation, a visit to a big city — and then do a bit of research to decide where to go. Well, recruiting top executives is a lot like taking a dream vacation. You don't just buy a ticket and hope it all works out. You need to do a bit of research first.

Yes, research is often laborious — even tedious. But it's through research — and only through research — that you can tightly target your prospects. Research lets you hone your message and deliver it to exactly the right person. And, thanks to research, you can speak knowledgeably about that person, his industries, and his challenges, enabling you to emphasize the positive aspects of your opportunity. In this way, you develop a relationship with the prospect. You become a trusted advisor — someone he'll happily refer to others.

REMEMBER

In-depth research may be time-consuming upfront. But in the end, this level of research will *save* you time. Why? Because in addition to helping you identify qualified candidates, research helps you to weed out unqualified ones — *before* you waste precious hours interviewing them. (As an added bonus, this also helps you limit the number of people who know you're hiring, which helps you maintain a higher level of confidentiality.)

Look, hope is all well and good. But it's so unpredictable! You need a more reliable way to efficiently and effectively find just the right person for the job — and research is the only way to achieve that. Like time-management guru Alan Lakein says, "Planning is about bringing the future into the present so that you can do something about it now."

REMEMBER

In our experience, when an executive recruiting effort fails, it's usually because of a lack of good research. No question, good research gives you the ultimate competitive advantage!

Texas Hold 'Em or Fantasy Football?

Most recruiters looking to hire talent limit themselves to a game of Texas Hold 'Em, blindly accepting the talent they're dealt from a limited deck of prospects. That is, instead of seeking out top people, they often settle for the best of the lot who are actively looking for a new position.

Exceptional recruiters take a different approach — one that's more like fantasy football. In other words, like a fantasy football team owner, these recruiters scout out — in other words, they *research* — the best players and draft them onto their teams. Indeed, fantasy football serves as a great model for conducting candidate research. Here are a few key parallels:

>> **Adopt an abundance mind-set.** In "real" football, NFL team owners must operate within certain rules. For example, they must abide by the salary cap, meaning they're limited in how much they can spend on talent. Also, they can't recruit a player from another team if that player is under contract, a practice called *tampering*. But fantasy football team owners don't give a hoot about salary caps or tampering. For them, it's all about drafting the best talent, regardless of where they are. They take what we call an *abundance mind-set*. Executive recruiters can — and should — do the same. They should consider every executive to be "available," all the time. (We call this approach "adopting an abundance mind-set.") Don't just pick the low-hanging fruit; identify which executives are the best, and set your sights on them.

>> **You can be your own scouting department.** The most successful fantasy football team owners are research junkies. Whether they're looking for offense, defense, or bench strength, it's all about the data — completions, attempts, yards, touchdowns, and interceptions. Top executive recruiters share this obsession. By parsing as much data as possible, converting this information into intelligence, they can continuously recruit top talent.

>> **You identify who you want, before you even see them.** When a fantasy football team owner looks for a quarterback, he knows he wants another Peyton Manning or Cam Newton. In other words, he knows what the "ideal" quarterback looks like, and he looks for someone who shares those same qualities. The same thing happens in an executive search. The best recruiters identify their "ideal" executive and then create detailed performance profiles of all top candidates to identify the best fit — even before they meet with them. This intelligence also enables the recruiter to compare performance among various groups and individuals, as well as against a host of variables such as company size and maturity, geography, market position, and even company culture.

>> **You embrace data.** In fantasy football, every NFL player's performance information is available online for analysis and scrutiny. With the click of a mouse, you can find statistics on every quarterback, running back, wide receiver, tight end, kicker, left tackle, running back — you name it. Whether you're looking for offense, defense, bench strength, completions, attempts, yards, touchdowns, interceptions — it's all there. The same goes for candidates for an executive search. The Internet offers a rich vein of information about all sorts of top talent. You can also find data that enables you to compare one executive with another or evaluate them against a host of variables such as company size, geography, market positioning, brand maturity, and even company culture. The bottom line? You can compile a great deal of information about each candidate, and reduce a large list of potential candidates to a manageable number of all-stars.

>> **You recognize that all players (and people) have patterns.** Top fantasy football team owners recognize patterns among their players. For example, they know who fares better in rain or snow and who favors grass over artificial turf. The same goes for executive recruiters. They find out everything they can about potential candidates, from the time they left college to the present day, to identify patterns. Then they ask themselves: Do the conditions under which this candidate was wildly successful currently exist in the organization for which I'm hiring?

>> **You know it's not just a game.** Many fantasy football team owners view the game as a simple pastime. But the best team owners are deadly serious about the game, spending countless hours pursuing even the slightest edge over the competition.

TIP

Yes, you should try to find the very best candidates, no matter where they are. But it doesn't hurt to start by searching for candidates who already live near the worksite. Then expand the search outward in concentric circles, like a bull's-eye. A tightly targeted search focused around local geography can reduce the time and expense associated with relocating an executive.

Your Step-by-Step Research Guide

We get it. Research is critical. But how do you do it?

As a first step, you should create a candidate road map — even if you've done similar searches in the past. (After all, no two searches are ever the same!) This road map lists all the places your need to "go" during your research to find top candidates.

Based on our experience, here's what your road map will likely include, in this order:

>> Your search committee as a group

>> Individual search committee members

>> Former candidates in your own database of previous searches (see Chapter 8 for more information)

>> Candidates you've already hired (specifically, candidates in similar roles or at the same company as the one you're hiring for now)

>> Colleagues

>> Public databases (free and paid)

With your prodding, these sources can help you develop an extensive list of names. When you have that list in hand, you can conduct further research into the industries and companies these candidates work in.

REMEMBER

When we say *prodding,* we really mean *asking good questions.* Good questions bring good insight! And the more insight you have, the less time you'll spend "kissing frogs" in search of that "prince" of a candidate.

Meeting with the search committee

With your candidate road map complete, you're ready to start building your list of candidates — starting with a meeting with your search committee. Your goal is to pin down the following information:

>> What companies are the best sources of executive talent that suit your needs?

>> Where does this talent profile currently reside? In which industries? Who are the competitors? Who are the direct suppliers and vendors? Who are the indirect suppliers and vendors?

>> What functional position(s) do they hold?

>> What specific titles are associated with this role?

>> What trends or events might attract talent to your company?

>> What trends or events — for example, takeovers, mergers (rumored or actual), or industry consolidations — might drive them from their current company or industry?

The answers to these questions will help you build your list of candidates.

Meeting with individual committee members

Before you adjourn your meeting with the entire search committee, arrange to call or meet with individual members to pick their brains one-on-one.

In these one-on-one discussions, you'll ask a series of questions. Phrasing is important here, so you'll want to ask these questions verbatim:

>> **Given what you know about the role we need to fill, where do you think the ideal candidate is now?** This question is designed to identify industries and companies where the ideal candidate might work now. At this early stage,

you're not looking for names of people (although it's never a bad thing if you get some). What you're trying to do is leverage your subject's experience to home in on where the ideal candidate might work (or worked in the past) or what groups that candidate might belong to. For example, if your subject says something like, "I'd look at ABC company" or, "Good people seem to come out of XYZ school," you're on the right track.

WARNING

Notice that this question does *not* ask, "Who do you know who would be good for this position?" In our experience, this will cause your subject to a) instantly lump you into the same group of clueless recruiters who have asked that question a hundred times and b) answer, "I don't know." That would be a shame, because, more often than not, subjects *do* know — they're just turned off by such an obvious question. We can't emphasize this enough: Don't alienate a rich resource by taking this tired approach!

» **If you were me, who would you call?** Answers to this question could include one of two types of people: potential sources of referrals or potential candidates. If your subject offers up a potential source, find out as much as you can about that person. That way, you'll be better prepared to probe her for information later on.

If your subject suggests a potential candidate, get as much background information as possible. Ask your subject:

- Why is _____ a good fit for the role? (By *fit,* we don't just mean his skillset and experience; we mean whether he would fit with the rest of the team.)

- How will _____'s experience help us achieve our objectives?

- Why might this opportunity be of interest to _____?

Many highly successful executives pride themselves on being "master networkers" — and odds are, at least some members of your search committee share this quality. Often, they've been able to climb the corporate ladder thanks in part to referrals by others, and they're happy to return the favor. Even better, you can generally rely on referrals from these higher-ups. These people won't waste your time by referring their completely unqualified brother-in-law.

» **Who's the most connected person you know who might be able to help me? (Only ask this question in certain circumstances.)** Some people (specifically, small-minded, shallow egomaniacs) might consider this question somewhat loaded — like, you don't think they're powerful or important enough to be able to help you themselves. So before you ask it, you may need to "read the room," so to speak. If you feel like the question won't be received well, then skip it. But if you feel like your subject is secure enough in his personhood to answer it, ask away. In our experience, this question often prompts the subject to offer up all kinds of ideas!

If you don't know your subject well enough to predict how he'll react to this question, and you feel like his answer to the second question yielded enough information, you can skip this question altogether.

In our experience, most search-committee members will have already given these questions a lot of thought, and will be more than ready to answer them. Still, to elicit your subject's unvarnished wisdom, you'll want to keep these points in mind:

>> ***How* you ask is as important as *what* you ask.** Use a casual tone of voice to convey your genuine curiosity. In our experience, when people believe that you think what they're telling you is interesting, they'll talk your ear off — and that's what you want! The idea is to build a rapport and gain trust. That way, you can ask more pointed questions as the discussion progresses.

Watch your tone. Don't let your voice betray boredom or skepticism. If it does, rest assured that your subject will quickly terminate the conversation. And if that happens, chances are, you won't be able to restart it — then or anytime in the future.

>> **Let your subject think.** After you ask each question, be silent and let him think. Your silence here is important. You want *him* to fill that void, not you!

>> **Ask follow-up questions.** Often, during a discussion like this one, each answer will reveal new lines of questioning. At the very least, you can — and should — ask why your subject has answered the way she has, where else she might look, or who else she might suggest. Just don't ask so many follow-up questions that you annoy her!

>> **Say thank you.** Each time your subject makes a suggestion, take a moment to thank him. And of course, thank him at the end of the call or meeting.

The bottom line? You want to ask these questions in a such a way that you invite a casual — yet insightful — conversation. If you do, you'll find that people will gladly spend as much time with you as you need. Oh, and this approach also helps set the tone for their cooperation once the interview process starts.

After your individual discussions with members of the search committee, rank their suggestions, placing the people you think will be most helpful at the top and the ones you think will be least useful at the bottom. Then email the list to your subject. After she has had time to think about it, follow up to see if the subject agrees with your rankings. Also ask the subject to introduce you to each person on the list, either by phone or by email.

Seeking help from former candidates and from colleagues

You'll approach people from previous searches, candidates you've already hired, and colleagues in much the same way you did the individual members of the search committee, asking the same questions and keeping the same points in mind.

Scouring public databases for candidates

Discussions with members of the search committee, people from previous searches, candidates you've already hired, and colleagues will yield your preliminary candidate list. But you'll want to scour several databases to find additional candidates, as well as information about various industries and companies.

With regard to potential candidates, you'll want to find out the following:

» Who are your competitors' top executives?

» Which of these executives have already demonstrated that they can do what your position requires?

» Which of these executives would be able to "blow the doors" off your opportunity?

» What can you find out about each of these executives? Specifically, you want the following information:

- Responsibilities
- Accomplishments
- Strengths and weaknesses
- Track record
- Career aspirations

» Why might these executives be interested in your opportunity?

TIP

To answer these questions, you need to get a sense of each executive's span of authority, as well as that of the team he manages. That's the only way you'll know if he meets your needs.

So, what databases should you use? This section offers a couple suggestions.

ZoomInfo

Most people like to save the best for last. Not us. We're going to give you the best *first.* So, what's the best database tool? Easy. It's ZoomInfo (www.zoominfo.com). For more than a decade, we've used ZoomInfo every single day. ZoomInfo uses automatic summarization to reduce information from hundreds of thousands of news and information sites into summaries, which retain the most important points of the original document. ZoomInfo also offers handy features that enable you to set alerts and gather intelligence from social media sites like Facebook and LinkedIn (discussed next), as well as tools for sharing profiles among coworkers. We simply cannot overstate ZoomInfo's power, breadth of information, and ease of use!

LinkedIn

LinkedIn (www.linkedin.com) is another research staple. It's easy to use and enables you to slice and dice data in all sorts of ways.

The site constantly evolves, with new tools added on a regular basis. Some of these tools are designed specifically for recruiting (although these are not available to those with a free account). In addition, you can join various LinkedIn groups for recruiters and search professionals. These include the following:

>> Researchers in Executive Search (www.linkedin.com/groups/3366840)

>> Executive Search Research Consulting Group (www.linkedin.com/groups/2011700/profile)

>> Research Methods for Search Professionals (www.linkedin.com/groups/4258769/profile)

For more information on using LinkedIn in your recruiting efforts, read *People as Merchandise: Crack the Code to LinkedIn Recruitment* by Josef Kadlec. (Spoiler alert: David penned the foreword for this book. And the cover quote comes from none other than Barbara Corcoran of *Shark Tank* fame.)

For more information on using ZoomInfo and LinkedIn, see Chapter 12.

Researching companies

At this point, you likely have an extensive list of names and titles. But this type of list offers about as much insight as the white pages of old: not much. Many recruiters and HR types have begun using the terms *search research* and *name generation* interchangeably, but these terms are not synonymous!

Executive search research is a much more in-depth affair. It yields valuable information and insight than a simple list of names and titles. It involves the diligent and continuous investigation of

>> Which companies are winning and why?

>> Who are the leaders driving the bus?

With search research, it's about the context. You don't just study a company's end result; you examine how it got there. Was it skill? (Or was it luck? Like one of our clients likes to say, "Even turkeys can fly with a strong backwind or a good kick in the feathers.")

What tools do you have to research companies? You can start with ZoomInfo and LinkedIn. In addition to offering information about employees (including executives), both these sites offer insights into thousands of companies. In addition to these, there are several other databases to help you research companies, including privately held companies, publicly held companies, start-ups, and nonprofits.

To research privately held companies, start here:

>> *Businessweek* (www.businessweek.com)

>> Dun & Bradstreet (www.dnb.com)

>> *Forbes* America's Largest Private Companies (www.forbes.com/largest-private-companies)

>> Hoovers (www.hoovers.com)

>> ThomasNet (www.thomasnet.com)

WARNING

Privately held companies are the hardest companies to research because these companies don't have a strict requirement to report to anyone but their limited shareholders.

Thanks to the increased reporting requirements dictated by the 2002 Sarbanes-Oxley Act, publicly held companies are easier to research. Still, it requires work. Here are the best sources of information about public companies:

>> Dun & Bradstreet (www.dnb.com)

>> CorporateInformation (www.corporateinformation.com)

>> Edgar Online (www.edgar-online.com)

>> Financial Web (www.finweb.com)

>> *Fortune* 500 (www.fortune.com/fortune500)

>> LexisNexis (www.lexisnexis.com)

If the company you need to research is a start-up, here's where you need to look:

>> Alltop Startups (http://startups.alltop.com)

>> BIIntelligence(www.businessinsider.com/intelligence/bi-intelligence-all-access-membership)

>> CB Insights (www.cbinsights.com)

Finally, Quintessential (www.quintessential.com) offers a collection of resources and tools to help you find information about nonprofits.

TIP

Can't find what you're looking for? Contact the professional association for the industry in question. For help finding relevant associations, visit ASAE: The Center for Association Leadership at www.asaecenter.org.

Researching industries

As a final step, you need to get a handle on the competitive landscape of the candidate or company's industry (or industries). A great jumping-off point is the list of industry portals at www.virtualpet.com/industry/mfg/mfg.htm. (We know. Weird name.)

You're not limited to online resources, though. Several print resources remain relevant:

>> *U.S. Industrial Outlook* (U.S. Bureau of Industrial Economics)

>> *Almanac of Business and Industrial Financial Ratios* by Troy Leo (Prentice-Hall)

>> *Annual Statement Studies* (Robert Morris Associates)

>> *Annual Survey of Manufacturers* (U.S Bureau of the Census)

>> *Industry Norms and Key Business Ratios* (Dun & Bradstreet Credit Services)

>> *U.S. Industry & Trade Outlook* (The McGraw-Hill Companies and the U.S. Department of Commerce/International Trade Administration)

>> *Standard & Poor's Industry Surveys* (Standard & Poor's Corporation)

TIP

Still at a loss? Call your local librarian. These professionals are well versed in research. In fact, they may even have time to do a bit of it for you!

OUTSOURCING RESEARCH

As we say earlier, in-depth research is tedious and time-consuming. If you find you simply don't have the bandwidth to do it right, you can outsource the job. To find firms that handle this kind of work, use your favorite search engine to search for the following:

- (executive search research) firms
- (executive search research) consultant

If you do farm out this job, you should still conduct some preliminary research on your own. That way, you'll get a good idea what you need from the search firm and where it should focus its efforts. Also, be sure to

- Meet the researcher who will do the work.
- Insist that the researcher demonstrate her advanced research capabilities.
- Require the researcher to provide a search road map, preferably on paper.
- Hold weekly meetings so she can update you on her findings.

Chapter **12**

What Is This Sourcer-y? Sourcing Candidates

When we started out as professional recruiters in the 1980s (yes, we know — it was practically the Stone Age), the Internet wasn't a thing. Well, it *was* a thing — the U.S. government began developing an early incarnation of it, called ARPANET, in the 1950s — but it hadn't yet entered the public sphere.

These days, with so much information at our fingertips, it's easy to forget how difficult it used to be to do, well, much of anything. That includes sourcing. Recruiters were severely limited in their choice of sourcing tools. If you were looking for clients, your source was the yellow pages. If you were sourcing candidates, you used the white pages and collected business cards at networking events to build your Rolodex. You also ran ads on your local newspaper's classified page or, if it was a really important job, in the newspaper's careers section. And of course, there was always the phone, which was both inexpensive and immediate.

To handle these tasks, many professional recruiters — retained recruiters, not contingency firms — partnered with professional researchers. These researchers did the bulk of the heavy lifting needed to find and qualify potential candidates, including extensive phone work, and were prized by recruiters for their ability to inject intelligence and insight into any search. The quiet backbone of every great executive recruiting practice, researchers often made the critical difference in the recruiter's ability to connect with a prospective candidate. Together, the recruiter and researcher were their own dynamic duo.

Then, in the mid-1990s, came the World Wide Web. For employers, getting on the web was a little like finding nirvana. The web made it faster, easier, and cheaper to connect with job hunters directly without the need for a professional recruiter. All they had to do was post an ad for the job on the company website or any of a number of burgeoning job sites and wait for candidates to click it. This was way better than going to the trouble of securing and paying for an outside recruiter and waiting for the researcher to pore through newspapers, magazines, journals, directories, and microfilm machines for prospects! Not surprisingly, many recruiting firms — particularly ones that were more transactional in nature — were forced to close shop.

There was just one problem: Although the web made it quick and easy for employers to find job hunters who wanted to be found (in other words, active candidates), it did not address the fundamental need to source prospects who were not actively looking — that is, passive candidates. It's no wonder hiring managers soon realized that using their websites and job boards to post positions offered little strategic advantage in terms of recruiting top executives. That gave those professional recruiters who survived an edge — and it's one they still use today. In this chapter, we explain how the professional recruiters of today source top candidates.

Back to the Future: Modern Sourcing

These days, top executive recruiting firms scour countless sources for outstanding candidates — both active and passive. To achieve this, many firms employ two types of investigators:

>> **Researchers:** These professionals focus on targeted industries, companies, and functional positions, compiling competitive intelligence from a multitude of sources.

>> **Sourcers:** These investigators, who rose to prominence in the early 2000s, use the phone, Internet, or both to find detailed bios or résumés of candidates who fit the position profile.

So, what's the difference? Put it this way: Researchers can source, but not all sourcers can do full-spectrum research, including competitive intelligence. In our experience, sourcers tend to stick with the phone or Internet to locate potential candidates.

COMPETITIVE INTELLIGENCE

The sourcing phase is about more than just finding potential candidates. It's also about gathering competitive intelligence. This includes industry trends, global trends, and information about the labor market. It also includes intelligence on a specific company, including information about its products, processes, and people; organizational charts; and news about patents, trademarks, and IP assets. Taken together, this information helps the researcher — and later, the recruiter — grasp from the outside what's happening inside an organization. This, in turn, makes it easier — and more fruitful — to approach and recruit senior executives who work there.

REMEMBER

It's not that executive recruiters are unable to perform the research and sourcing functions. In fact, some recruiters — particularly those who have been in the business for 20 years or more and remember the old ways of sourcing — handle all three roles: researching, sourcing, and recruiting. Others, however, believe these activities may not be the best use of their time. For example, David's firm, Perry-Martel, employs both researchers and sourcers — often, several of each on a single project. These professionals work in support of the firm's recruiters, who handle all client-facing activities, including interviews.

One more thing: Researchers and sourcers source, and recruiters recruit. In other words, once it's time to make a live connection with a targeted executive, the recruiter takes over.

Sock It to Ya: Sourcing's One-Two Punch

You know who does the researching and sourcing, and you know how they do it. But in what order should it occur? Our advice: Start by gathering as much high-level information as you can about the target industry, companies, and individuals. The Internet will be your primary resource, but you can use print resources, too. Then follow up by phone to ferret out any details that elude you online. This one-two punch will yield the best results, enabling the sourcers to hand off a rich selection of résumés, bios, and target lists to the recruiter.

During both of these phases, you'll be talent-mapping various companies and specific departments. *Talent mapping* means discovering who works with which executives and in what capacity, including their duties, responsibilities, and titles. Talent mapping during (or before) a search enables you to pinpoint exactly who to target when recruiting for a particular skill set or experience.

Annual events like SourceCon, which gather sourcers from all over the world to hone their craft in real-time competitions, have brought online sourcing to mainstream recruiting, all but guaranteeing the profession will continue to advance.

High-level sourcing

There are loads of resources for high-level sourcing both online and in print form — so many, in fact, that you might drown in the data you compile. To stay afloat, use this list of key resources as your water wings:

» **Google** (www.google.com): This is an obvious starting point (duh). You'll learn how to execute effective searches on Google later in this chapter.

   For free intelligence on an industry, company, or individual, updated daily, set up a Google Alert (http://alerts.google.com).

» **Wikipedia** (www.wikipedia.com): If individuals or companies are sufficiently notable, you may be able to read up on them in Wikipedia.

» **Company website:** If your search efforts uncover a company worth exploring for potential candidates, visit its website.

» **Glassdoor** (www.glassdoor.com): Research companies, jobs, salary information, and inside connections here.

» **LinkedIn** (www.linkedin.com): LinkedIn offers tons of intelligence about companies and individuals.

» **LinkedIn groups:** There are a bajillion LinkedIn groups — so many it's almost statistically impossible you won't find one worth mining for candidates. These include:

   • *Industry groups:* These include groups for, say, the software industry, the food service industry, the banking industry, and so on.

   • *Functional groups:* Functional groups might include groups for marketing, sales, finance, and so on.

   • *Specialty groups:* These groups are more granular, focusing on a specific role. Examples might include social media marketers, supply chain managers, or what have you.

» **LinkedIn SlideShare** (www.slideshare.com): Experts in various fields post presentations, infographs, and documents on this site. If you're looking for an executive who is one such expert, you may find one here.

» **Google+** (http://plus.google.com): This is yet another source of information about companies and individuals. More and more companies have established a presence on Google+, and others are sure to follow. Even if a company *doesn't* have a presence on the site, you can find out what people have to say about it.

» **U.S. Bureau of Labor Statistics** (`www.bls.gov`): The U.S. Bureau of Labor Statistics maintains loads of data that can prove valuable during an executive search.

» **Business newspapers:** There are the obvious ones, of course — the *Wall Street Journal, Fortune,* the *Financial Times,* and so on. But in addition to these, there are many regional business papers. The vast majority of these publications are available online.

» **Industry-specific periodicals:** You'll find loads of these — for example, *Manufacturing Today, Industry Week, Manufacturing Automation, Quality Magazine* . . . the list goes on. Many of these publications are available online, although some may be print-only.

» **Industry association websites:** Newsletters and reports from industry associations — not to mention their member roles — are a great source for potential recruits. Be sure to check these during your search.

TIP

To find relevant industry associations, try searching online or perusing the *Encyclopedia of Associations,* the *National Trade and Professional Associations Directory,* the *Encyclopedia of Business Information Sources, Directories in Print,* and the *Guide to American Directories.* (Note that some of these tomes are available in print only — meaning you may need to visit your local library to get your hands on them.)

» **CI Radar** (`www.ciradar.com`): This site enables you to uncover competitor presentations, research, competitive analysis, and so on. The site automatically collects, filters, and scores each document for relevance based on your industry or market.

» **Online directories**: Online directories — for example, PeopleSearch (`www.peoplesearch.com`) — enable you to find the home phone number of executives you'd like to reach outside normal business hours. Many of these directories are compiled by actual humans, making them more accurate than websites composed of unverified links.

For help using the Internet to source candidates, see the section "Wooly Boolie: Using Boolean Logic to Simplify Sourcing" later in this chapter.

TIP

If you don't have any researchers at your disposal, try calling your local library for help. Many libraries employ business librarians, and they can save you a ton of time. If you don't have access to a librarian and you're really stuck, then call a reporter who specializes in the area or function you're recruiting for and ask for guidance. She might say no — but she might not. (As an added bonus, developing a relationship with a reporter may result in her calling you for your own insights for articles she's working on.)

Ferreting out the details by phone

Sourcing online enables you to gather high-level information about the target industry, companies, and individuals. In contrast, sourcing by phone allows you to uncover additional details about these targets.

REMEMBER

Sourcing by phone doesn't just let you fill in any gaps from the online search. It may also uncover new prospects, because not every company is online.

A good online sourcer can sniff out just about any type of information you can imagine, just by calling a company's main line and speaking with the receptionist or switchboard operator. This includes

>> Names of key people

>> Position titles.

>> Reporting relationships

>> Expansion plans

>> New products

REMEMBER

Really, there's not much a trained telephone sourcer *can't* find out!

It isn't always the receptionist who spills the beans. You'd be shocked — *shocked,* we tell you — by what most PR departments are willing to share with a stranger on the phone. Salespeople eager to land a new account are likewise very chatty. It's amazing what insight you can glean from a five-minute phone call!

If you get to the point where you've called the reception desk so many times that the receptionist knows your voice, try calling the accounts payable department. Personnel in this department are accustomed to dealing with angry suppliers looking for money. If you call and apologize for getting the wrong line (that's a ruse, obviously) and tell them what role you're trying to reach, odds are they'll not only provide you with the name of that person, but even put you through to the person's extension.

Wooly Boolie: Using Boolean Logic to Simplify Sourcing

Long before the Internet — heck, even before there were telephones — an English mathematician, educator, philosopher, and logician named George Booth devised what's now called *Boolean logic*. Boolean logic is a way of representing relationships between two things.

Originally, Boolean logic was used in the study of algebra. These days, it also applies to Internet searches. By using Boolean logic in searches conducted in search engines such as Google, Yahoo!, and Bing, sourcers can uncover top talent that may otherwise go unnoticed.

To apply Boolean logic in an Internet search, you use logical operators between search terms. These include (but aren't limited to) AND, OR, NOT, and AND NOT. For example, suppose you wanted to find a software engineer. Typing **(software AND engineer)** would enable you to view results containing just software engineers, rather than also containing links pertaining to mechanical engineers, electrical engineers, railroad engineers, and so on.

TECHNICAL STUFF

LinkedIn is constantly changing. That means the user interface we describe in the next few pages may be different by the time you read this. If that's the case, check www.executiverecruitingfordummies.com/downloads for an updated guide to using Boolean search strings on LinkedIn.

HELP WITH BOOLEAN SEARCH STRINGS

Yes, you should learn the "why" and "how" behind constructing effective Boolean search strings. But sometimes, you just need a little head start to get going. To help with this, here are a few web-based solutions for creating Boolean search strings, courtesy of Dean Da Costa, author of a popular blog called "The Search Authority."

- **SourceHub by SocialTalent** (http://source.socialtalent.co): This tool enables you to create Boolean search strings for specific job openings and run them one a variety of websites, including LinkedIn, Twitter, Facebook, Google+, Google, and Indeed.

- **TalentSonar Boolean Search String Generator** (www.talentsonar.com/tools/boolean-search-generator): This is another quick and easy tool generating tight Boolean searches. This free tool takes the guesswork out of Boolean search creation.

- **Hiretual** (www.hiretual.com): This is an extension for the Google Chrome web browser that enables you to build Boolean search strings to search both LinkedIn and other social sites. It also gives you the ability to save profiles and download them as a CSV file.

We asked renowned sourcing trainer Josef Kadlec to supply an example of a Boolean search used during the sourcing phase. Josef is the author of *People as Merchandise: Crack the Code to LinkedIn Recruitment.* Josef provided the sample LinkedIn and Google searches discussed in the following sections.

Sample Size: Conducting a Sample Search

To help you get the hang of using LinkedIn and Google to search for candidates, let's run a sample search.

Suppose you're looking for an executive who meets these four critical criteria:

>> The candidate is a chief financial officer with a designation.

>> The candidate has raised either debt or, preferably, equity.

>> The candidate has experience working at a start-up.

>> The candidate lives in New York City.

Searching on LinkedIn

Your first search stop — especially for a C-suite hire — is LinkedIn, a social network for professionals that boasts more than 480 million professional profiles, with more posted every second.

Why LinkedIn? Simple. Unlike other social media sites such as Facebook, Instagram, Twitter, Snapchat, and so on, LinkedIn is designed specifically for the sharing of professional information. True, most people don't visit LinkedIn or update their profiles anywhere near as often as they do on other social media sites, but that's okay. All you're looking for at this juncture is static data — in other words, information on people's profile pages.

To expedite your search, LinkedIn offers an Advanced People Search feature. Notice that the Advanced People Search dialog box (shown in Figure 12-1) contains several fields. You may be tempted to just fill in all these fields at once and click Search, but resist that temptation! Otherwise, if you get zero results, you won't have any way of knowing which parameter is the bottleneck. And, you may accidentally eliminate people who may, in fact, be good matches.

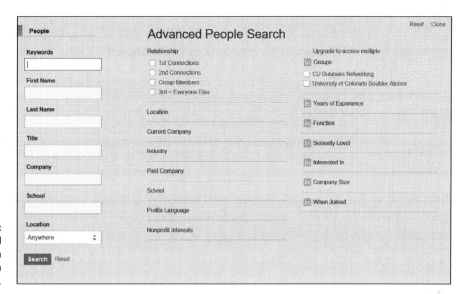

FIGURE 12-1:
The Advanced
People Search
dialog box in
LinkedIn.

Instead, your goal is to find all potential candidates in a systematic manner. Follow these steps:

1. **Direct your web browser to** www.linkedin.com **and click the Advanced link next to the search box at the top of the page.**

2. **To identify all possible CFOs on the site, type** CFO **in the Title field.**

But don't stop there. One by one, add other relevant titles and terms to describe the position — for example, **chief financial officer** or **VP finance**. Separate each of these with the OR Boolean operator and press Enter or Return when you're finished. Here's an example of what your search string might look like:

CFO OR "chief financial officer" OR VP finance OR EVP finance OR "vice president finance" OR "chief finance officer" OR finance director OR financial director

REMEMBER

Why the quotation marks around *chief financial officer, vice president finance,* and *chief finance officer?* Simple. You're searching for those exact phrases; adding quotes ensures Google treats each phrase as one expression. Omitting the quotation marks around *chief financial officer,* for example, would result in hits that include chief+financial, chief+officer, and financial+officer, which is not what you're looking for. (No quotes are needed around the other multi-word phrases because those are limited to two words only.)

TIP

Wondering how we came up with the additional titles and terms? By nosing around LinkedIn. During other searches for a CFO, we perused the results to see if any contained other relevant terms. You can do the same for your searches.

On the right side of the screen, LinkedIn displays the results of your query, with links to profiles of individuals who match your search criteria. On the left is a narrow pane, shown in Figure 12-2, that contains the same set of fields as before. You'll enter additional information in these fields to refine your results.

Keywords

First Name

Last Name

Title

CFO OR "chief financial of

Current or past ⬍

Company

School

Location

Located in or near ⬍

Country

United States ⬍

Postal Code

[   ] Lookup

Search Reset

FIGURE 12-2:
Refine your
results in this
pane.

3. **In the field that appears immediately below the Title field in Figure 12-2, choose Current from the list.**

4. **From the Location drop-down list, select Located In or Near.**

5. **In the Country field, choose United States.**

6. **To narrow your results to CFOs that have successfully raised money and have worked at a start-up, try typing the following search string in the Keywords field, leaving the Title, Location, and Country fields as they are:**

    raised (funding OR funds OR money) (start-up OR start-ups)

TIP

Notice the parentheses in the search string. On LinkedIn, you can add parentheses around AND or OR statements to combine terms. In this example, using the parentheses enables you to search for the word *raised* plus the word *fund, funds,* or *money,* as well as the word *start-up* or *start-ups,* in one stroke. You can also place quotation marks around multiple terms to find an exact match. For example, you might type **"technology company"** to return profiles that contain that exact phrase.

This reduces the number of profiles shown significantly.

7. **Specify New York City as the location.**

    To do so, type **10001** in the Postal Code field. Then choose 25 mi (40 km) from the Within drop-down list. This will limit your results even further.

    At this point, you could just screen those 19 profiles one by one and contact the ones that make the cut. But before you do, ask these questions:

    - Could there be a CFO on LinkedIn who raised money for a start-up but did not mention that in his profile?

    - Could there be a CFO on LinkedIn who lives in or commutes to New York but does not include a New York postal code in her profile?

    - Could there be a CFO on LinkedIn who does not currently have a job?

    - Could there be a CFO who does not have a LinkedIn profile?

    If you answered yes to any of these questions, your work is not done. It's time to drill down further.

8. **Change the drop-down list below the Title field from Current to Past Not Current.**

    In this way, you can find people who were, say, CFOs in the past but now serve as officers in finance. Or, change the drop-down list to Current or Past to see everyone who has served as a CFO, both now and in the past.

9. **Play around with the terms in the Keywords field to loosen up the search.**

    We suggest deleting the start-up keywords. After all, it's possible someone mentioned she raised money without specifying that it was for a start-up. Your search string should look like this:

    > raised (funding OR funds OR money)

10. **Maybe a candidate in New York chose not to state his postal code, but did indicate his location in the text on his profile. To find these people, delete the entry in the Postal Code field. Then alter the search string in the Keywords field to read as follows:**

    > raised (funding OR funds OR money) (New York OR NY)

TIP

For those who want to become LinkedIn search experts, Josef has developed a special talent-sourcing methodology. He calls it the LinkedIn Onion Search. To learn more about it, visit www.slideshare.net/JosefKadlec/linkedin-onion-search.

Searching on Google

There is life — lots of it — beyond LinkedIn. To find it, you can perform what we call an *X-ray search.* An X-ray search enables you to use a search engine such as Google or Bing to find résumés from several sources, including Twitter, GitHub, Stack Overflow, XING, Google+, or any other website (including LinkedIn), all at once.

In this section, we explain how to perform an X-ray search using Google. (We chose Google because it's the most widely used web-based search engine on the planet.) To start, direct your web browser to www.google.com. Then, in the search box, enter the following search string.

> (CFO OR "chief financial officer" OR VP finance OR EVP finance OR "vice president finance" OR "chief finance officer" OR finance director OR financial director) (raised start-up) (new york OR NY) intitle:cv OR intitle:resume filetype:pdf OR filetype:doc OR filetype:docx OR filetype:rtf –sample

REMEMBER

Yes, this search string looks long and complex — and it is. But the more complex your query, the finer your results.

The Boolean logic used here works very much like that used on LinkedIn. There are some syntactical differences, though. Basically, this search string will return pages that contain the following:

- » The terms *CFO, chief financial officer, VP finance, EVP finance, vice president finance, chief finance officer, finance director,* and/or *financial director*
- » The terms *raised* and *start-up*
- » The terms *new york* and/or *NY*
- » The terms *cv* and/or *resume* in the page's title
- » Pages of file type PDF, DOC, DOCX, or RTF
- » Pages that do not contain the term *sample*

TIP

As noted in the last bullet, you can search for pages that do not contain a particular keyword. You do this by preceding the keyword with a hyphen. For example, the following string returns only those pages that do not contain the term *specialist, consultant, expert, trainee, intern,* or *associate.* This type of search is missing one key feature, however: the ability to specify Current versus Past, as you can on LinkedIn. Oh well. Nothing's perfect.

financial OR finance –specialist –consultant –expert –trainee –intern –associate

SOURCING IN ACTION

Recently, we worked with a crack unit of six researchers and two sourcers (one online and one telephone) on an executive search for a CFO for a beverage start-up in New York City. To start, the team segmented the search by four key factors (in order of importance):

- Industry
- Experience raising debt and/or equity
- Chartered Accountant designation
- Public company experience

We completed the search in near record time. In just seven weeks, we reduced a field of 32,079 potential CFO and VP finance people to just 438 prospects. We then pared that group down even further to just 43 viable targets. From that, we identified and interviewed 7 fully qualified candidates, passing our top two along to the search chair and client. One of these received — and accepted — the offer. That's good teamwork!

Keep It Going: Sourcing on an Ongoing Basis

Some people wait for someone to vacate a position before they start sourcing for it. But in truth, you should be sourcing all the time, with or without a vacancy. That way, you'll be ready when the need arises.

REMEMBER

Anytime is the right time to recruit if you understand how to leverage your assets.

Where should you direct these ongoing sourcing efforts? To find out, read on.

Cruising alumni networks

People you went to school with or who you've worked with in the past can be prime sources for leads. Often, you can find these people among school or work alumni groups. One way to find these groups is to search for them using your favorite search engine. (Type the name of your school or the company in question and the word *alumni*.) Or, look for them on LinkedIn. There, you'll find thousands of groups for university and college alumni (including sports teams), corporate alumni, and military service. (On a related note, you can also find online groups for members of social clubs, such as Toastmasters, Knights of Columbus, and so on.)

Reaching out to your extended network

You and your company are already part of a vast network of professionals who have a vested interest in your success. We're talking accountants, attorneys, bankers, and venture capital groups, not to mention all your suppliers, loyal customers, and members of trade associations in your industry. Ask them for leads! More often than not, they'll be happy to help. Even better: In addition to suggesting who to approach, these contacts can also tell you who to avoid.

Keeping track of the competition

There should be one senior person in your organization who actively scouts the competition. This person should

>> Know when a competitor's best people are ripe for change, such as when stock options vest or a new product is late to market

>> Know about upcoming acquisitions, which may or may not be welcomed by existing staff

>> Know when a competitor lays off staff

TIP

One slick move is to target talent that is still employed after a layoff and offer them the chance to work with you. Trust us: The best time to tempt someone is when she's pondering her future! By taking this approach, you gain top talent and rob your competition of critical resources while they're at their most vulnerable. Sneaky? Perhaps. But effective.

How do you find this info? For starters, follow your competitors on LinkedIn. Check updates from key employees, track new hires and promotions, and note who has departed and where they've gone. Also, track press releases and any other information the company wants to share.

If a competitor is publicly traded, you can also use Google Finance (http://finance.google.com) to stay abreast of what's happening. You'll find news stories, blog posts, even income statements there.

Building your brand

One of the best ways to land top talent is to build your brand. That way, you make *them* come to *you*.

"Okay," you're thinking, "but how?" One way is to put your senior leaders on display. Farm them out to speak at trade shows. Have them write opinion pieces for trade publications. (Hire a writer if you have to.) In other words, turn them into rock stars to cultivate a positive impression. Then stand back and watch the résumés pour in.

Look, everybody who's anybody wants to play with the best of the best. People want to be on Danica Patrick's pit crew, on Steph Curry's team, or in Serena Williams's player's box. You get the idea. If you want to draw talented executives — the best of the best — then your existing senior staff must be the best of the best, too. (Added bonus: Having the best of the best on staff is also a plus when you're negotiating compensation.)

Stacking your bench

Every great sports team has a roster of highly skilled bench players, just waiting for their opportunity to shine. Often, these players are A players. They'd be starters on any other team.

You, too, should have a strong bench — solid leaders who stand ready at the sideline. These people aren't employees — yet. They're talent that you (or HR) have scouted at industry functions, conferences, and trade shows, or who applied for positions when there weren't any but showed great promise nonetheless.

When you spot a "bench player," keep track of him. As you assess and balance your team's strengths and weaknesses, a starting position just might open up.

Powering up HR

A highly skilled human resources group that takes a proactive approach to sourcing and recruiting can save you time and money. Make sure your HR function

>> Understands how to use social networking sites to share information about your company with potential candidates

>> Is aware of alternative resources for identifying talent, like Hoovers, ZoomInfo, LinkedIn, Facebook, and Google

>> Invests in state-of-the-moment training on sourcing and recruiting techniques

>> Allies with marketing to draft job postings that sell the "sizzle and the steak," so to speak

4

Locating and Evaluating Candidates

Chapter **13**

Recruit Reboot: Recruiting Top Candidates

Enough with the preliminaries! Now that you've nailed down a succinct and engaging job description (and it's gotten the okay of everyone on the search committee), created an enticing position profile, prepped your confidential candidate brief (CCB) questionnaire, completed your market research, and sourced prospects through various means, you're ready to start recruiting. That means paring down your list of potential candidates, calibrating your needs, and reaching out to anyone who makes the cut — in other words, doing the fun part! That's what this chapter is all about.

Passive Aggressive: Passive versus Active Candidates

There are two main types of candidates in the labor market: active candidates and passive candidates.

An *active candidate* is someone who happens to be looking for a job at the exact same time you're recruiting for one. He may be on the market for any number of reasons, like the following:

>> He's employed, but his current employer offers limited growth potential.

>> He's employed, but his current employer is unstable.

>> He has been let go for business-related reasons, like outsourcing.

>> His employer went out of business.

>> He has been fired.

In contrast, a *passive candidate* is someone who is not currently looking for a job. Some passive candidates won't even *discuss* a new opportunity. Others, however, may be persuaded to consider one if it's sufficiently compelling — although they won't seek you out to learn about it.

Engaging a passive candidate requires a personalized approach. Luckily, the intelligence you gathered during the research and sourcing phases should give you an idea how to engage her in conversation. But if she turns you down, don't burn any bridges. You may be able to match her with a different opportunity down the road. (We talk more about approaching passive candidates later in this chapter.)

REMEMBER

You want to attract the best candidates, period — not just the best candidates looking at career ads, trolling job boards, responding to that poorly disguised phone call from a recruiter asking, "Do you know anyone who might be interested in this position?"

YOU'RE FIRED!

David here. Don't assume that if someone's been fired, it's a mark against him. It may say more about the "firer" than the "firee." Perfect example: I was fired from my first job as a headhunter when my boss objected to paying me 50 percent of the $84,000 in deals I closed while on my honeymoon, saying I "got lucky." The next week, I started working with a competing firm down the street. Six months later, I became that firm's top biller. A year after that, in 1988, after billing $758,000 but having my earnings capped at $52,000, I formed my own search firm with partner Anita Martel — and I've never looked back.

Few organizations, or even third-party recruiters, pursue passive candidates. After all, convincing someone who likes her current job to consider taking a new one is a lot of work. But in our experience, it's totally worth it. Here's why:

>> **You won't have to compromise.** Your chances of finding a passive candidate with the exact skillset you need are way higher than finding an active candidate who's a perfect fit.

>> **They're solid producers.** Passive candidates have the talent and work ethic to get the job done. That's why they already have a great position.

>> **They won't try to "sell" you.** Passive candidates buy first and sell later. That is, they take the time to assess the fit before proceeding. And they're less likely to inflate their qualifications to fit the role because, well, they already have a job they love.

From a purely statistical standpoint, it's unlikely that your ideal candidate is available and actively looking at the exact time you need to fill the position. That's why you need to consider passive candidates in addition to active ones. Passive candidates, which represent a huge, largely untapped pool of high-quality executives, aren't superior to active candidates per se; they just have different motives based on their employment status. That's why your recruitment strategy must appeal to both groups. You can't afford to overlook *anyone.* Our advice? Assess the person first. Then consider her current employment situation.

TIP

These days, it's all about branding. That's the best way to draw not just active candidates, but passive ones, too — that is, the ones who *aren't* looking for a job just now. Position your company as a leader, and they'll find out!

THE IMPORTANCE OF "SELLING" YOUR COMPANY

The more recognizable your company brand, the easier it is to attract candidates — especially active job seekers. But that's just the beginning. In addition to fostering positive brand recognition, companies must sell prospects on the idea of working for them, especially as the talent pool shrinks and demand for top people increases. That's why we recommend sales training for HR professionals whose focus is talent acquisition. True selling is identifying a customer need and then fulfilling that need — which, when you think about it, is what recruiting is all about, too. By proactively building relationships and asking effective discovery questions (not interview questions), savvy HR pros can discover what motivates a potential candidate personally, professionally, and financially — and identify how their company can meet those requirements.

A-Listers: Paring Down Your List

Thanks to your research and sourcing activities (or if you hired a consultant, *his* research and sourcing activities), you should have some or all of the following:

>> A list of internal prospects from your organization's "farm team," which you've grown over the last several years

>> A stack of résumés and/or applications (if you advertised the position)

>> A list of referrals from your trusted network of colleagues

>> A "hot list" of prospects who have been referred by the search committee

>> A list of potential targeted prospects who came from your research and sourcing efforts (or those of your consultant)

In this section, you learn how to sift through this mountain of information to pare down your list of prospects. At the end of this exercise, you'll be left with two groups: a "yes" group of potential candidates and a "no" group of individuals who don't make the cut. (Note that there is no "maybe" group. Anyone who is a "maybe" should go in the "yes" group for the time being.)

WARNING

In recruiting, rejecting someone you should have interviewed is far more common than hiring the wrong person. Don't make this rookie mistake!

Assessing your farm team

First, you'll assess your *farm team* — that is, any interested parties who currently work for the organization. That means studying each person's résumé and, if available (and you're permitted access), his employee reviews. You may also compare each prospect's résumé to his LinkedIn profile to ensure consistency and gather any additional intelligence.

TIP

In our experience, internal prospects rarely bother to update their résumés for a position in their current company. (Maybe they assume they'll be interviewed automatically?) To find out if an internal prospect omitted something from his résumé that may be of real value to the role, send him a position profile and a CCB.

You'll divide these potential candidates into two groups: a "yes" group and a "no" group.

After you sort through the list of potential internal candidates, send anyone who makes the cut a link to a psychometric assessment. The results of this assessment will help you decide which prospects to pursue.

We use Great People Inside (www.greatpeopleinside.com) to assess internal candidates at this juncture. It's cost-effective, and it works. During the final stage of the interview process, as you're preparing to make your selected candidate an offer, you'll also use an emotional intelligence assessment tool. For that, we use the EQ-i tool from Multi-Health Systems, Inc. (http://tap.mhs.com/EQi20.aspx). This one-two punch covers all your bases.

What about the "no" group? Inform these people, preferably in writing, that they don't meet your needs. While you're at it, print out a copy of this rejection letter along with any notes about them, staple it to their résumés, and keep it all on file in case you can use them in the future. Oh, and don't dilly-dally. Nobody likes to be strung along. Not only does this help to ensure the continued loyalty of these internal candidates, but it frees you from having to respond to a continuous stream of unnecessary phone calls, emails, and other correspondence as people follow up on their applications.

If you're so inclined, you can provide a brief summary of steps they can take to improve their qualifications for the next time around.

Sifting through résumés and online applications

Sifting through résumés and online applications submitted by external prospects isn't so different from assessing those submitted by internal ones:

1. Divide them into a "yes" group and a "no" group.

2. Have the "yes" group undergo the aforementioned psychometric assessment from Great People Inside.

3. Immediately inform the "no" group, preferably in writing, that they don't meet your needs.

4. Maintain a file on each "no" group member for future use.

Evaluating referrals from your network

Evaluating referrals from your network isn't so different from assessing your farm team or appraising outside prospects — *if* the referral came with a résumé. But what if it didn't — which is often the case? No worries. Just check the prospect's LinkedIn profile (assuming she has one). If it features a résumé or career summary, print it out and review it as you would any other prospect's. While you're there, see if the prospect is currently employed, if she's connected to the person who referred her, and whether the referrer has written a testimonial about the prospect (or vice versa). This will help you clarify the working relationship between the referrer and the prospect.

CANDIDATE EXPERIENCE

We keep harping on the importance of responding to prospects in a timely manner. This is all part of what's called the *candidate experience*. Candidate experience isn't so different from customer experience; both affect how people view your organization.

The candidate experience has always been a big deal. But thanks to websites like Glassdoor (www.glassdoor.com) — which enables people to comment on companies where they've worked or applied for employment the same way they might share their experience at a restaurant, store, or other business — candidate experience is more important than ever. Indeed, candidate experience has become a critical differentiator for organizations that vie for talent in today's hypercompetitive market.

There's even a special award for companies that offer an excellent candidate experience: the Cande Award, issued by a nonprofit called the Talent Board. The Cande Awards may not affect recruiting at the most senior levels because executives rarely comment publicly on their candidacies. However, they may affect the hired executive's ability to recruit a stellar team — which may influence whether they join your organization today. Best to start offering a stellar candidate experience now, if you don't already!

For more information on candidate experience, see Chapter 14.

REMEMBER

Odds are, referrals from your network won't come with an updated résumé. That's because most referrals are passive candidates. As discussed in Chapter 10, requiring these prospects to submit an updated résumé at the outset will either slow the process to a snail's pace or cause the prospect to opt out altogether. (That's why you created a CCB instead.)

In addition to reviewing the prospect's résumé (or not), you should also contact the person who referred her. Ask these questions, in this order, and take notes as she answers:

>> Why, specifically, do you think [prospect's name] would be an outstanding [position's title]?

>> How do you feel [prospect's name] would work with [the hiring manager and any other relevant executives]?

>> Why do you think [prospect's name] might be interested in this role?

REMEMBER

This question is important. You're asking it so you can gather intelligence that will help you craft the opening statement you'll use if you decide to contact the prospect. Trust us: It's to your advantage to understand what might attract the prospect to your organization and/or what's pushing her away from her current job.

>> Is [prospect's name] aware that you've referred her for this position?

>> Is it okay if I mention this conversation with you if I decide to contact [prospect's name]?

If the answer is yes, then do mention the conversation if you speak with the prospect. If it's no, ask the referrer why, and honor his request.

Finally, during this conversation with the referrer, decide whether you will, in fact, pursue the prospect, and inform the referrer of your plans. If you decide *not* to pursue the prospect, but the prospect knows about the referral, determine then and there who will call the prospect to notify her of your decision. (In our experience, this news is best delivered by the person who made the referral.) Then make sure said notification actually occurs.

REMEMBER

As always, if you're not sure about a prospect, err on the side of caution and put her in the "yes" group.

Checking the hot list

Dealing with your *hot list* — referrals from members of your search committee — is just like evaluating referrals from your network. You review their résumés (or not) and check their LinkedIn profiles. You'll also quiz the referrers about the prospects — indeed, you'll ask the exact same questions.

There's just one difference: When a search committee member refers a prospect, she often assumes you'll interview that person no matter what. She expects you to take her word that the prospect is both interested and qualified — especially if she provides the prospect's résumé. As a result, assessing these prospects is a delicate exercise. Still, we urge you to ask the same questions you directed to the referrals in your own network. This will reveal — to you, and to the person who referred the prospect — whether he is, in fact, qualified for the job. If in doubt, or if you're being squeezed by politics, err on the positive side by putting the prospect on the "yes" list.

TIP

After you speak with the search committee member about the prospect, send her a handwritten thank-you card to thank her for her help. Also call her after you speak with the prospect (assuming you do) to let her know how things went.

Following up on your targeted list

Your targeted list is composed entirely of prospects who not only have not applied for the position, but may not even know the hiring organization exists. That means you'll need to contact each prospect personally, one at a time, to assess his interest.

WARNING

Alas, most recruiters fail to make this personal contact at this stage. Instead, they send form emails through vehicles like LinkedIn, which allows them to "touch" a lot of people but in a superficial way. Trust us: This practice represents a sure path to failure. It's akin to spamming and it does *not* work.

Before you go to all that trouble, though, review any documentation you have on each prospect, such as his bio, résumé, LinkedIn profile, or ZoomInfo summary, to cull the list. Then ask the person who sourced and compiled the list one important question about each remaining prospect. (If you compiled the list yourself, use this question to confirm whether each remaining prospect is indeed worth pursuing.)

> Why do you think [prospect's name] would make an excellent [title of position] for our organization?

The point of this exercise is to assess how the prospect's skills and experience line up with the position profile and how his accomplishments map to the needs of the role. If the fit's not there, the prospect is a "no."

REMEMBER

A list of names without this corresponding intelligence is about as useless as an umbrella in a hurricane. Identifying why you should contact each prospect will save you a ton of time.

After you've pared down this list, check around to see if people on the hiring team know anyone on the list. If they do, chat them up to get a better understanding of the prospect's potential and to develop a strategy for contacting the prospect to ensure a warm reception. Maybe they could introduce you to the prospect, or maybe they could contact the prospect to endorse you, the role, and/or the organization.

Bench Press: Benchmarking Your Search

Having culled your list of prospects to a manageable number, you're ready to start "hunting heads," right?

Wrong.

Before you begin contacting prospects, there's one more thing you need to do: Set a benchmark or standard. In executive-recruiting terms, that means choosing one prospect to serve as your gauge in terms of skills, experience, and most important, fit. This benchmark is your ideal candidate — your perfect ten. You'll then interview that candidate as you would any other.

Choosing and interviewing a benchmark candidate is important for three reasons:

>> **It helps you avoid hiring the wrong person.** This is a big deal. As noted by executive search expert Kevin Kelly in the *Financial Times,* "Forty percent of executives hired at the senior level are pushed out, fail or quit within 18 months." Translation: These executives weren't the right people for the job. The numbers are even worse for workers who are promoted into an executive role for the first time. According to the Corporate Executive Board, 50 percent to 70 percent of these new executives fail. Of these, 50 percent "quietly struggle," while 3 percent "fail spectacularly."

TECHNICAL
STUFF

This failure rate is astounding — but it's also predictable. That's because today's young executives are required to assume senior roles at an accelerated pace, despite lacking the experience, knowledge, relational maturity, and emotional maturity to sustain success. And of course, lack of training and development doesn't help. According to one ten-year study of executive performance, during which researchers interviewed some 2,600 Fortune 1000 executives, 76 percent of respondents described their companies' formal development processes as "not helpful" or "minimally helpful" in preparing them for an executive role. In addition, 55 percent described the ongoing coaching and feedback to help them in their executive roles as "minimal, if any." Finally, 45 percent noted they had "minimal understanding of the challenges they would face in an executive role." (This is consistent with our own findings during 1,500 executive search assignments over a combined 50 years.)

>> **It shortens the duration of your search.** Choosing a benchmark candidate requires a bit more work upfront — about three hours or so — but it can reduce the amount of time it takes to conduct your search, sometimes by 50 percent or even more. The bottom line? Yes, benchmarking takes a little extra time upfront, but it will save you time in the long run and help to guarantee you don't waste energy on the wrong candidates. Benchmarking is a little like setting a haystack on fire to quickly find the golden needle within!

>> **It enables you to crystallize your requirements.** Interviewing the benchmark candidate helps you to hone the job description, position profile, and CCB — as well as focus the thinking of the search chair and search committee — to more accurately reflect your needs. It also gives you insight into what constitutes the right "chemistry" (which is important, considering chemistry is the leading reason for rejecting candidates). In this way, you calibrate a common understanding of the ideal candidate.

It's likely — though not guaranteed, of course — that your benchmark candidate will be asked back for more interviews and may even wind up being your top candidate (or at least a strong contender at the end of your search).

Choosing the benchmark candidate

Your benchmark candidate isn't someone you choose at random. Instead, she's someone who is

» Known by you, your search chair, or your executive search professional

» Deemed to be both qualified and a cultural fit

The benchmark candidate should match up with at least 80 percent of your technical parameters and 95 percent of your fit-related soft skills (although this is not a hard and fast rule).

If you hired an external recruiter, he should have no trouble picking a benchmark candidate. Indeed, the moment he finishes writing the position profile, he should begin mentally matching candidates he already knows with the role.

Approaching and interviewing the benchmark candidate

You approach the benchmark candidate as you would any other: by recruiting him, screening him, and speaking with him in person or over the phone to pique his interest in the role; sending him the position profile; and gathering his CCB (which you'll compare to the position profile as well as his résumé, if available, and/or his LinkedIn profile).

Refer to Chapter 10 for more information about the position profile and CCB. As for piquing the candidate's interest in the role, that's covered later in this chapter.

After dispensing with these preliminaries, you're ready to interview the candidate in earnest. You conduct this interview exactly as you would the search chair interview, which involves you, the candidate, your consultant or executive recruiter (if you have one), and the search chair, as discussed in depth in Chapter 14. The primary objective of this interview is to confirm that you and the search chair agree on what constitutes an ideal candidate — especially in terms of fit. An added benefit is that you have a chance to bond with each other as partners working toward a common goal.

FIT HAPPENS

Skills and experience are just check boxes in the candidate's CCB. The real wildcard is fit. Even if it prolongs the search process, you must pinpoint the desired fit and calibrate your search parameters accordingly. Otherwise, you'll wind up wasting time on marginal candidates or, worse, hiring the wrong person. When you know exactly what you're looking for in terms of fit, the "never going to work" candidates become painfully obvious. Note, however, that when we say *fit,* we don't necessarily mean *fit in.* In fact, you may be looking for the exact opposite. For example, if you're in a shift, turnaround, or reboot situation, someone who fits in might be exactly what you *don't* want.

The benchmark interview also gives you a chance to gather feedback from the candidate. This feedback may drive you to adjust the position profile or revise the questions you ask when gathering each candidate's CCB. In our experience, the most common of these changes relate to educational requirements versus years of experience, industry-specific competencies, the necessity (or not) for relocation, and compensation. You want to make these changes now, before you begin your recruiting campaign for real.

A benchmarking interview is a bit like a dry run. It lets you validate your requirements before taking your search to the market. But it's more than that. It's also your first real interview with the person you think is your strongest candidate. You want to impress her as much as she wants to amaze you. Her experience with you and your organization is critical. For more on candidate experience, see Chapter 14.

WARNING

You know the candidate is your benchmark — but the candidate shouldn't. Don't tell her that others are being measured against her. Doing so gains you nothing, but could cause you to lose her as a candidate if she thinks you're playing games with her. That's not your intention!

After the interview

Shortly after the benchmark interview, while you still have the details fresh in your mind, meet with the search chair to discuss the following:

» How closely do the candidate's skills and experience match those in the position profile?

» Are you and the search chair on the same page with regard to the requirements for the position?

>> Is the candidate a good fit?

>> Has the interview with the candidate revealed any gaps in the position profile?

>> Are any calibrations or adjustments needed?

If the benchmark candidate is on target, then you're good to go. If, however, you realize that you're way off in terms of skills, experience, and fit, then you and the search chair must discuss the job description, position profile, and CCB until it's clear what's wrong with them and how they should be fixed. Then, select a new benchmark candidate, and start over.

WARNING

In our experience, it's very rare that the recruiter and search chair misjudge fit more than once. If they do, it may be worth replacing the recruiter, the search chair, or both.

Head Case: Headhunting Prospects

You have a long list of prospects and you've successfully conducted the benchmarking interview. That can only mean one thing: You're ready to headhunt. *Headhunting* means identifying the best-qualified candidate with the highest potential interest in the shortest amount of time.

Making initial contact

As a first step, you must make direct contact with each person on your list (discreetly, of course). "That's easy!" you're thinking. "I'll just email them." Yeah, no. It's true that using email or other forms of technology to connect with prospects can quickly whittle your carefully researched long list down to a handful of interested parties. But are these the *right* interested parties? Probably not. Most likely, the best candidate didn't bother to respond.

To improve your odds of landing the right candidate, you must personally phone each person on your list. Your objective with this initial call is twofold:

>> To introduce yourself

>> To persuade her to allow you to email her the position profile

REMEMBER

The initial phone call is all about opening the door for a second call.

The first time you call, you'll almost certainly get the candidate's voicemail. When you do, leave an intriguing message and your private number so she can call you back.

What do we mean by *intriguing message?* Here's an example. Once, there was a senior executive that both David and his client were hot to talk to. (To say they were "punching above their weight class" would be an understatement.) The executive in question, Mr. Richard Crutchlow, had been (among other things) the first president of Oracle Canada and was renowned for his sales prowess. He was also, it turned out, renowned for his tendency to bite the heads off recruiters.

David hit on an effective strategy for making contact with Crutchlow. Instead of having his head bitten off, he would hand it over on a silver platter. He called him, and left this message on the executive's voicemail: "Mr. Crutchlow, my name is David Perry. I'm phoning you today to apologize." David then recited his phone number and hung up. A few minutes later, Crutchlow called him back. "Apologize for what?" he said. "I don't even know you." David was ready with his reply. "That's why I'm apologizing," he said. "I know who you are, and I know what you've done, and until now I've never had a good reason to call you. For that I apologize!" Crutchlow stayed on the line, and met David's client a few days later. Shortly thereafter, they closed a deal — and his client's stock rose from 69¢ to $7.10 in record time.

If the prospect doesn't phone you back, don't give up. It may take half a dozen calls or more to make contact. (David's personal record is 51 calls to one prospect.) That's a small price to pay to reach a great candidate!

When you finally do make contact — either because the executive has phoned you back or because you've continued your attempts to reach her — you must act quickly to avoid a quick "No, thank you, I'm not looking" followed by a dial tone. You need to quickly establish a peer relationship in order to have a fruitful discussion. That means having a script at the ready.

Here's the script David uses. It's based on an approach he learned from recruiting guru Peter Leffkowitz at a seminar in 1986. These days, Peter leads a new in-house training group designed to transform a corporate talent acquisition division into a highly productive internal SWAT team of recruiters. He graciously agreed to tailor a script for the book:

> [Prospect's name], you and I haven't spoken before, so this call may come as a little bit of a surprise to you — especially because I have so much more knowledge about you than you do about me. Can I grab your focus for a moment?
>
> I head [title of your department], a fairly significant portion of the [name of your function] side of a Fortune 1000 organization (or your organization's position in the

marketplace). I/we have built a foundation of leadership that many in my/our industry (or in IT, accounting, business development, or what have you) consider to serve as a role model for other companies in the [industry or operational sector]. I/we have built that recognition because of one single focus that I/we have: to isolate and cherry-pick the strongest, most creative (or out-of-the-box thinking), and perhaps unappreciated, executive leadership.

My name is [your name], and I drive the [company or department] of [name of your organization].

Pause. . . .

Are you still good time-wise? If not, what are two times that work for you in the next two weeks? I'm not in a rush. This could be an important conversation for us both.

Pause. . . .

You're good? Okay. Let me take some of the mystery out of this.

I (have a team of folks who) have spent some time quietly vetting a handful of [title of the role you're recruiting for] that I/we think have more horsepower than their companies are tapping into. Of course, that's a highly subjective opinion, but that opinion primarily comes from other leaders I/we have respect for.

I'd like to find out your thoughts on that, and, depending on your thoughts, see if you might have an interest in — with utmost confidentiality — exploring a role with [name of your organization] that might make you feel whole professionally. What are your thoughts?

If the prospect responds positively, continue with this:

I'd love to tell you about it. As a matter of fact, I have a detailed summary of the role I'd be pleased to send to you. But first, let me ask you a few questions.

Would you agree that you have a little more horsepower than is required to do your job?

In a utopian situation, where would you stretch your contribution?

Why hasn't that occurred?

Now you're into politics, philosophical differences, low ceilings, nepotism — even commute or travel or being closer to failing parents.

When that discussion is complete, David says:

I'm glad we took time to talk. I'd like to send you a copy of the position profile I prepared for you. What's your personal email address? Or I can FedEx it to your home if you prefer.

David has found that 99 times out of 100, prospects give him their private email addresses. Then, David quickly emails the position profile and politely asks the prospect to stay on the line until she receives it. (This is to ensure the message doesn't bounce back.) Then, he says this:

> I know you're busy, that you're not actively looking for a new position, and you most likely don't have a current résumé — and I don't want one, at least not now. If and when we speak in a few days, and it turns out you're interested in learning more, I'll send you a confidential candidate brief to complete in place of a résumé.

Often, the prospect asks David to go ahead and send the CCB. Then, David tells her that doing so is premature, because it contains privileged information. He explains:

> I'd prefer to take a follow-up call from you after you've had ten minutes of quiet, uninterrupted time to review the position profile.

Next, David asks the prospect when she thinks she'll have a chance to review the position profile, and when he should circle back to gauge her interest and answer any questions she may have.

Finally, before ending the call, David repeats his name and offers his telephone number so the prospect can write them down. He also provides an email he uses especially for recruiting and invites her to look him up online by giving her his company's web address and the URL for his LinkedIn profile.

WARNING

At no point during this initial contact should you engage the prospect in further conversation. There's no point until she has read the position profile. The one exception is if she asks how you got her name. Typically, your answer will be, "You were identified by our research team as someone of high interest because. . . ." Then fill in the "because" with an honest explanation.

David has used this same basic script for 30 years, and it has served him well. It's honest, respectful, and deliberate — non-salesy and matter of fact. He has modified it, of course, but its essential message has remained the same.

If you're looking to come across as professional and sincere — and you are — you should develop a similar script and use it. After you do, read it out loud to a colleague you respect. Did he perceive anything off-putting about the language or tone? If so, adapt your script as needed.

TIP

For more help piquing the interest of senior executives, read *Pitch Anything: An Innovative Method for Presenting, Persuading, and Winning the Deal,* by Oren Klaff (McGraw-Hill). Although the author's approach — which is unique and not the least bit smarmy — focuses on grabbing the attention of an investor during a formal presentation, his principles are transferable to this initial call.

RECRUITING FOR UNUSUAL ROLES

What if you're recruiting for a role that's really foreign to you — say, something that's highly technical or scientific? Fear not. You can determine whether the prospect is fully versed in the field by asking two or three qualifying questions. As for what those questions are, well, it depends on the position. Your best bet is to ask the hiring manager to provide them. (While you're at it, ask him to provide the answers.)

Here's an example of two such questions that David used during a search for a chief technology officer for a satellite company:

- What are the tradeoffs between power and bandwidth?

- How does this affect capacity satellite payload and traveling wave tube amplifiers?

These questions made it easy for David to separate the "truly-ares" from the "wannabes." This approach will work for you as well.

It's up to you when you ask these types of questions. You could do it at the end of the first call or the second. David likes to ask in passing at the end of this first call, just before he hangs up, but you should do what's comfortable for you.

(Dis)qualifying the candidate

When the prospect has had time to review the position profile, call him again. Your goal with this call is not to qualify the prospect, but to disqualify him. By the end of this call, you'll either want to convert this person from a prospect to a candidate or cross him off your list.

REMEMBER

This call isn't about selling the job. It's about you gaining an understanding of who this candidate is as a person, leader, and contributor, and what's important to him.

When you connect — again, it may take a few tries (but hopefully not too many, now that you're no longer a stranger) — start with this:

> Have you had an opportunity to review the position profile I sent you? If so, do you have any questions I can address or would you prefer I call you back at another time that's more convenient?

Assuming the prospect is free to talk, dive right in. Field any questions he may have, answering them as best you can. If you notice the prospect's questions are particularly incisive or in depth, take it as a good sign — it likely means he's interested in the position.

After you've exhausted his questions, try saying the following:

> I don't have any specific questions for you at the moment. However, I'd appreciate it if you could roll me back to when you first got out of college and take me through your career up to now — that is, if you have the time.

You'll find that most prospects do have the time. Some may even talk almost continuously for as long as an hour. No matter how long he speaks, your job is to listen — *actively* listen. That means no interrupting. It also means using your emotional intelligence to pick up on unspoken clues that may hint at a more complicated story — in other words, reading between the lines.

REMEMBER

You need to understand what makes the prospect tick — the types of challenges he rallies for, the types of people he works best with — all the while relating your newfound intelligence to the position's requirements (especially with regard to fit, as defined by your benchmark interview). In our experience, a person's character can be distilled from the patterns that reappear throughout his life. Specifically, you're looking to discover if he has a strong *internal* locus of control (that is, he tends to believe he controls the outcome of events) or a strong *external* locus of control (in other words, he thinks external circumstances dictate the outcome of events). You'll be able to assess this if you ask him to step you through his career story from the beginning to the present day.

Really, you're like one of those CIA psychologists, who examine the speech patterns of world leaders for clues about their personalities.

Specifically, listen for the following:

>> Are there recurring themes in his career?

>> How does he address controversy?

>> How does he tackle new challenges?

>> Does he respond to situations in ways that will work in this organization?

>> How did his contributions positively affect the organization (or not)?

- » What types of people does he work best with?
- » Did he grow as a result of his accomplishments?
- » Is he adaptable?
- » Is he ambitious?
- » Is he resilient?
- » Does he focus on execution?
- » Does he have personal issues that may influence his performance?

Also, as the prospect details each career move, consider these questions:

- » Did the move make sense?
- » Did his reasons for leaving make sense?
- » How clearly did he see the situation?
- » Has his career progressed in a steady fashion?
- » Does it seem like he makes the same mistakes over and over again?
- » What does his length of tenure at each company tell you?
- » Are there holes in his story?
- » Were there specific aspects of each job he liked?
- » Were there specific aspects of each job he didn't like?
- » Do any similar negatives exist in your company?

REMEMBER

You already know the prospect is technically qualified for the job. What you're hoping to find out during this call is what makes him tick.

When you're up to speed on the prospect's career, it's decision time. Do you want to pass this prospect to the next point in the process? Or is it better to pass him by? In other words, given what you know about your requirements, is this prospect a good fit, and could this opportunity be the next logical step in his career?

Passing the prospect to the next point in the process

You like this prospect — a *lot*. But is the feeling mutual? That's what you need to find out — that, and what might motivate her to leave her current position and join your organization. These motivating factors typically fall into two categories:

>> **Pain factors:** A *pain factor* is anything at the candidate's current job that she's not 100 percent satisfied with and that may be pushing her away. Pain factors might include a change in senior management, rumors of an acquisition, or the company moving in a new direction. To identify pain factors, ask her these questions:

- Obviously, if you were totally satisfied at your current position at [name of prospect's current company], we wouldn't be talking today. What are some of the factors in your current work situation that you're not completely satisfied with? Why are these important to you?

- What are some of the factors you hope to find in a new employment situation that aren't present in your current situation? Why are these important to you?

>> **Gain factors:** A *gain factor* is anything that appears in your position profile or is revealed during your conversations that piques the candidate's interest in the role. To identify gain factors, ask her these questions:

- What are some of the factors that motivated you to talk with us today? What did you find attractive?

- What was it about the description of the mandate at [name of your company] that most interested you? (Repeat as needed to find additional points of interest.)

TIP

When the candidate sends you her CCB, see if it reflects these pain and gain factors. If so, that should give you some indication of how to keep her engaged throughout the interview process. It may also provide insight as to how to craft and offer a deal.

Next, ask the prospect if you can send her the questionnaire for the CCB. Explain that this is in lieu of an updated résumé, and that you want to send it to her because you think she's a great fit. Then wait for her response. Usually, the prospect will tell you how she feels about things right away.

Finally, end the conversation on a cordial note and explain the next steps — namely, that your next conversation, which will be a face-to-face meeting, will be driven by how responsive the candidate is. Also explain that the decision to move forward and investigate the opportunity rests with her.

Passing the prospect by

As we like to say in the recruiting biz, "Many are called, few are chosen." And it's true. Only a few candidates will advance beyond this second call to a face-to-face interview. Indeed, it's not unusual to cull several hundred prospects into a handful of top candidates during this phase of the search.

If this prospect is a no-go, let him know right away, and explain why. Be truthful and direct, but gentle. It's only fair to the candidate — no one likes to be left hanging. And remember: The candidate you reject for an opportunity today may be ideal for one tomorrow (or could refer someone who is), so act accordingly. After his conversation with you, he should feel as if he's the "one that got away."

What's next?

Obviously, you don't just make these calls to one prospect. You make one or both of them to every contact on your list.

After you finish, decide who you want to meet and why. You're looking for no more than eight to ten people. Invite them for face-to-face interviews. (Chapter 14 talks about this and subsequent interviews in great detail.) From here on out, you'll spend your time interviewing only those prospects you know are viable candidates — people who will excel in the role if you offer it to them!

Chapter **14**

Interview Interlude: Interviewing Top Candidates

You've nailed down a precise and accurate job description. You've composed an enticing position profile that highlights the job's potential for your target audience. And you've crafted an impressive confidential candidate brief (CCB) — one that will both intrigue candidates and engage them in a dialogue about the role (without requiring them to submit a résumé). In other words, you know what the ideal candidate looks like. Now, whether you're part of the internal corporate hiring team or an external recruiter, you're ready to identify that ideal candidate among your many prospects by interviewing them.

Executive interviews are different from regular interviews. For one thing, there's more at stake. For another, executive interviews must place special focus on revealing the candidate's personal qualities. Yes, the candidate's knowledge, skills, experience, and track record are vital. But we can't stress enough the importance of evaluating the candidate's personal qualities to ensure a cultural fit within your organization.

What personal qualities are we talking about? Here are a few examples:

>> **Leadership attributes:** All key leadership roles require individuals who can develop a plan, assemble a team, and lead the team to work the plan.

>> **Work ethic:** The best leaders have a work ethic that's second to none. Moreover, they possess extraordinary stamina. These people will do whatever it takes to get the job done!

>> **Intelligence:** An effective executive is super smart, in terms of both raw intelligence and emotional intelligence. They also have solid intuition. This enables them to quickly make good business decisions under pressure, often without having all the details.

>> **Passion:** Passion, energy, drive, commitment — what we often call the "fire in their belly" — all these are requirements for a top executive. That's how they drive an energized and enthusiastic work force. Often, there comes a time during the interview process when the right candidate — your next great hire — develops a passion for the challenge and opportunity you've presented, and can articulate how she could contribute.

TIP

Watch closely to see how the candidate's perception of the opportunity evolves over time. You'll pick up clues about what's important to her, which you can use later to close the deal.

Not surprisingly, the interview process for key leadership roles will likely take considerably longer than it does for positions lower on the ladder. *Really* getting to know each candidate — which, given the stakes, is absolutely imperative — takes time!

REMEMBER

We're well aware that what follows describes a rigorous, formal approach to interviewing. Although we advocate making it as simple as possible for candidates to engage with us and discover details about the opportunity, we don't advocate you making it easy for them to join your organization — not at this level.

Stage Right: Understanding the Progressive Two-Stage Interview Process

We believe in making it easy for candidates to find out about your opportunity. But we *don't* believe in making it easy for them to join your organization. There's too much at stake! After all, you're not hiring a clerical worker; you're hiring an *executive.* To make sure you land the right person, we recommend that you thoroughly vet each candidate using a rigorous, two-stage interview process.

THE 80/20 RULE

Your goal in the interview process is to vet the candidate — and that means letting him speak. During all interviews in the two-stage process, let the candidate do 80 percent of the talking. That way, you can accurately assess his abilities and shortcomings. If you find yourself talking more than 20 percent of the time, zip it.

REMEMBER

Some people worry that a rigorous interview process might turn candidates off, but we've found the opposite to be true. And even if we hadn't, we'd *still* recommend a rigorous process. The obvious question, though, is what do we mean by *rigorous?* What we *don't* mean is dragging out the process for months on end or asking the candidate to jump through endless hoops. Instead, we mean ensuring that the candidate and key stakeholders have met a sufficient number of times, all parties feel comfortable with each other, all questions have been addressed, and the only thing left to discuss is the offer.

Stage 1: Identify, evaluate, engage

Stage 1 involves the following interviews, in order:

1. The benchmark interview

2. The initial contact

3. The screening interview and CCB

During this stage, you'll cull a long list of prospects — possibly more than a hundred candidates — to a short list of 20. Ideally, this takes about six to ten working days. (We cover these three interviews in Chapter 13.)

Stage 2: The five-part robust interview

In stage 2, you conduct the following five interviews, in order (see Figure 14-1):

1. **Face-to-face interview:** The candidate interviews face-to-face with the recruiter and consultant.

2. **Search chair interview:** The candidate interviews with the recruiter or consultant and search chair.

3. **Hiring manager interview:** The candidate interviews with the recruiter or consultant, search chair, and ultimate hiring authority.

4. **Search committee interview:** The candidate interviews with the recruiter or consultant, search chair, and search committee.

5. **Candidate presentation:** The candidate meets with the search committee to deliver a formal presentation.

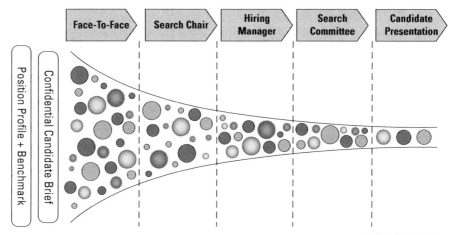

FIGURE 14-1:
The five-part
robust interview.

During this stage — which may take several weeks due to the number of players involved — you'll pare your short list of 20 candidates down to an even shorter list of two to three candidates. Then you'll pare *that* list down to your top choice. By the end of the interview process, the winning candidate will have spent more than a dozen hours answering (and asking) questions, and will have met with everyone involved.

Stage 2 interviews are typically done in person, face to face. In general, these interviews involve the candidate (obviously) and at least two interviewers. Why two interviewers? Two reasons: So that one can ask the questions and the other can act as a scribe, and to correct for any personal biases.

TIP

Formal interviews lend themselves to canned responses, can be practiced, and may gloss over important social behavior. Informal meetings on the other hand, may favor candidates who are spontaneous or charismatic but not as thoughtful, and may adversely influence your decision because they're likeable. To mitigate these problems, try using both types of meetings. In our experience, when you use this approach and script behavioral and situational questions into discussions, it always yields more useful information.

WARNING

Everyone has personal biases — including many we're not aware of. These biases, which might relate to gender, race, religion, or other characteristics, often guide our decisions about a candidate, even if they have no bearing whatsoever on the candidate's ability to do the job. To ensure you don't reject the best candidate due to personal bias, two interviewers should participate in all face-to-face interviews.

These interviews are typically formal in nature. That being said, it's a good idea to sprinkle some informal meetings in there, too — or at the very least to enjoy some informal moments during the interview process. That way, you can get a sense of the candidate's true personality and social skills. (That's why we suggest adding an informal component to interview 4, covered later in this chapter.)

The remainder of this chapter covers the different types of stage 2 interviews. (We talk about the stage 1 interviews — the benchmark interview, initial contact, and screening interview — in earlier chapters.) First, though, let's talk about how to prepare for these interviews and what to do afterward.

Preppy Handbook: Prepping for Each Interview

The interview process starts long before you meet the candidate in person. Here's what you need to do before any stage 2 interview:

>> Send an itinerary to the candidate (if the interview involves travel and/or multiple meetings).

>> Review documentation on the candidate and position.

>> Get the search committee up to speed on the candidate and the interview process.

>> Prepare documentation for the candidate.

Sending the itinerary

As soon as you've made all the arrangements for an interview that involves travel and/or multiple meetings for the candidate, send an itinerary via FedEx or express mail to the candidate's home address. The "home address" part is critical. If you send the itinerary to his work, someone else might open it, which is bad. And for the love of all that is holy, do *not* send the itinerary to the candidate via his corporate email account. Most companies monitor employee emails. If the upcoming interview will involve the search committee, also distribute copies of the itinerary to each member.

In addition to covering all travel arrangements (if applicable), the itinerary spells out the time, date, and venue for the meeting.

TIP

If an interview is expected to span more than a couple of hours, be sure to schedule regular breaks. Nature does have a way of calling at the most inconvenient times! Oh, and regarding the meeting venue: Avoid public or high-traffic areas. For confidentiality reasons, you don't want anyone who might recognize the candidate to see him!

The itinerary should also include

>> The name of the person who will greet the candidate upon his arrival

>> The name and title of the person who will conduct the interview(s)

>> What format the interview will be, and whether anyone will be joining via teleconference or video (both of which are generally unacceptable at this level except for in rare circumstances)

>> How long the interview will take

>> What information the interview will cover

>> What (if anything) the candidate needs to bring or prepare

WARNING

Avoid rescheduling interviews due to conflicts if at all possible. Yes, plans change, and it's impossible to prepare for every contingency. But you *can* take time upfront to schedule around existing plans and commitments, like meetings, work-related travel, and vacations. Rescheduling due to a conflict that could've been avoided won't help you make the best impression!

Reviewing documentation about the candidate and position

Before every interview, each participant should thoroughly review the candidate's résumé and any available ancillary information, such as the CCB. Depending on where you are in the interview process, they may also review notes, reports, or other feedback from previous interviews. And if the candidate has published any articles or white papers, participants should read those, too. If they discover anything that requires clarification, they should prepare interview questions accordingly.

It's a good idea to compare the candidate's résumé and CCB against her LinkedIn profile, to make sure there are no discrepancies.

Speaking of interview questions, interview participants should also review the interview guide created for this position. This guide contains basic qualifying questions, as well as questions for use by various members of the hiring team, including the search chair, the ultimate hiring authority, and the search committee. (Chapter 10 discusses the interview guide in more detail.)

Getting the hiring team up to speed

Before every interview, connect with all members of the hiring team to brief them on

>> Why they should interview the candidate

>> The candidate's interest, concerns, and fit

>> Areas where the candidate might be lacking in relevant experience

>> How they should welcome the candidate

Ultimately, what you're trying to do here is explain to the hiring team why you consider the candidate to be right for the role and why the candidate is interested in the position. This consistent transparency helps to ensure you hire the right candidate for the job.

Preparing documentation for the candidate

After their initial meetings, most candidates will download and review any publicly available news and reports about your company, such as its 10-K report, 10-Q report, 8-K report, proxy statement, Schedule 13D, and Form 144. What they *won't* be able to access, but may be very interested in reviewing, are internal newsletters or any comparative studies you might want to share. As part of your attempt to "sell" the candidate on your company, it's a good idea to make this information available to her. Oh, and if the candidate would need to relocate in the event she accepts the job? Now's a good time to provide materials about the community, including information about housing and schools. (Your local government and Chamber of Commerce are good resources for this.)

If the candidate fails to review the publicly available materials we mention, we'd think twice about hiring her. Her failure to perform proper due diligence on the company could be a sign of carelessness.

Afterburner: After the Interview

After each stage 2 interview, you must assess the candidate. You're not looking for perfection, obviously. But you do want to decide whether you think the candidate was prepared, convincing, credible, compelling, and logical, and whether he spoke well. You and anyone else on the hiring team who participated in the interview should also discuss what transpired during the meeting. Try answering these three questions:

>> What has the candidate accomplished that is relevant to the company's goals?

>> How does his experience meet the company's needs?

>> Is the candidate's story credible and convincing?

Finally, you should note any concerns you have about the candidate and flag any issues that may require further investigation.

TIP

If you're working with a consultant, this person should spearhead these post-interview efforts. At a minimum, she should provide ongoing feedback after debriefing both the candidate and the interviewers.

GUT CHECK

Yes, we know. Your gut feeling about a person is neither logical nor scientific. But you're not Mr. Spock, and this isn't the USS *Enterprise.* Inexperienced interviewers should *not* rely on gut instinct during the interview process. But if the interviewer is, say, an executive with 20-plus years of experience, she can — and should — listen to her gut. If you're worried about any unconscious biases you may have, remember these key points:

- The functional spec meets the needs of the business plan, and the candidate meets the criteria listed in the functional spec.

- The candidate is already known to be outstanding. He has been systematically courted for this role by search professionals for weeks or even months, or he has enjoyed a strong business relationship with a key member of your search team for even longer than that.

- Everyone who has vetted the candidate has the organization's best interests at heart and would not put forth a candidate who was not top-notch.

In other words, it's okay to check your gut when you know the candidate meets all the key criteria.

During these follow-up meetings, don't be afraid to consider how you *feel* about the candidate. What does your gut tell you?

With this information in hand, the interviewers indicate "go," "stop," or "need more information" about the candidate. They then write an interim candidate assessment report and submit it to everyone else involved in the search.

Face Time: Conducting the First Face-to-Face Interview

Participants: Candidate, recruiter, consultant (if applicable), and scribe (optional)

Time: Two hours

When you conduct this interview, you may find yourself experiencing *déjà vu*. That's because this interview is similar to the screening interview you conducted in stage 1. The difference? This interview is *much* longer.

REMEMBER

If you did engage a consultant, he should be by your side for the remainder of the interviews.

The objective of this interview is to compare the accomplishments, experience, and skills outlined in the candidate's résumé and CCB with the position profile, to look for inconsistencies, and to identify patterns of success or failure. You'll also:

>> Assess the candidate's communication skills.

>> Judge fit, as per the benchmark interview.

>> Gauge the candidate's executive presence.

>> Perform a deep dive on the candidate's leadership style.

>> Evaluate the candidate's adaptability.

REMEMBER

When you conduct each of the interviews discussed in this chapter, one person asks the questions and another takes notes. (You can switch up who does what, as desired.) If you have a scribe, taking notes is that person's role.

Getting the candidate's story (again)

The first half of this interview is about getting the candidate's story (again). First, though, you want to welcome the candidate, thank her for coming, ask if she has any questions for you, and answer those questions truthfully and to the best of your abilities. If the candidate asks a question you don't know the answer to, tell her you'll find out and follow up. (Then do that.)

Welcome the candidate, thank her for coming, and ask if she has any questions before the start of every stage 2 interview, not just this one.

With these preliminaries out of the way, you're ready to begin. Start by saying something along these lines:

> Could you please take us through your career again, like you did during our phone interview, but this time allowing us to ask you some questions along the way? I'd like it if you could start with your first job out of college and work up to the present time.

As the candidate speaks, ask probing follow-up questions that focus on her contribution, leadership, adaptability, personal style, and fit. In particular, ask these five questions as she discusses each stop on her career journey:

>> **How did you find out about that job?** Most people find out about job openings on job boards, company websites, or social media sites, like LinkedIn. But top executives aren't "most people." When it comes to employment, great leaders don't seek; they're *found.* You're looking for someone with a history of being hunted. Otherwise, she probably doesn't have the skills or experience you need.

>> **Why did you take that job?** Top performers know why they wanted a particular job. They have a plan, and they seize any opportunity that advances it. Just don't be surprised if the candidate's answer *doesn't* mention titles or money. Those are secondary measures of success. These execs understand — and actively seek — what motivates and challenges them.

>> **What did you learn in that job?** Ultimately, you ask this question to see whether the candidate was successful in the job or if she failed. If it's the latter, you want to know whether the candidate accepts blame for that failure or lays it on everybody else. Either way, you're looking to find out what lessons the candidate learned and how she applied them. If the candidate's answer to this question doesn't translate to your requirements, ask additional questions to ascertain how she learns and, more important, whether she's committed to continuous learning.

>> **What did you accomplish in that job?** Obviously, the candidate's answer to this question reveals her accomplishments. But it can also reveal whether her accomplishments grew in size and complexity over time. And, perhaps more important, it can help you assess her leadership style and management skills.

Narcissistic, command-and-control types generally reveal themselves in their answer to this question, taking credit for saving the world single-handedly, without the help of a team of some type. Unless the role specifically calls for this type of person (and few do), they're to be avoided at all costs.

>> **Why did you leave that job?** Good people do leave for a better opportunity or more money. But they also leave because an employer is too demanding, the company has moved in a new direction, or (most commonly) they don't like their boss or co-workers. Whatever the candidate's answer, record it (you'll need to verify it if she becomes your top choice), and resist the temptation to ask for more details. Instead, pause for a few seconds to give her the opportunity to explain if she wishes. And most important, don't be judgmental. You're not looking for a saint.

Too many underwhelming executives are hired simply because they were at the right place at the right time. To weed out these poseurs, you need to do more than listen to candidates talk about what they've accomplished; you need to home in on the details to find out how things *actually* got done. If a candidate can't describe this in detail, then odds are she wasn't the architect of the achievement, and instead benefited from a halo effect. As one client used to say, "Even a blind squirrel finds an acorn once in a while!"

When you're caught up on the candidate's work history, follow up by asking her these two critical questions:

>> **What are your proudest accomplishments?** Most people will stick to work-related triumphs, but you're also interested in what she has achieved outside of work. The point here is to get a sense of how she establishes goals and faces adversity — in her professional *and* personal lives. Sacrifices made for personal achievements say a lot about a person's character.

>> **What is the one thing you would change about your current company if you could?** If the candidate can immediately list her dislikes, if the list contains more than a few complaints, and if she cites similar frustrations when talking about other places she has worked, consider it a red flag. Double red flag if the same conditions apply in the role you're recruiting for.

Follow up on patterns that concern you. Some people never take ownership, always seeing things as someone else's problem. They'll say things like, "That project was above my pay grade." Others refuse to take responsibility for failures, making statements like, "They threw me under the bus!" Still others consistently spar with their bosses, peers, or employees. "We just didn't get along," they'll say. These types of comments are a clear DEFCON 2 alert to not proceed further with this candidate. If you hire her, these patterns are unlikely to change.

By now, skills and experience are a given. At this point, you're looking for patterns of behavior and thoughtful answers to assess culture and fit.

Fact-checking the candidate's story

The first hour of this interview is about getting the candidate's story. The second hour is about fact-checking that story. You want to confirm that what the candidate said during this interview matches what he said during the recruiting and screening calls and on his CCB and résumé. If you note any inconsistencies, question him on them. This is important! You need to understand his story correctly.

Even though this portion of the interview is about fact checking, the tone should be "normal business conversation," not "interrogation." You're courting the candidate, not cross-examining him!

First, cover the basics. That way, the details don't come back to bite you. This will also establish some checkpoints for the reference calls to come. For each previous job, starting with his first one out of college, ask the following:

>> **Dates:** What were the candidate's exact dates of employment? Were there any gaps between jobs? If so, find out why. If the candidate sat idle for a significant period of time, it could be a red flag. Yes, he might have been taking classes or consulting, both of which are fine. But it could be he was on the golf course — in which case, not so much.

>> **Hierarchy:** Find out how the company was organized and how the candidate fit in. Also pin down who he reported to, who his peers were, and what he did. If the candidate held many titles within the organization, confirm them all, and see whether each new role was a promotion or a lateral move. All of this will provide you with a clearer picture of the candidate's real responsibilities.

>> **Authority:** What was the candidate's span of authority? How many people were on his team? Did he make changes to his team? If so, why? What was the outcome?

>> **Contribution:** It helps to know what shape the business was in when the candidate joined. What problems did it face? What were its top three short- and long-term objectives? How effectively did the candidate contribute to the achievement of those objectives?

>> **Performance:** How did the business perform compared to the plan? How did it perform compared to the previous five years? What impact did the candidate have on the company's overall performance? How did his accomplishments affect the business?

You should expect 100 percent consistency in the candidate's answers to these questions. If you notice a discrepancy, try calling the candidate out by injecting a punctuated pause into the conversation. It will quickly become obvious whether the candidate intended to be deceptive. If you catch the candidate in a lie — even a little white one — then you must remove him from the running.

Closing the interview

If you're interested in advancing the candidate to the next round of interviews, at the end of this interview do the following:

» Confirm the candidate's interest in proceeding to the next interview, with the search chair.

» Confirm the candidate's interest in the role as currently spec'd out, if offered.

» Note any concerns.

» Ask if the candidate has any outstanding questions.

Essentially, even though it's just your first interview with the candidate, you're using these questions to jump-start the offer process by uncovering potential stumbling blocks or even deal-killing issues (for example, if the candidate's compensation expectations — or yours — are way out of line).

REMEMBER

The last thing you want is for your top candidate to become a reluctant bride at the end of your courtship. You want to "close the deal," so to speak. To do so, offer continuous feedback throughout the interview process — including after every interview. Oh, and be quick to address any issues the candidate may flag, no matter how trifling they may seem to you. For more on closing the deal, see Chapter 16.

Chair Up! Conducting the Search Chair Interview

Participants: Candidate, recruiter or consultant (if applicable), search chair, and scribe (optional)

Time: Two to three hours

This interview is designed to further assess the candidate's suitability for the role.

Getting the candidate's story (yet again)

The purpose of this meeting is, once again, to get the candidate's story. This time, however, you're looking for the abridged version. Ask the candidate to spend 10 to 15 minutes detailing her career, starting with her first job out of college and working up to the present time. This gives the recruiter (now listening to the candidate's story for the umpteenth time) a chance to check it for consistency. At the same time, it offers the search chair additional insight into the candidate's background, beyond what appears in her résumé and CCB.

REMEMBER

This discussion could provide a clue as to the candidate's level of interest. For example, if she draws analogies from past experience or offers her own insights unprompted, that's a good sign that she has thought seriously about the role and can see herself accepting it if offered.

Next, it's time to assess the following:

>> The candidate's ability to deliver the desired outcomes

>> The candidate's interpersonal skills

This assessment will likely take two hours or so.

Assessing whether the candidate can deliver the desired outcomes

No matter what job you're hiring for, you need to know the candidate can deliver the goods. That means drilling down on one or two of the professional accomplishments listed in his CCB or discussed in a previous interview. Also ask him to flesh out the details of one accomplishment in his personal life. The candidate's work-related accomplishments will likely give you a sense of how he operates within a team, while his personal ones might tell you how he does with more solitary activities.

Listen carefully while the candidate speaks, and don't interrupt except to ask for clarification if necessary. Ask yourself:

>> What can we glean from the language he uses to tell the story? Does he tell it in an interesting manner that holds our attention? Does he try to talk over our heads, or is he able to converse in a more common, everyday fashion? Does he drop names in an attempt to impress us?

If a candidate uses lots of five-dollar words, it's a good indication that he's incapable of communicating well with those outside the executive suite — which is not good. Executives must be able to communicate with anyone, from people on Wall Street to the rank and file at a town-hall meeting.

>> Is the candidate a team player, a team leader, or both? Does the candidate seem to gravitate toward one of these traits — team player or team leader — exclusively?

>> Is the candidate a lone wolf?

>> Does the candidate have the ability to adapt to situations?

>> Will the candidate's style work with the company's culture?

Next, ask the candidate to tell you about a time when things didn't go as planned. This time, as the candidate speaks, consider these questions:

>> How does the candidate explain the situation?

>> Does the candidate take responsibility for the outcome, or does he blame someone else?

>> Is the candidate quick to throw others under the bus, or does he rise to the defense of the team?

Finally, find out how the candidate defines success. Ask him:

>> How do you define success?

>> Do you believe you've been successful? (This is a fairly general question, so it's not unusual for the candidate to answer by saying, "Yes and no." If that happens, drill down for specifics.)

>> Did you succeed in achieving your performance objectives this year?

>> What specifically did you do?

Finding out how the candidate defines success is important. You won't know if you should kick your interview partner under the table unless you ask this question!

Determining whether the candidate has solid interpersonal skills

Now you're ready to assess the candidate's interpersonal skills, as well as her leadership style and her approach to goal setting. To draw out this information, use these prompts:

>> **Describe an experience from your past that demonstrates that you're an effective change agent.** The candidate's response will help you assess the candidate's flexibility and adaptability.

>> **Tell us about a specific time when staff reductions required restructuring of the workload.** Follow up by asking how she did the restructuring, who she involved, and how and why she involved them. The candidate's response will help you gauge her interpersonal effectiveness.

>> **Tell us what you've done to create an atmosphere of trust and empowerment within your sphere of influence, and what tangible results you've seen as a result of your efforts.** The candidate's response will reveal her approach to organizational stewardship.

Finally, probe the candidate regarding her personal ambitions. Try asking these questions:

>> What life goals have you set for yourself?

>> By what standards do you measure your personal success?

>> What plans do you have for self-improvement and personal development?

Answering the candidate's questions and wrapping up the session

Devote the next 45 minutes to an hour to fielding any questions the candidate may have. As before, answer any questions you can, and promise to follow up on any you can't.

Finally, wrap up the session by asking the candidate these two key questions:

>> **Why do you think you're a good fit for this opportunity?** The candidate's answer to this question will help you assess how well his past accomplishments align with this position.

>> **What's your plan for making our organization better?** Unless you're dealing with a government agency, what you're looking to find out here is how the candidate will make the organization money, save the organization money, and/or improve its efficiency. This is true to some degree even for nonprofits.

Closing the interview

If you're interested in advancing the candidate to the next round of interviews, then at the end of this interview, ask the same questions you asked at the end of interview 1 (see the earlier "Closing the interview" section). Also do the following:

>> Discuss compensation, including any "golden handcuffs" in effect.

>> Identify what type of counteroffer she would accept from her current employer to remain.

Next steps

After this interview, you're ready to start referencing and fact-checking on an informal basis. We suggest using a specialized CRM program like Invenias (www.invenias.com). With Invenias, which is designed specifically for recruiters, you can easily see which of your existing contacts may know the candidate. You can also use Invenias to search LinkedIn and ZoomInfo for people who have worked with the candidate in the past. You can then use Invenias to build a reference list. (For more on checking references, read Chapter 15.)

WARNING

It's okay to build a reference list, but don't start contacting these references just yet. At this stage of the game, you must maintain confidentiality. Otherwise, you can kiss the (very upset you blew his cover) candidate goodbye.

Hire Rise: Handling the Hiring Manager Interview

Participants: Candidate, recruiter, consultant (if applicable), search chair, and ultimate hiring authority

Time: Two to three hours

By now, the candidate has been thoroughly vetted. She has made it this far because the recruiter, consultant, and search chair believe she'd be a great fit for the job. But it's the ultimate hiring authority who has to work with the candidate day in and day out, so he's the one who needs to make the final call. That's what this interview is about: ensuring the ultimate hiring authority likes the candidate and can work with her. It's also a chance to assess the candidate's systems thinking and creative thinking, as well as her leadership style.

Assessing the candidate's systems thinking

You can gauge the candidate's systems thinking by asking him to talk you about a specific decision he made within his organization that had unexpected consequences outside of his organization. Then follow up by asking the candidate how he dealt with those consequences.

TIP

We recommend that you let the search chair ask these questions. That's because most likely, the search chair has served in one or more corporate executive positions, which required him to make these types of judgments on a daily basis.

Gauging the candidate's creative thinking

Next, you want to get a sense of the candidate's creative thinking. Ask these questions:

>> What approach do you take to improve performance?

>> How, specifically, do you identify problems?

>> What strategies do you use to measure the impact of a problem?

>> How do you deal with problems?

>> How do you measure your success or failure in dealing with problems?

>> Describe a problem you dealt with from its initial identification to its resolution.

TIP

Have the ultimate hiring authority ask these questions. He'll work most closely with the new hire and will be responsible for her results.

Evaluating the candidate's leadership style

Executives often favor a command-and-control leadership style. This approach, however, often doesn't work with today's knowledge workers. For this reason, it's important to get a sense of the candidate's innate leadership style. That means reviewing his level of self-awareness, candor, flexibility, and humility.

The U.S. Department of Veteran Affairs (VA) offers solid guidance on how to assess these qualities. It suggests asking the following prompts and questions:

>> Everyone makes the occasional poor decision or does something that just doesn't turn out right. Give an example of when this happened to you.

>> What did you learn?

>> What would you do differently?

How the candidate responds to these questions will help uncover any narcissistic tendencies that would interfere with his ability to get the job done.

Closing the interview

Once again, if you're interested in advancing the candidate to the next round of interviews, ask the same questions you asked at the end of interview 1 (see the first "Closing the interview" section in this chapter). Also do the following:

>> Hammer out all compensation-related issues once and for all.

>> Ask the candidate for references. You'll follow up on these *after* the interviews — but only if the search team decides to extend the candidate a job offer (assuming her references are satisfactory, of course).

TIP

If there are issues the candidate doesn't want you to know about — she has a drug or alcohol problem, her demeanor is more sand than substance, she has family issues that regularly interfere with work, she has a short temper, she blames others for her own failures, and so on — then hopefully, her references may bring them to light sooner rather than later.

Finishing the Search Committee Interview

Participants: Candidate, recruiter or consultant (if applicable), search chair, and search committee

Time: Three to four hours

This interview, called a *panel interview,* is not just a meet-and-greet; it's more of a make-or-break. It's the hiring team's last chance to vet the candidate. In fact, this interview is *so* important, it's actually *two* interviews — one formal and one informal.

The point of the formal interview is to identify something — anything — the recruiter, consultant, search chair, and ultimate hiring authority may have missed.

This interview is conducted without the ultimate hiring authority present. More important, the search committee conducts this interview without knowing the results of the ultimate hiring authority's interview. That way, they're forced to develop their own opinion instead of simply following along with the boss, as some are apt to do.

The consultant or search chair should design the base interview questions for each of the search committee members and/or review all questions to be asked, mostly so there's no unnecessary duplication of questions. One-on-one meetings are encouraged with individual committee members so both the interviewer and interviewee can dig more deeply into specifics functional or departmental issues the panel would have little interest in.

The informal interview, which typically takes place over lunch, is meant to expedite bonding and buy-in — both critical aspects of the close.

REMEMBER

Ultimately, the purpose of these meetings is for the search committee to confirm the candidate's fit and help decide whether he's the right person for the job.

Prepping for the interview

Not surprisingly, given the stakes, these interviews involve a bit of prep work upfront.

Earlier, we talk about how before every interview, each participant thoroughly reviews the candidate's résumé and CCB, notes and reports from previous interviews, articles and white papers published by the candidate, and so on. The same goes here — except in this case, the search chair facilitates matters by consolidating all this information, along with a meeting itinerary, into a single packet and sending a copy to all the committee members for review (preferably to their home addresses).

The search chair then meets with the search committee to pose this question:

> Given what we know about the candidate and what we need to achieve by staffing this role, what do we want to find out about this candidate personally and professionally that we don't already know?

Based on their answers to this inquiry, the search chair, the consultant, and members of the search committee will draft questions designed to draw out this information. (The consultant should review these questions before the interview to make sure there are no duplicates.)

It's a good idea for the consultant or search chair to train members of the search committee on effective interview techniques — for example, training them to ask hypothetical questions or discuss problem-solving scenarios to find out how the candidate might handle this or that situation, training them to avoid illegal interview questions, and so on. This training should include tactical coaching, as well feedback mechanisms to enable search committee members to share their insights and impressions during the interview.

Conducting the formal interview

At the beginning of the formal interview, the search chair introduces the candidate to each member of the search committee. After that, each member of the search committee poses one of the questions he or she drafted for the interview. While the candidate answers, other committee members take notes. (This is standard practice for search committee interviews.)

The most productive search committee interviews are structured, planned in advance, and executed with rigor.

Meeting informally

After the formal interview, adjourn for lunch. This should take place off-site, in neutral territory. The idea is to get the candidate to let down her guard.

When choosing a lunch spot, take into account any dietary preferences or concerns the candidate, chair, or members of the committee may have.

Why is this is important? Simple. If the candidate is going to divorce her current company and maybe even relocate far away from friends and family, she needs to feel an emotional connection with the search chair and committee — one that goes beyond mere courtesy. In other words, she needs to bond, and she simply can't do that if her guard is up.

Next steps

Immediately after the meeting, while everyone's thoughts and impressions are still fresh, there should be a discussion that ends in a go or no-go decision.

This meeting may last several hours and involves conducting an open discussion of the same issues you've considered at the end of each interview.

REMEMBER

During this discussion, listen to your gut. Don't be afraid to consider how you *feel* about the candidate. Yes, we know, "Feelings are neither scientific nor logical." But this isn't the USS *Enterprise* and you're not Mr. Spock. So do a gut check before making the final decision. During the post–interview meeting, ask the following questions:

>> **Do you trust this candidate?** This is a yes-or-no question. You must also be able to say *why* you feel the way you do. If you're going to proceed with this candidate, the answer must be a unanimous *yes.* If anyone answers *no,* a discussion is in order. The holdout must clearly explain her rationale. The discussion ends when everyone agrees the candidate is a no-go or the holdout has been made to understand why she is incorrect in her assessment and changes her mind. There can be no hung jury here. If there is, it will undermine the candidate's legitimacy.

>> **Has the candidate made you a believer in his candidacy?** Why or why not? Is more information required?

>> **Do you honestly believe your company would be better off if this candidate were to come onboard?** Why or why not? Is more information required?

>> **Are the concerns raised about the candidate relevant to the job in question?** If so, you'll need to conduct another interview to address them. When you do, dig into the candidate's answers and settle the issue once and for all. (Note that it may not be necessary for the entire committee to attend this interview.)

REMEMBER

A negative answer to the first question is a showstopper. A negative answer to the last question necessitates that you conduct another interview, dig into the candidate's answers to your questions, and settle the matter once and for all.

Don't expect to be able to cover every issue without exception. Just be certain you understand in detail the job and environment in relation to the skills, background, and personal qualities of the finalist candidate. Doing so will put the odds of success in your favor.

After this post–interview meeting, the consultant debriefs the candidate and, if applicable, floats a trial offer.

REMEMBER

At this point, no further information about the candidate should be needed. If there are still areas of concern, the ultimate hiring authority, search chair, and consultant must discuss the best way to handle it (although frankly, if this is the case, it means the consultant hasn't done his job well).

Present Tense: Carrying Out the Candidate Presentation Interview

So far, during each successive stage of the interview process, you've assessed the candidate's fit, his skills in relation to the tasks associated with the job, and his interest in the job. By now, you're likely completely convinced which candidate is the right one for the job. But the truth is, you've never actually seen him in action. That's why we recommend you ask him to prepare and deliver a formal presentation before the recruiter, consultant, search chair, and search committee. If you're looking to fill a role in sales or marketing, ask the candidate to prepare a 20-minute presentation for a fictitious new account. For non-sales and marketing positions, ask the candidate to present his 30-/60-/90-day plan.

This presentation is important, but it's not a test. There are no right answers. Yes, what the candidate says during the presentation is significant. But what's more notable is how he prepares for the presentation. This will give you a fairly accurate snapshot of his work habits and leadership style. Specifically:

>> Did he ask for the right amount of help or guidance? If, during the presentation, you notice obvious gaps of information that could have been filled had the candidate asked, it may indicate a working style that's, well, stilted.

>> Did he act like a lone wolf or an armchair general? Is being a lone wolf or an armchair general an asset or a liability in the role you're staffing?

Watch closely and take notes. You're not looking for perfection, but you do want to assess whether the candidate is prepared, convincing, credible, logical, and compelling. These are the same factors your customers will consider when they do business with this candidate!

After the presentation, the hiring team meets to compare notes. Find out the following:

>> Does everyone feel the same way about the candidate?

>> Are the reasons for their selection or disqualification of the candidate appropriate?

>> What further questions (if any) need to be asked?

>> Do the candidate's goals and skills align with the requirements of the role?

>> Based on the candidate's presentation and his delivery of that presentation, do you believe he's sincerely interested in the opportunity?

REMEMBER

The candidate presentation offers insight into how the candidate thinks, strategizes, organizes, handles pressure, communicates, presents, and thinks on his feet.

Candidate as Customer: The Importance of Candidate Experience

Your search team has invested loads of time and money into developing a short list of candidates. So, the last thing you want to do is blow it now, during the interview phase. That means providing a positive experience for the interviewee.

The number-one way to ensure a positive candidate experience is to set — and adhere to — a protocol for following up after each interview. Timely follow-up is crucial not just with candidates still under consideration, but for those who have been eliminated from contention. This is especially important in the final stages of the hiring process. Failure to provide timely feedback to candidates shows a lack of organization or interest on your part and may result in your losing your first — and maybe even your second — choice for the position!

TIP

It's the job of the consultant to follow up with candidates after each interview. If you've secured a consultant, have him submit a report that details how each of these follow-up conversations went. That way, your corporate image won't be tarnished by a careless consultant failing to follow up with an important candidate!

You can't just look out for your strongest candidates, though. You must do it for the weaker ones, too. After all, candidates you pass on might be in a position to buy your company's product or service or to recommend it to others. Or there may come a time when you want to recruit them for a position for which they're better suited. Or it may be that you want to partner with, buy from, or hire one of their friends. If you treated them poorly during the interview process, you can rest assured that none of this will come to pass!

TIP

Regardless of whether you offer a position to a candidate or not, you must treat her in a way that reflects positively on you and your firm. Our advice? Treat every candidate the same way you would the CEO of your largest corporate client.

Try imagining each candidate as a customer. Think about it: If you have a great customer experience, you'll probably buy from that company again and tell at least some of your friends about it. And if you have a *bad* customer experience?

Well, you probably *won't* buy from that company again — and you'll tell everyone you know about it. The same goes for candidate experiences.

REMEMBER

The executive hiring process is a lot like a courtship — especially now. Given the scarcity in today's market, companies incentivize top executives to stay put. If you want them to jump ship, you have to entice them — to *woo* them. This will do more to help you negotiate a final deal than anything else (including money).

One more thing: We've seen countless unskilled interviewers focus on finding reasons to disqualify a candidate — even someone who has been vetted as thoroughly as a bodyguard for a criminal mastermind. Although such caution is understandable, it must be checked. Otherwise, the candidate might start looking for reasons to disqualify *you.*

IN THIS CHAPTER

» Recognizing the importance of reference checks

» Identifying who should conduct reference checks

» Formulating a plan of attack

» Reaching the best references

» Knowing what questions to ask

Chapter **15**

Point of Reference: Checking References

References are the glue that binds the two other major hiring variables — résumés and interviews — together. By themselves, résumés and traditional interviews are unreliable. Résumés can be intentionally misleading, and interviews are a crapshoot. In the end, both are merely tools you use to gather data. Only by conducting reference checks — actually contacting the people the candidate has worked with — can you verify that data.

In this chapter, we show you how to go about checking a candidate's references. You'll learn how to formulate a plan to complete this task, identify who you should call, and steer the conversation, as well as what questions to ask.

Identifying the Two Big Questions Reference Checks Will Help You Answer

Checking references is critical in helping you to answer two main questions:

>> **Can the candidate do the job?** By checking references, you can get a better read on the candidate's *real* abilities — not just what the candidate *says* he can do.

>> **Is the candidate a danger to others or to your company?** Answering this question is critical from a safety standpoint. Hiring an unstable candidate can place you, your employees, and your customers in harm's way — mentally, physically, or financially. It can also leave you open to a negligent hiring lawsuit.

REMEMBER

Checking references can help you determine whether the impression you have about the candidate's ability to do the job is accurate.

Can the candidate do the job?

Checking references is your best opportunity to determine whether a candidate can, in fact, do the job for which he has applied. Specifically, checking references enables you to confirm the candidate's

>> Track record

>> Skills

>> Competencies

>> Specific responsibilities

>> Team/unit performance

>> Individual performance

>> Dominant leadership style

>> Management skills

>> Communication style

>> Interpersonal skills

>> Strengths

>> Areas for improvement

Is the candidate a danger to others or to your company?

You can't be too careful when it comes to your hiring practices. In our experience, most hiring managers don't stop to consider the potential dangers in their hiring choices. And unfortunately, violence in the workplace is all too common. If such an incident were to occur at your place of business, your company could very well be liable — especially if you failed to check the perpetrator's background. Indeed, every year, American companies are held liable for crimes committed by their staff, including theft, assault, and even murder.

WARNING

If an employee has a history of misconduct indicating a propensity for criminal behavior, and if an employer could have discovered that history through a background investigation, then that employer could be held liable for any resulting injuries in the event of a workplace attack. Failing to adequately investigate before hiring can expose the employer to liability for injuries, pain, and suffering, and even punitive damages. Failing to conduct such a check — a practice called *negligent hiring* — could put your whole firm at risk.

NEGLIGENT REFERRALS: BE CAREFUL WHO YOU RECOMMEND

Employers can also be held liable for giving a false reference about a potentially dangerous employee — something called *negligent referral*. Some years ago, Allstate Insurance Company faced a negligent referral lawsuit. The wrongdoing allegedly occurred when Allstate wrote a letter of recommendation for an employee, stating that he was let go as part of a corporate restructuring. In fact, the employee had been fired for bringing a gun to work.

The man's new employer, Fireman's Fund Insurance Company, claimed that it had relied on the letter from Allstate in its decision to hire the man. In January 1993, the man shot five Fireman Fund co-workers in the company's cafeteria, killing three of them, before fatally shooting himself. One of the survivors and the families of those who were killed filed a suit against Allstate.

The one positive outcome from this tragedy was legislation designed to prevent such an event from happening again. Thirty-five U.S. states have passed laws to protect employers by granting them immunity from civil liability for *truthful, good-faith references*.

Bottom line: When you're called upon to provide a reference for one of your former employees, be completely honest about why she was let go. And when you're checking references for potential new hires, make sure you fully understand the circumstances under which that person left his previous employer.

Of course, criminal behavior is not limited to just violent behavior. There's also theft. According to the American Management Association and the U.S. Department of Justice, employee theft and dishonesty cost U.S. businesses between $60 billion and $120 billion per year. Perhaps even more stunning, the "average" employee embezzles $125,000 over the course of her career. (Imagine what an *above*-average employee could do!) This figure does not include the billions that employers spend each year on security guards, security systems, and loss-prevention initiatives. Nor does it include the $36 billion employers spend each year in response to workplace violence.

TIP

Like former Intel CEO Andy Grove said, "Only the paranoid survive." It's wise to be prudently skeptical — even paranoid — about candidates, lest you discover someone has "put lipstick on a pig." A hiring mistake at this level is not easy to fix and many cause a great deal of harm before it's discovered.

Who Should Do Reference Checks? (Hint: The Hiring Manager)

For executive-level hires, checking references is a "do-it-yourself" project. It's the one job that should *not* be delegated. Although there are many ways to outsource reference checks, none of them should be used for executive-level hires.

The ultimate hiring authority must personally check the candidate's references. Why? Because no matter how thoroughly prepared someone else may be, the hiring manager is in the best position to drill down on answers that appear vague or off the mark. Only the hiring manager understands the intricacies of the job well enough to ask additional questions — questions that may not occur to others, and that may help to ensure the wrong person is not hired.

REMEMBER

If and only if the hiring manager is on his death bed should references be checked by someone else.

Besides, as we've said, if you're the ultimate hiring authority, your counterpart at the candidate's present and previous firms will likely be more open to speaking with you personally than some third party who's simply going through the motions. In our experience, most employers follow the Golden Rule: "Do unto others as you would have them do unto you." Most executives are simply less likely to lie to their peers.

TIP

CEOs should speak to CEOs, presidents to presidents, managers to managers, and so on. The camaraderie afforded by your respective positions will prompt a more honest response. Be prepared for real candor here. The higher up you go in the company hierarchy, the more candid the responses will be.

Formulating a Plan

Checking references is key to guaranteeing a quality hire — but only if you do it correctly. You can't just call the people on your candidate's list of references and expect excellent results. To check references effectively, you need a plan that is both thorough and executable. It must contain all the steps needed to ensure you get the best possible information to make your hiring decision.

So, what are these steps? Here goes:

1. **Identify who you need to speak to at each of the candidate's former organizations (and in some cases, her current employer) to verify and validate the information you gathered during the interview stage.**

    These people may include (but are not limited to) the following:

    • Supervisor

    • Peers

    • Subordinates

- Clients

- Suppliers

2. **Set up a phone meeting with each reference ahead of time.**

   Don't expect to barge unannounced into someone's busy day and conduct a quality reference check. Tell each person how much time you'll need.

3. **Send each reference a copy of the job description or position profile ahead of time so he or she can review it before your meeting.**

   This step saves you time during the meeting and enables the reference to think of specific examples ahead of time.

4. **Pinpoint what you want to know about the candidate that each reference is in a position to reveal.**

   What information do you need to verify (beyond skills and experience) that relates to the position for which the candidate is being considered? What information will help you decide whether the candidate is the right fit — for example, her attitude, level of motivation, or leadership style?

5. **Determine which questions will likely uncover the information you need and write them all down in order of importance.**

   That way, even if you run out of time or the reference is called away before you conclude the call, you'll have as much vital information as possible right away, and you'll know where to start when you call back to finish the conversation.

Who You Gonna Call?

David here. Back in the day, I had a friend who spent nearly $1,000 — an entire month's pay (yes, I'm that old) — on stereo speakers. But when he hooked them up, he discovered that the music didn't sound any different than before. It was just way louder. Incredibly, his record sounded much better on *my* system, which was considerably less expensive. Why? Because although my speakers were cheap, I had spent $200 on a top-of-the-line needle for my record player. (Record players. Remember those? If not, Google them.) Because the needle makes first contact with the record, it affects the quality of the sound that is delivered to the speakers.

Along these same lines, who you contact in the course of a reference check will affect the quality of the information you received. In fact, who you contact is even more important than the questions you ask. You could have the most rigorous reference check known to humankind, with the best possible questions, but it won't help you one bit if you ask the wrong people. As they say, "Garbage in, garbage out."

REMEMBER

When asked for references, most candidates stack the deck in their favor, filling their list with people who are ready and willing to sing their praises. And can you blame them? If you really wanted a plum role, like the one you're recruiting for, wouldn't you do the exact same thing? If you're faced with such a list, it's imperative that you dig deeper to find those references who will give you an accurate appraisal of the candidate's abilities.

So, who can give you the most objective information about a candidate? Here's a hint: not his priest, best friend, drinking buddy, spouse, or mother. Instead, you need to talk to people who can judge the candidate's ability to do the job for which he's being recruited.

REMEMBER

Don't rely on personal references. Relatives and friends are of very limited (if any) value to you. Their opinions can't possibly add any insight into the candidate's work habits on the job. His buddies don't know what he's like to work with. Character references have their place, but not here. They're seldom of value unless they come from individuals who, for example, sit on the same board of directors as the candidate and have known the candidate for more than a few years.

DEAD TREES

Be wary of all letters of reference provided directly by a candidate. Prewritten references can be very misleading. Many are written at the time of termination. Firing a person is a very sensitive task. Often, employers try to soften the blow by writing letters of recommendation that are heavy on praise, with few (if any) negatives. Worse, some candidates may even have written these letters themselves.

Several years ago, David was suspicious of some letters of reference that a candidate had provided from his overseas employers. Specifically, David was concerned by the resolution of the photocopies. They were quite hazy. (So was the candidate, frankly.) He managed to sneak a peek at the file this candidate left on David's desk, only to find that the "originals" he had photocopied for David contained signature blocks that had been cut and pasted onto corporate letterhead. In other words, the candidate had simply written his own letter and pasted the president's signature in the appropriate place.

Presumably, this fellow was betting that David wouldn't call his former employer in the United Kingdom — or that if he did, the chairman of this multi-billion-dollar company wouldn't take his call. In any event, he bet wrong. David did a full background check on him, and it turned out he truly was a thief and a liar. In fact, Interpol was interested in his whereabouts. You just can't make this stuff up!

As you probably know, a person's past job performance is a good predictor of his future performance. In other words, if the candidate did a great job at ABC Company, chances are, he'll do a good job for you. So, you want to talk to people who have recent, first-hand experience with the candidate *on the job.* These people fall into two major categories: direct references and indirect references.

Direct references

Direct references are the references given to you by the candidates themselves. The most useful references come from people who are (or have been) professionally involved with the candidate on a day-to-day basis. These include the following people:

» Supervisors

» Peers

» Subordinates

» Clients (when appropriate)

GOOD REFERENCES VERSUS GREAT REFERENCES

As Adam Kaplan, founder of Kaplan Executive Search, has said, "There is a big difference between a good reference and a great reference, and as a recruiter you must listen for this because it could mean the difference between hiring average and hiring greatness." Here's an example of a good reference:

> I'm happy to tell you about Jane Smith. I worked with Jane for 5 years. Jane was a great asset to my team. She did a good job motivating her salespeople. Under her leadership, our sales grew.

Now, that's not bad. But compare that with this *great* reference:

> Of the 15 sales managers I've supervised, Jane Smith is by far the best. She knows her salespeople individually, and as a result, they perform for her at their highest level. I have never seen a happier and more productive sales force than I did when Jane was running ours. I would hire her again in a heartbeat!

Clearly, you're looking for a great reference!

TIP

One of the main reasons you should take notes during interviews with candidates is so you can fact-check later. Assuming you did as we suggested, your notes should contain the names of individuals who worked with the candidate on "such-and-such project." Be sure to contact those people in addition to the others mentioned here to make sure the candidate did, indeed, work on the project and that his contributions met expectations.

Supervisors

The best possible information about the candidate will come from his current boss. For example, the candidate's direct supervisor can tell you

>> If the candidate consistently meets key performance indicators (KPIs)

>> How to motivate the candidate

>> The candidate's leadership and management skills

>> The candidate's strengths and weaknesses, as related to his role

>> Insight into the candidate's character

Don't just limit yourself to the candidate's previous direct supervisors, however. The candidate's previous boss's boss — for example, the board chair — may have a different perspective about the VP of sales than the president or CEO, so it's a good idea to talk to that person, too. Check with your HR department to see if you need the candidate's permission first.

WARNING

Don't call the candidate's current boss unless the candidate has expressly indicated that you may do so. And even if the candidate *does* give you permission, check with your legal department for any paperwork the candidate may need to sign ahead of the call. If you cause a negative change in the candidate's current employment status by performing a reference check, you'll likely be responsible for financial damages. Worse, if word gets out that you make a habit of this practice, people will think twice about talking with you about positions in the future. Rumors about these types of *faux pas* spread like wildfire and can impede future hires.

Peers

The qualities most in demand today — leadership skills, communication skills, a bias toward action, and passion — are the ones the candidate's peers are probably in the best position to comment on. That's why we typically check at least two peer references for every supervisory one. A candidate's peers can give you a true picture of his strengths and weaknesses as they pertain to his job function and how he supports the business unit.

TIP

Ask the candidate's peers to rate the candidate not just against his peers, but against other people who formerly held the candidate's position — just in case there is someone better out there to recruit instead. (Call us ruthless! But you have to be.)

Subordinates

No one understands better than a candidate's direct subordinates whether that candidate is pulling his weight. Subordinates also know where all the "bodies" are buried — you know, those projects that were never quite completed or the one that cost the company $1 million to fix. Frankly, next to the candidate's boss, the candidate's subordinates will provide the most insight into his character. As with peers, we typically conduct two subordinate reference checks for each supervisory one.

TIP

Find out if any dedicated subordinates followed the candidate from his last gig . . . and if they're likely to do so again when the candidate makes his next move.

Clients

Talking with your candidate's clients can be most interesting. Clients likely know what this person is like when he's *not* in the office. They can tell you if the candidate makes promises that he (or the company) can't possibly keep, just to close a deal. Clients can also fill you in on how the candidate resolves matters when something goes wrong. Finally, they can tell you whether the candidate is a good ambassador for his current employer.

360-DEGREE FEEDBACK

No one person will be able to give you all the information you need to make an informed decision about a candidate. To get a complete picture, you need to speak with the candidate's boss, peers, subordinates, and clients. Each reference offers a distinct perspective. For example:

- The candidate's direct boss assigns his responsibilities, so that person will know exactly what types of projects the candidate has handled in the past.

- The candidate's peers know what an overachiever he is (or isn't).

- The people who work directly for the candidate — that is, his subordinates — know everything about the candidate that his boss and peers don't.

- A candidate's clients may be able to tell you things about the candidate that people in the office know nothing about.

This type of 360-degree feedback is enlightening.

THE HR DEPARTMENT: THE LEAST USEFUL SOURCE OF REFERENCES

Notice that we did not list the candidate's HR department as a source for a direct reference. That's because the HR department invariably offers the most frustrating and, we would argue, irrelevant references. Why? Two reasons:

- **HR doesn't work with the candidate on a daily basis, so it can offer only second-hand knowledge or anecdotal information.** HR won't be familiar with the candidate's day-to-day performance unless he's a superstar or a complete dud.

- **Most HR departments are hesitant to reveal anything, no matter how true, that might lead to legal action.** If HR does choose to comment, it's usually just to tell you, "Yes, he worked here." Obviously, that doesn't cut it. (And by the way, if the candidate *is* a superstar or a dud, HR may try to intentionally mislead you — tricking you into either passing on the candidate or hiring him, respectively). Seriously, talent management is HR's job, even if it means managing a loser out of the organization and into the unwitting arms of a competitor.

Indirect references

You aren't limited to checking the references given to you by the candidate — the so-called direct references. You can also check what we call *indirect references.* These include sources in the candidate's industry and in any relevant professional associations. Contacts at firms that are direct or indirect competitors of the candidate's firm can also provide useful information. All these sources will likely be more objective about the candidate. In addition, it's unlikely they'll have received any coaching from the candidate. (Not that a candidate would ever coach his references, mind you. . . .) Even if these sources know the candidate by reputation only, you'll be able to get a fix on whether the reputation is a good one.

It's also a good idea to run a keyword search for the candidate on the Internet. LinkedIn is a good place to start (assuming, of course, that the candidate has set up a profile page on that site). On LinkedIn, you can see "endorsements" of your candidate by others who have worked with him. These endorsements and other information on LinkedIn may also enable you to fact-check the candidate's accomplishments. (*Remember:* Put the candidate's name in quotes to find profiles of people with his first and last name. Keep in mind that there are many Bob Smiths in the world. Don't automatically assume the page you're looking at is for *your* Bob Smith.) If the candidate doesn't have a LinkedIn profile, then by all means, run his name through a search engine.

REMEMBER

Checking indirect references may take a bit more work on your part, but it will be worth it. Fortunately, the greater the candidate's visibility in the industry, the easier this is to do.

Steering the Conversation

At the outset of your conversation with each reference, job number one is to establish trust and set the stage for a frank discussion. That means briefly introducing yourself, establishing a rapport, and assuring the reference that you'll never reveal the contents of the conversation to the candidate — all using a congenial tone. This will go a long way toward putting the reference at ease and ensuring that he lowers his guard and speaks freely. (A little flattery will help with this, too.)

Next, describe your role, and offer a brief overview of the job you're trying to fill. That way, the reference will be better able to compare the job on offer with the one the candidate held with his company. (To expedite this step, you can send the position profile to the reference before the call.)

WARNING

Respect the reference's time. In other words, don't ramble on. If you do, you can be sure he'll cut the conversation short long before you get the information you need!

At this point, you're ready to start asking questions. Your goal is to find out as much about the candidate as you possible can. What is she like? Is she pleasant to be around? Is she flexible? Adaptable? How are her leadership skills? Her interpersonal skills? Will she be suitable for periodic promotion?

First, however, you need to pin down a few basics. If your reference served as the candidate's supervisor, start by asking these questions:

>> **Did she report directly to you? If so, for how long?** If the answer to this question is less than one year, find someone else to talk to. One year is just too short a period to form a valid impression.

>> **Did you complete or contribute to her performance appraisals? If so, how many did you do?**

If, on the other hand, the reference is a peer or subordinate of the candidate, ask this question:

Did you work directly with the candidate as part of a team? If so, for how long? Longer is better.

Now you need to confirm with the reference what you already know from the candidate's résumé and your interview notes. Here's what to ask:

» Could you please verify the candidate's dates of employment?

» What was the candidate's function or title?

» Could you please verify the candidate's earnings? Does this number include bonuses, overtime, or incentives?

» How long did the candidate work for your company?

» Who did the candidate work for before joining your company?

REMEMBER

This last question is important. It may reveal whether your candidate did a stint somewhere else but neglected to tell you about it. This may indicate that there are other things that have slipped the candidate's mind.

Notice how simple these first several questions are, how easy they are to answer. All you're asking for here is facts. There's no pressure on the reference to share his opinion — yet.

REMEMBER

You'll get better responses to your more probing questions if you ask the simple ones first.

After the reference answers these basic questions, ask yourself: Are his answers consistent with the candidate's? If so, then you're ready to proceed with the next round of questions. These questions will enable you to establish how well the reference knows the candidate:

» How would you describe your relationship with the candidate?

» How often did you interact with her? Daily? Weekly? Monthly?

» How would you describe your relationship outside work?

With this information in hand, it's time to really get down to business. First and foremost, you want to ask why the candidate left the organization. Be direct. Say, "Why do you think she left the organization?" Then, quickly ascertain whether the reference's answer jibes with the one provided by the candidate. If it doesn't, you may have a problem, or may need to inquire further.

FINDING OUT THE *REAL* REASON THE EMPLOYEE LEFT

If you *really* want to know why the employee left, try asking these questions from recruiter Jim Durbin to elicit the truth:

- Why isn't the employee working for you anymore?
- Was there anyone better?
- Is it true that the employee left because she was never going to get your job?
- When the employee left, were you surprised?
- Did the employee have other offers when she accepted your position?
- What did the employee's references say when you checked them?
- What is your vesting schedule for options?

The answers to these questions may reveal whether the reason the employee gave for leaving was, indeed, truthful.

Beyond that, you'll want to ask questions to uncover your reference's opinions on the candidate's background, personality, skills, and performance. Start with these basic subjective questions:

- » What were the candidate's strengths on the job?
- » Were there areas in which she needed improvement?
- » Was she dependable?
- » Was she a team player?
- » How would you compare her work with others who held the same job?

Also ask the reference to comment on specific points that the candidate discussed during her interview. For example, you might ask the following. (Again, you'll want to compare the reference's answers with those provided by the candidate.)

- » In your opinion, what was the candidate's biggest accomplishment at your company?
- » In what areas would the candidate benefit from constructive coaching or mentoring?

>> This position requires interaction with *x* types of co-workers or customers in *y* types of situations. How does that compare with what the candidate did for you? How well do you think she would handle these types of interactions for our company?

Don't be afraid to ask pointed questions regarding any areas of concern.

REMEMBER For additional question ideas, see Table 15-1. Note that many of these questions are very similar to questions you'd ask the candidate herself.

TABLE 15-1 ## Suggested Questions

Category	Question
General	How would you assess the candidate's ability to predict needs early on?
	How quickly can the candidate process information?
Communication and creativity	How would you describe the candidate's oral and written communication skills?
Day-to-day performance	During the time the candidate was employed at your company, how well did she progress?
	Can you comment on the candidate's level of ambition and on the candidate's ability to actually reach her goals?
Employability	Would you recommend the candidate for the following position: [company, product line, position, responsibilities]?
Interpersonal relations	How well did the candidate get along with her superiors?
	How well did the candidate get along with her peers?
	How well did the candidate get along with her subordinates?
	What do you think of the candidate as a person?
	How would you describe the candidate's relationships with people?
	How did or might the candidate deal with a difficult boss?
	How opinionated is the candidate?
Work performance	Do you think the candidate clearly understood her job function?
	How was the quality of the candidate's decisions and judgments?
	Was the candidate able to anticipate and prevent problems?
Technical skills	Are the candidate's technical skills up to date?
	Did the candidate possess any areas of expertise?

(continued)

TABLE 15-1 *(continued)*

Category	Question
Personality characteristics	Are you aware of any personal problems that interfered with the candidate's ability to do her job?
	Are you aware of any of the candidate's efforts at self-improvement?
Management skills	Was the candidate responsible for management decisions?
	For how many people was the candidate responsible?
Leadership style	Would you describe the candidate as a leader or a follower?
	If you would describe the candidate as a leader, what type? Autocratic? Democratic? Free reign?

REMEMBER

Every executive-level reference will be different depending on the skills and experience you're looking for. That means you'll need to develop and ask a unique series of reference questions that reflect the role's requirements.

Then, of course, there are those questions that are specific to the role and/or function of the job in question. For example, if you were hiring a VP of sales, you might ask these questions as well:

>> How would you rate this candidate's ability to pick winners when it comes to hiring salespeople?

>> How were leads obtained and distributed to salespeople she managed?

>> How effectively did the candidate work with the VP of marketing?

>> Was the product or service in question a technical or emotional sale?

>> Was the candidate's performance/income based on volume or gross margin?

>> Did the candidate achieve her KPIs on a regular basis? What were the KPIs?

TIP

WARNING

If applicable, also ask about the candidate's relationships with vendors, customers, and professional colleagues. These questions do the following:

>> Establish the working relationship.

>> Focus on broad information.

>> Home in on what you need and want to know.

If you find that the reference was quick to answer the more general questions but pauses before answering the more specific ones, then he's probably really thinking about the answers. If, however, the reference is unable to answer questions as they become more specific, or if he offers wishy-washy responses, then he may not be a qualified reference.

IN THIS CHAPTER

» **Putting together the compensation package**

» **Negotiating the deal**

» **Delivering the offer**

» **Dealing with counteroffers**

» **Drafting a solid employment agreement**

» **Onboarding**

» **Retaining talent**

Chapter **16**

Happily Ever After: Sealing the Deal

Y ou've found your ideal candidate. You've contacted his references and conducted the necessary background checks. Your industrial psychologist says he's a "great fit." Your search committee and chair have given him a resounding thumbs up. You've even been to dinner with him and his significant other. All that's left is to develop and negotiate an offer, right?

Well, no. As you've learned, the *best* time to start the offer process is during the very first interview, shaping the offer in any discussions that follow. That way, you can uncover potential stumbling blocks or even deal-killing issues (for example, if his compensation expectations — or yours — are way out of line). But assuming you've addressed all these issues, it *is* time for you to assemble the compensation package, negotiate the details, and extend a final offer — in other words, to close the deal. You also have to start thinking about how you'll get your new hire up to speed, and how to retain him over the long haul. That's what this chapter is all about.

Pay Up: Calculating Compensation

Compensation may not be the deciding factor for an executive considering making a move. But it can still be a highly effective lever for prying her loose. If nothing else, a solid compensation package can persuade an exec to at least consider the other components of your offer.

For every executive compensation package, there are several key considerations:

>> **The candidate's current compensation package:** You'll find this out from the candidate during various recruiting, interview, and debriefing sessions. At a bare minimum, your compensation package must be better than the one the executive already has, as must other features of the job (challenge, opportunity, visibility, and so on).

>> **Market rates for comparable positions:** You can bet the candidate will have researched this using sites like Glassdoor (www.glassdoor.com), which includes information about thousands of companies, often from the people who work there; Vault (www.vault.com), which posts salary surveys for entire industries; and others. You should do the same! This is one situation where your best defense is a good offense.

TIP

Employees are concerned about salary, but long-term incentives are also a factor. Long-term incentives tied to key performance indicators (KPIs) are good for both the employee and the company. Companies that include these incentives in their compensation package attract high-quality executives who don't want to leave.

>> **Rates of pay for peer-level executives in your company:** The new hire should earn the same base salary as her peers in the company.

>> **Your company's compensation policies:** Depending on your organization's compensation policies, if the base salary doesn't cut it, you may be able to use a signing bonus to sweeten the deal.

>> **The candidate's bottom-line salary:** You need a real-live number here. "In the ballpark" doesn't count. This number should include not only the candidate's salary, but the monetary value of her benefits package and the value of real perks.

Other compensation factors may include variations on the following:

>> Future professional growth opportunities

>> The degree of risk in your company

>> Future reward potential (for example, bonuses or equity appreciation)

>> The amount of dislocation in the candidate's life

>> How badly the candidate needs the job (or doesn't)

>> How interested the candidate is in joining your company

>> The amount of risk you're taking in hiring that candidate

There may also be idiosyncratic wants or desires that defy logic or objectivity but could be deal breakers. We've seen requests that range from periodic round-trip tickets to visit a child at college to a jet-fuel gas card.

REMEMBER

You've been transparent (we hope) throughout the interview process regarding the position and compensation. None of that's changed. All you're doing now is putting everything on paper so there are no misunderstandings.

Compensation tips

Here are a few general tips when it comes to compensation:

>> **Agree on power before pay.** Lots of people think that a person's title determines his salary. But in fact, his responsibilities — and the power that comes with those responsibilities — are what governs how much an employer is willing to pay. The greater the level of responsibility, the richer the pay packet! So, before you start tossing around numbers, you want to pin down exactly what responsibilities the new executive will have. That means agreeing on — and documenting — the position's title, reporting structure, authority, accountability, number of direct staff, committee responsibilities (if any), and specific performance standards.

TIP

Performance standards should not be subjective. They should be both observable and measurable. For example, don't say, "Increase sales." Say, "Increase sales by 15 percent in 12 months." Otherwise, performance measures become open to interpretation — making your bonus subjective, as well.

>> **Cover benefits before salary.** Start compensation talks by bringing up benefits — stuff like insurance, professional fees, vacation, and whatnot. Be sure to show the entire value of the package. This will help you to build up some good will before you get into salary talks.

TIP

Decide on salary last. That way, the candidate will understand his total compensation — benefits plus salary. It's a big number!

>> **Focus on the candidate's unique needs.** Different candidates have different needs. One might need extra stock options. Another might need a signing bonus. Or a particular candidate might have more unusual needs. Maybe he

owns a horse. In that case, you could offer to orchestrate the horse's relocation. Or maybe his spouse needs a job. If so, you could try to place that person in the company, too. Or maybe the candidate wants to work remotely — at least for a while. For example, if the candidate doesn't want to relocate until his kids are done with high school, you might allow him to work remotely for a set period of time. We recently closed a $4.2-million deal by agreeing to *not* move the candidate for a full four years!

» **Offer psychic cash.** *Psychic cash* is anything that has psychological value to the candidate. Examples of psychic cash include intangibles, like industry leadership, fast growth, stability, challenge, and so on. Psychic cash might include tangibles, too — like a company vehicle, access to the company jet, access to exclusive events or retreats, paid education, sabbaticals, and more. Really, psychic cash can be almost anything you can think of (assuming it's legal, of course). We've seen a company purchase a classic cherry-red Gibson ES-335 hollow-body guitar for use as psychic cash! Sometimes, you'll find that psychic cash is worth more than actual cash. It proves to the candidate that you really listened to his needs. Trust us: Psychic cash can help close deals!

» **Ensure the offer is competitive.** Of course, *competitive* is a relative term, and all candidates are different. Still, you must ensure that your offer is competitive with the outside market and equitable internally.

» **Set firm, clear expectations.** Successful compensation packages are structured to reinforce the position's KPIs, as defined by the job description and highlighted in the position profile. Great candidates simply won't accept a compensation offer where the expectations are a moving target.

» **Make sure the candidate fully understands your total compensation program.** We sometimes find that a company has a better benefits program than the candidate or even the hiring manager realizes. Other times, we've seen situations where the company's first offering isn't as attractive as the candidate thought it was. Either way, you must explain the minutiae of your compensation package — we mean every single feature and its intended benefit — to the candidate.

REMEMBER

Successful offers account for the needs of the individual, as well as those of the company. In our experience, when deals are struck that favor one over the other, the relationship is often short lived!

Assembling a compensation checklist

Together, all these factors — and others — will comprise your proposed compensation package. To ensure you don't miss anything, use the compensation checklist in Table 16-1.

TABLE 16-1   **A Compensation Checklist**

Compensation Item	Current Value	New Offer	Comments
Monetary			
Base salary			
Annual bonus			
Equity			
Stock options			
Commissions			
Profit sharing			
Subtotal			
Incentives			
Retirement benefits			
Deferred compensation			
Financial-planning assistance			
Income splitting			
Signing bonus			
Subtotal			
Benefits			
Bridge the healthcare plan*			
Paid vacation			
Automobile allowance			
Medical			
Dental			
Life			
Disability			
Travel			
Subtotal			

(continued)

TABLE 16-1 *(continued)*

Compensation Item	Current Value	New Offer	Comments
Perks			
Paid parking			
Professional dues			
Onsite daycare			
Home office			
High-speed Internet			
Technology tools			
Continuing education			
Tuition forgiveness			
Wellness programs			
Training days			
Club memberships			
Travel consideration			
Sabbaticals			
Flex time (flexible working hours)			
Subtotal			
Relocation assistance			
Moving expenses			
Realtor fees			
House-hunting trips			
Short-term housing			
Short-term living allowance			
Bridge loan			
Low-interest loan			
Forgivable loan			
Company purchase of homes			
Spousal career assistance			
Subtotal			

Compensation Item	Current Value	New Offer	Comments
Severance			
Lump-sum severance			
Insurance continuation			
Outplacement			
Relocation assistance			
Subtotal			

Before the executive joins, your HR department must inform your insurance provider that you will need to bridge the executive's current healthcare package.

We complete a compensation checklist for each candidate throughout the hiring process. That way, we have all the notes we need in one place.

By their very nature, executive compensation packages are one of a kind. This is one area where the one-size-fits-all approach just won't cut it!

Everything's Negotiable: Negotiating Like a Pro

Good news! We literally wrote the book on negotiation. The only problem? We didn't write it for you. *Guerilla Marketing for Job Hunters 3.0*, by Jay Conrad Levinson and David E. Perry (Wiley), is for people on the other side of the negotiating table — employees making a move. The information in that book gives job seekers a distinct edge. But don't worry. In *this* book, we nullify that advantage.

The negotiation process is important — and it's not something you want to skip. Your candidates expect to negotiate, and if you deny them the pleasure of doing so, it will turn them off. After all, fishing's no fun when the fish just jump into the boat!

How you handle final negotiations will reveal to the candidate how much you value her as a person. That doesn't mean you should cave — it just means that you want the prospective hire to see that you're considerate of her position.

Preparing for negotiations

Research buys leverage. Before you open any negotiation, you must conduct research. That means creating a checklist of what the candidate needs and expects. We don't just mean needs and expectations with regard to salary. We're talking about the complete package — including her personal situation. Does the candidate have a spouse or significant other to consider? Does she care for aging family members? Are there child-custody issues? (This last one's a big one.)

WARNING

If you fail to identify the candidate's needs and expectations, you may find that in the rush and excitement of closing the deal, you make unnecessary (and budget-blowing) compromises. Or you may blow the deal altogether. Both of these are bad outcomes!

NEGOTIATING THROUGHOUT THE HIRING PROCESS

Throughout the hiring process, float a few trial balloons to gauge the candidate's interest and to gather the intelligence you need to make the final offer. Ask questions like the following:

- If we make you this offer, will you accept it?

- What will it take for you to accept the offer?

- How could we structure this deal to make it acceptable?

- What would be fair-market compensation for someone like you in this location?

By the time the candidate enters the second round of interviews, you should also cover his current compensation, incentives (including all nonvested equity and stock grants), severance clauses, golden handcuffs, noncompete parameters (if any), earlier-than-scheduled compensation review, guaranteed minimum first-year bonus, and any other perquisites.

As you step through the hiring process, listen for comments like, "My spouse won't relocate," "We have a son in high school," "My noncompete hasn't expired," "I have a large bonus that I won't be paid for six months," or "My stock options are only partially vested." These are red flags. You should discuss them immediately — as soon as you find out about them. Also, watch for comments like "We're a two-income family," "My daughter has two horses," or "I'll need to buy a new car." These aren't deal breakers; they're bargaining chips. With these, the candidate is setting the table for future negotiations.

The good news is, you've likely done much of this legwork during the recruiting process. Indeed you've used this understanding to move the candidate through each stage of the hiring process. With this information at hand, you can link the candidate's dreams and aspirations with the position you want to fill, whether that means more power, more responsibility (with the accompanying authority), more visibility, more money, or something else.

REMEMBER

When it comes to making an offer, you want to play to win. It's like this: It's the bottom of the ninth. You have two outs, the game is tied, no one's on base, and you're at bat. If you strike out or fly out, you're done. Walking or getting a base hit would be better — but only marginally so. Really, you have only one surefire option here: to give it all you've got and hit a home run. The same goes with recruiting. When you're about to make an offer to your top candidate, don't hold back. Give it everything you've got. Will you hit a home run every time? Well, no. Nobody bats a thousand. But if you swing for the fences every time, you increase your odds of success.

Choosing the negotiator

If you've been working with an external recruiter, you have an important decision to make: Who will handle negotiations — you or him? Often, the external recruiter handles negotiations. That being said, we concede that many recruiters lack the depth of knowledge and breadth of skills to negotiate a complete package. You'd be wise to gauge your recruiter's negotiating skills before handing that responsibility over.

There are other problems with using your recruiter to negotiate. First, it's usually in the recruiter's best interest to offer as much money to the candidate as possible because this number is tied to his own compensation. Second, some recruiters might be more interested in closing the deal as quickly as possible than in hammering out the best possible terms. If either of these happens, you'll need to grab the reins.

TIP

Our advice? Have the recruiter launch trial balloons at the beginning of the negotiation. That way, if the candidate becomes agitated, any complaints will be directed toward the recruiter, not you. Then you and the candidate can unite in spirit to throw the recruiter under the bus as you conclude the negotiation. Don't worry — the recruiter understands that it's all just part of the game. As long as he still gets paid, he'll be happy.

Projecting a positive attitude

Many business deals are short lived. They're transactional in nature. For example, suppose you're buying a car. In this type of deal, you might reasonably thump your fist on the salesperson's desk as you attempt to negotiate a concession. After all, you'll likely never see that salesperson again!

An employment negotiation is another matter. These types of negotiations are relationship driven — and the relationship can last a lifetime. That's why you can't afford to be arrogant, uncompromising, or aloof. Sure, you might gain some advantage in the short term — but at what cost? Don't forget: There may be a time when the tables are turned. If that happens, don't be surprised if the candidate is as arrogant, aloof, and uncompromising with you as you were with her.

So, how *should* you approach the negotiation? A positive attitude is key. But you must strike a balance. That is, you don't want to appear so excited that she assumes you'll pay more than she's worth to you, but you don't want to run her off by appearing indifferent. We suggest an air of detached enthusiasm.

Oh, and if you're negotiating in person, be aware of your body language. Telegraph what you want the candidate to see. Smiling and placing your palms face up on the table are signs that you're open and receptive to what she's saying. Furrowing your eyebrows and closing your fists conveys the opposite message. If you need to compose yourself, take lots of bathroom breaks!

TIP

Drink lots of water during a face-to-face negotiation — but skip the coffee and alcohol.

Breaking an impasse

Sometimes, negotiations come to an impasse — especially if you didn't follow our advice about starting to structure the deal from the very first interview. To keep a negotiation alive, and to demonstrate your sincere interest in coming to a mutual agreement, try asking these questions:

» Are you flexible on salary, signing bonus, annual bonus, and so on?

» Would you consider other dimensions of the package beyond the annual salary and job title — for example, signing bonus, annual bonus, vacation, retirement plan, equity, and so on?

» How can we structure the compensation package to make it acceptable?

This is a time when you really need to use your active listening skills. As you listen, repeat each point the candidate makes back to him so he knows you've understood him correctly. (It's okay to paraphrase.) Resist the urge to sell the candidate on the company during this discussion. Instead, listen to his concerns and tell him what you'll do to try to resolve matters in his favor and will get back to him. Then do that.

TIP

In case negotiations with your first choice break down completely, stay in touch with your second choice to ensure he remains enthusiastic!

Special Delivery: Delivering the Offer

In addition to an employment agreement, you'll also want to craft an offer letter for the winning candidate. You'll open this letter with a salutation, following by something along these lines:

> This letter confirms our recent discussions regarding your employment with [full legal name of the entity]. Listed below are the particular terms of this offer.

Next, you'll lay out the terms. These will likely include the following:

- » The position's title
- » The name of the executive the new hire will report to, along with that person's full title
- » The start date
- » The full base salary
- » Details regarding the bonus, including what (if any) amount is guaranteed
- » Information about any 401(k) or profit-sharing programs
- » Information about benefits, vacation, and holidays
- » Contract information
- » Conditions

Finally, the offer letter should be signed by the hiring manager.

Some companies are great at delivering offers. One company we worked with sent the offer letter by courier, accompanied by a high-gloss copy of the company's annual report that featured a forward-thinking "Thank you!" for the candidate's upcoming contributions. But that wasn't all: The delivery also included a dozen long-stemmed roses for the candidate's wife. This personal touch really showed the candidate how much the company valued him.

GETTING BUY-IN FROM THE SIGNIFICANT OTHER

It's not enough to get the candidate's buy-in. You must also get her significant other's. *Remember:* You're just relocating an executive. You're uprooting her entire family!

Right out the gate, find out whether the candidate's significant other or family has any special requirements — think special schools, access to medical care, or help with ageing parents (not an exhaustive list by any means). If you can't accommodate these needs, it may be a deal breaker. Also inquire about the significant other's career considerations.

As the hiring process progresses, invite the candidate's significant other to meet the senior team and *their* spouses. A dinner party is a good way to do this. This is especially helpful when the candidate's significant other works inside the home. Introducing him to your "executive family" helps him visualize his new social environment, making the move less unsettling.

You don't have to go that far when delivering your offer. But whenever possible, you should have someone make the offer in person. Apart from being able to get an immediate signature, this approach enables you to walk the executive through the entire package and explain each item to him. Also, whenever you can, go out of your way to meet with the executive's spouse or significant other (if applicable) to answer any questions before those questions snowball into concerns.

Counter-Intuition: Dealing with Counteroffers

Remember all those times we say to check in with your candidate to make sure you are both on the same page with regard to your opportunity and what it would take to persuade her to seize it? Well here's one reason why: so you don't have to deal with a counteroffer. In other words, if you've piqued the candidate's interest by properly pitching your opportunity, and you've identified and met all her needs, then that candidate won't be tempted to stick around at her current job no matter *what* she's offered.

Still, you can rest assured that the candidate's employer *will* attempt to keep her, and you should prepare the candidate accordingly. First, tell the candidate to take your offer home and discuss it with her significant other (if she has one — and by now, you should know if she does). Next, ask her to return the offer signed and witnessed. Then say the following:

> You're going to get a counteroffer from your former employer. I know you told us you wouldn't accept a counteroffer under any circumstances, but the pressure on you is going to be intense.

Follow this statement with a pause to give the candidate an opportunity to talk about why she won't accept a counteroffer. Then recap her reasons. Next, make each of the following points, pretty much in this order:

» "[First name], understand that it's easier for your former employer to keep you with a counteroffer than replace you. That's because the real cost of recruiting your replacement is not just the recruiter's fee but the cost of lost opportunities."

» "Sure, they'll give you the raise now, but that just gives them more time to launch a silent search to find your replacement."

» "You'll be the first one bumped if the company hits a rough patch because you betrayed it."

» "Your boss's leadership is now going to come into question, especially if anyone else has left in the last few years. That'll hurt her chances for advancement or at least it'll have the board questioning her management skills."

» "You're out of the leadership inner circle the moment you resign because you've broken their trust."

Usually, that does the trick.

But what if, after all that, the candidate *does* come back with a counteroffer? Simple. To quote Tony Soprano, "Fuhgeddaboudit." Never counter a counteroffer. Look, you already made your absolute best offer, and you know it meets the candidate's needs. If she comes back looking for more, it's time for you to walk.

David here. Very early in my career, a heavy construction company enlisted me to recruit a VP of engineering and chief estimator. We had real trouble finding the right candidate. Eventually, we settled on a guy who lived 2,000 miles away whom the president of the company liked. (Me, I wasn't sold on him, but whatever.)

After a protracted negotiation, my client and the candidate agreed to terms and settled on a start date, and the candidate resigned from his current position. A week or so before the candidate was set to move, he called me to ask if the client would sweeten the deal with a new truck. (Can you smell trouble?) My client happily agreed. The next day, he asked for an interest-free loan to buy a bigger house in his new location. Again, my client happily agreed. This went on for the better part of a week, one request after another.

About an hour after the moving truck containing all the candidate's worldly possessions had left his house, I got another call from the candidate. To be fair, what he asked for was pretty innocuous. But when I called my client to ask him what he wanted to do about it, I could hear the exhaustion in his voice. "I don't know," he said. "Should I do it or not?" I explained I was merely a conduit and had no professional opinion. "Well, what's your *personal* opinion?" he asked. So, I told him. "Given the way this candidate has behaved during our negotiation, I'm worried he might destroy the relationships you've built up with your subcontractors by squeezing them for every last nickel. If it were me, I'd cut him loose." Fifteen minutes later, I called the candidate back, informed him that my client had given him two weeks' notice, and that we had turned the truck around.

TIP

All that being said, stuff does happen. Sometimes there are extreme circumstances, like the candidate's wife who asked for a divorce and filed for sole custody of the children on the same day you made the offer.

Agree to Agree: Composing a Solid Employment Agreement

For any new hire, you need a solid employee agreement. An employment agreement is a document that details both party's rights, duties, and obligations as employer and employee. An executive employment agreement could be a simple 2- or 3-page affair or a 50-page tome.

The employee agreement typically starts with some boilerplate text, like this:

This employment agreement (the "Agreement") is made as of the [date] day of [month and year] (the "Agreement Date"), by and between [full legal name of the entity] with and on behalf of its wholly owned subsidiary, [full legal name of the entity] (the "Company"), and [full legal name of the candidate] ("Executive").

Then you'll want the agreement to spell out the following:

>> **Employment services:** Here's where you outline the terms of employment, the position and duties, and whether the new hire will have any responsibilities with regard to the board.

- » **Compensation:** This section of the agreement lays down the base salary, incentive compensation, employee benefit plans, vacation time, and covered business expenses.

- » **Termination of employment:** In this part of the agreement, you explain issues pertaining to termination of employment. These include voluntary resignation, termination by the company with or without cause, changes in control, removal from any boards or positions, additional vesting, the execution of the separation agreement, and excess parachute payments.

- » **Confidentiality and restrictive covenants:** Here, you define policies with regard to confidential information, non-competition, non-solicitation, non-interference with business relationships, equitable modification, and remedies.

- » **Post-termination obligations:** By this, we mean return of company materials and executive assistance.

- » **Miscellaneous:** As you might guess, the miscellaneous section features a hodge-podge of points, such as notices, withholding, successors and assigns, no waiver, severability and survivability, execution in counterparts, governing law and waiver of jury, construction, and any amendments.

And of course, you'll need to leave room for the appropriate signatures — the new hire's as well as that of the hiring authority.

All Aboard! Onboarding

The executive recruiter isn't responsible for onboarding the new employee. But he is responsible for checking in periodically to make sure everything is running smoothly.

We suggest you circle back with the candidate on these milestones:

- » After the candidate's first week

- » After her second week

- » After her first month

- » After her second month

- » Every quarter thereafter for the rest of the candidate's first year on the job

We also urge you to set up a similar appointment schedule with the search chair so you can hear his side of the story. Specifically, you want to see how well the candidate is fitting in, how she's faring on her 30-60-90 day plan, and how her department has responded to her leadership.

Finders Keepers: Retaining Top Talent

Nearly 100 percent of our executive searches conclude successfully — and if you follow our process, yours will, too. But that's not where the story — or your job — ends. In other words, you've *found* the talent; now you need to *keep* it.

Keeping top talent is no small feat. Competition for the best and brightest is fierce. After all the effort and expense of acquiring a top performer, the last thing you want is for that person to abandon you for another suitor!

The new hire's first hundred days will be your bellwether. To ensure you get off to a solid start, the search chair should follow up with both parties — the new hire and the ultimate hiring authority — to make sure objectives have been met and promises have been kept.

TIP

For guidance during those crucial first hundred days, read *The New Leader's 100-Day Action Plan: How to Take Charge, Build Your Team, and Get Immediate Results,* 4th Edition, by George B. Bradt, Jayme A. Check, and John A. Lawler (Wiley).

But honestly? Talent retention starts way before those first hundred days. You should be focusing on talent retention even before the hire, during the recruiting and interview process. That means considering the three C's of talent retention — challenge, communication, and compensation — right out of the gate.

REMEMBER

When it comes down to it, the most important thing you can do to keep headhunters at bay is to keep all the promises you made to the new hire while you were courting her — even the ones that weren't documented.

Challenge

If you want to keep your executive talent, you need to provide a stimulating and challenging environment. That means doing the following:

>> **Conveying the company's goals, vision, and mission:** Key executives need to know where they fit into the big picture. That way, they can position and plan for their own success. To achieve this, you must put measurable

performance goals in place, with a formal review process to gauge performance at realistic intervals. Even better, ensure that these company goals line up with any personal goals an executive might have.

>> **Expecting excellence:** It's no surprise that top executives want to work with the business equivalent of a Tom Brady or LeBron James. Healthy egos thrive in an environment that not only recognizes excellence, but expects it. You can encourage these types of executives to join — and remain at — your firm by making your company a magnet for exceptional employees. When you earn a reputation for top-level performance, you can bet that top talent will want to join you, and that your current staff will never want to leave.

>> **Allowing creative license:** When executives are challenged to reach tough goals, their satisfaction increases. But when they're allowed to find their own ways to reach them, it goes through the roof. Sadly, opportunities for this type of creativity quickly disappear as the new hire is absorbed by your company's "system." Don't let that happen!

>> **Helping them to grow:** Get to know the goals of your key executives and work together to develop a career plan for them. This will go a long way toward building lasting relationships with your employees. As an added bonus, it will help your company develop a reputation for fostering excellence in people. This will bring even more good candidates your way.

>> **Giving them room to fail:** To *really* flourish, key performers need an environment where they can fully apply their talents and creativity to their job — and where they won't be punished if something they try doesn't work. And take comfort: These folks contribute a lot — brain power, education, experience, creativity, energy . . . the list goes on. They'll be right more often than they're wrong!

Communication

Good communication is what enables you to spread your company's goals, vision, and mission; convey your expectation of excellence; and encourage creativity — thereby increasing retention. That means doing the following:

>> **Having two-way dialogue:** Successful communication requires a two-way dialogue. Don't just talk to your talent; listen to them, too. Rest assured: The best performers will go where they will be heard. If you want them to stick around at your company, then you must actively listen when they speak — during the hiring process and beyond.

>> **Giving positive reinforcement:** What's the main reason people change jobs? They don't like their managers. But the *second* main reason is a lack of recognition. Yes, financial incentives are important. But for many, honest praise is even better than a raise. A pat on the back may well be the most effective talent-retention strategy going — and it couldn't be easier to do!

>> **Giving people the power to make decisions:** Everyone wants a voice and a responsive ear at work — none more than top talent. Indeed, for these executives, involvement in key decisions is mandatory. If you don't involve them, they'll be gone in a heartbeat.

Compensation

In addition to using compensation to attract top talent to your company, you can also use it to retain them. Here are two compensation tools to consider:

>> **Over-the-top rewards:** If an executive's performance really blows your socks off, an over-the-top reward is in order. Cash, gifts, an invitation to dinner, airline tickets, a weekend getaway, a fishing trip with the boss — all these rewards will help foster a long-term relationship.

TIP

If an executive really rocks performance-wise, it's often due at least in part to an extremely supportive spouse. So, if you decide to reward that executive, recognize her spouse, too. Send them both on a relaxing getaway or invite the pair to dinner. Trust us: A spouse who feels appreciated is less likely to encourage his partner to jump ship for a new opportunity!

>> **Long-term financial ties:** Long-term financial ties make it expensive for executives to leave before you want them to. As such, these may well be the most important component of any compensation package. Consider staggering payouts or associating payouts with loyalty and longevity. Just be sure the incoming executive views these ties as a positive incentive rather than restrictive handcuffs!

5

The Part of Tens

IN THIS PART . . .

Focus on the key principles of effective executive recruiting.

Get tips for working successfully with the search committee.

Discover why you should use a professional recruiter.

Chapter **17**

Ten Key Principles of Effective Executive Recruiting

E xecutive recruiting is a complex process, but a few key principles apply across the board. Keeping these points in mind will help you land the right person for the right job, every time.

Remember It's Always a Seller's Market

The best executives — the ones you're looking to hire — already have jobs. Good ones. Indeed, the best and brightest in any industry rarely if ever look for a new job. But you want to find the best talent out there, not just the best among those looking for work! That means you have to build your team by skillfully targeting employees who work for your competitors. Establish a crack team of people to court them. Then create a rigorous interview process designed to get to know these executives and reveal positive details about your process. That's the only way to win in a seller's market!

Sell First, Buy Later

Very few business owners do an adequate job selling prospective candidates on their companies. For some reason, they assume everyone's as enthralled with their companies as they are! That's why you need to sell first and buy later. In other words, you must "sell" your business before you attempt to "buy" talent. Paint your business as a winner, and insist that everyone in the hiring process do the same. Most executives don't switch jobs for more money. They move for greater challenges and the opportunity to play on a winning team. Package your organization accordingly.

Be Opportunistic

Assign one senior person in your HR group the task of actively scouting the top talent in your industry. This person should keep his ear to the ground to find out when your competitors' best people are ripe for a change, such as when stock options vest, new products are late to market, or there has been a change in senior management. Recent or upcoming acquisitions are also prime opportunities. And if a competitor announces layoffs, have your HR rep call the people he has been tracking there — particularly the ones who survived the purge — and offer them the opportunity to work with you.

No question about it: The best time to tempt someone is while she's pondering her future. Your gain is your competitor's loss, at its most vulnerable time.

Use a Boutique Search Firm

Unbeknownst to most corporate hiring authorities, large executive search firms don't actually have a particularly extensive reach. And they're often spread too thin — meaning you have to compete for their attention. That's why we recommend using a boutique firm rather than a larger search entity. A boutique firm can bring knowledge, judgment, efficiency, and objectivity to your executive search. Plus, the better boutique search firms have a very high success ratio. Indeed, these firms guarantee success, working on your project until it's complete.

Be the First to Walk Away

Recruiting top talent requires considerably more time and effort than attracting the average performer. Give yourself room to get the deal done without the added pressure of time. That way, you maintain control of the process. It also gives you leeway to walk away if a candidate's expectations exceed your budget. When you walk away first, it increases the value of your business in the candidate's mind.

Build a Farm Team and Draft Only A-Players

Every great sports team has a roster of A-players waiting on the sideline, primed for the coach to send them in at just the right moment. Likewise, you must constantly assess and balance the strengths and weaknesses of your team. Long before you need to make a change, your HR group should be building your bench strength. Challenge your HR team to scout out top talent ahead of time and to systematically track these potential hires. One way to do this is to save attendee rosters from conferences and trade shows. Another is to connect with candidates who applied for positions when none were available, but showed great progress. Then keep in touch using a service like LinkedIn.

Seal the Deal with Psychic Cash

Everybody wants to be the best — to leave an impression on the world. If you can provide people with the things they need to achieve that goal — state-of-the-art technology, industry leadership, fast growth, stability, challenge, and so on — you're more likely to draw them in. We call these resources *psychic cash.* What's great about *psychic* cash is, you can use it to shift the conversation away from *actual* cash. If you make your (truly) best financial offer and supplement it with psychic cash, you exponentially increase your odds of landing top talent.

Leverage Your "Manning Factor"

Everyone wants to play on the team led by Peyton Manning. (Or Cam Newton. Or Tom Brady. Or Aaron Rodgers.) That means you need to channel your inner MVP. Build your personal brand and that of your business. Cultivate positive impressions. If you can convince top executives that you can help them win a Super Bowl, they'll be far more interested in working for you! This is also a good way to mint some psychic cash.

Qualify for Integrity

Actions speak louder than words. As you proceed through the hiring process, look for ways to judge the integrity of each candidate. When hiring, take Warren Buffett's advice: "Look for three qualities: integrity, intelligence, and energy. And if you don't have the first, the other two will kill you."

REMEMBER

Integrity — people either have it or they don't. And if they don't, you don't want them working for you.

Don't Hire a Liar

WARNING

Often, interviewers extend offers based on their first impressions, gut feelings, or chemistry, with little (if any) regard for the hard evidence that proves which candidate is right for the job. Don't do this! To ensure you don't wind up with an underperformer (or worse, someone who is ethically suspect), you must perform background and reference checks. Indeed, reference checks are the only way to sort out who really has the skills and who's just a smooth talker. Speaking with an executive's co-workers and direct reports during a reference check is the only way to obtain an accurate assessment of that prospective hire. Oh, and don't outsource executive-level reference checks. Check the references of every prospective executive hire yourself.

Chapter **18**

Ten Keys to Working Successfully with the Search Committee

I f human capital is the most essential factor in organizational success (and we think it is), then the executive search committee, guided by its chair, plays a pivotal role in the future of any organization. This chapter fills you in on ten cost-free ways to ensure that the search committee closes on everyone's first-choice candidate.

Identify a Clear Agenda for the Board

The search committee must negotiate with the board of directors to pin down the agenda. In this way, you ensure that all members of the search committee are focused on the same goals, and that they clearly understand the key competencies required for the new hire.

Agree on a Prioritized Sourcing Strategy

The executive search committee should agree on a well-defined yet diverse sourcing environment to build an adequate pool of potential candidates. Search committees that are willing to accept a broad, prioritized sourcing strategy will have the most success uncovering the best talent.

TIP

As you develop this prioritized strategy, picture the concentric circles on a dartboard, where the bull's-eye represents your sweet spot and the concentric circles are closely aligned industries.

Articulate the Organization's Return on Investment for Recruiting

All too often, organizations view the acquisition of staff as a simple byproduct of expansion. But the acquisition of key executives is an investment, like any other — and every investment should be measured by its return. That is, every new hire should have a demonstrative return on investment (ROI) that clearly justifies the time, effort, and cost involved. For executive-level hires, that ROI will be tied to strategy. Knowing how the executive will contribute to the bottom line is critical to understanding who to hire. It also helps to ensure that you tie hiring decisions to business needs, not candidate availability.

Set Realistic Expectations

Many boards want to hire executives who have held an equivalent position at a similar-sized or larger company — and rightly so. The problem? Most current executives are interested in taking on a new opportunity only if it's a move up the organizational hierarchy or with a company of greater size. That way, they know they're not simply making a lateral move.

TIP

The search committee must set realistic expectations for candidates. That means identifying what will motivate an executive to move to a new position. Motivators include the following:

>> The new role represents a move from a lower-potential opportunity to a higher-potential one.

- The new job represents a move from a general manager or functional role to a higher position, such as CEO. (This situation is common with multinationals, where general managers often act as division presidents.)

- The executive will be compensated more, including a complex equation of cash, equities, net present values, and opportunity costs.

- The executive perceives a strong cultural fit between herself, the board, and the company.

- The executive shares the founder's passion or vision for the company.

Do a Reality Check

The challenge of every organization is to give top executives a compelling reason to join — and a compelling reason to stay. In other words, finders must become keepers. To help with this, the search committee should do a reality check. Specifically, it should ask:

- Does the company have a captivating story that will appeal to the best and the brightest executives?

- Does the existing executive team inspire confidence?

- Does the company have a robust recruitment and interview process that enables you to move quickly when qualified and interested candidates are found?

- Is the company willing to adjust the position requirements if you can't find or attract what you had hoped for? If so, agree on those adjustments before you begin your search.

- If members of the search committee were in the place of their top candidates, would they accept the job? If the answer is yes, then proceed. Otherwise, continue working on the front end.

Be Consistent with the Messaging

The executive search committee's message to prospective candidates about the company and about its mission is vital to the project's success. As such, that message must be consistent, well supported, and attractive to the target audience.

Accordingly, if you use an executive search consultant, that person must be highly informed regarding the key elements of the company, including personalities of the senior management team, strategy and competitive position of the company, profit and loss, and corporate strengths and weaknesses. Be prepared to invest time in educating the search consultant.

Create an Emotional Link

Your prize executive will almost certainly become aware of other opportunities out there when he becomes engaged in your search — even if he wasn't actively looking when you first approached him. It's critical for your success that you recognize and plan for this eventuality from the start. In the end, the candidate will choose the company he feels most connected to. Your job is to make sure it's yours.

Conduct a Discerning Candidate Analysis

Understanding an executive's value system, prior achievements, and leadership qualities is part art and part science, and it requires complete commitment and participation. Here are some sound techniques and strategies to achieve this goal:

» Define criteria and best practices for determining leadership qualities, past performance, key competencies, and value systems.

» Observe candidate behavior during the courtship and interpret it to identify strengths, weaknesses, and motivations.

» Conduct reference checks, including early spot checks, to confirm a candidacy throughout the search, not just at the end of the process. You want to know sooner rather than later if there is a valid reason to exclude a candidate.

Negotiate a Successful Offer

The lead consultant is responsible for ensuring that all necessary data is available to structure an appropriate compensation package. This includes five critical categories of information:

>> The candidate's current employment terms, including cash, bonuses, timing of payouts, equity overhangs, noncompete agreements, and other disengagement liabilities

>> The compensation structures in the competitive marketplace, which is valuable for the board as well as the candidate

>> Other career options that the candidate may be considering

>> Expertise to create terms that work, taking into account personal needs, taxation advantages, the trade-offs of equity strategies that hit the P&L versus those that do not, severance and employment contract terms, and so on

>> The candidate's hot buttons, so as to present an offer that satisfies her complete hierarchy of needs

REMEMBER

Don't let the candidate think — even for a second — that you're looking for a deal. Move quickly when you've made your decision.

Let the Search Chair Close the Sale

In the final analysis, the search chair is the one who convinces the candidate there is a fit; articulates why the background, skills, opportunities, and challenges align; and explains how there is wealth to be made. This last point is critical, especially for funded ventures. Cap structures are often complex, and it's hard for newcomers to anticipate how much additional funding will be required and in how many tranches. Only the search committee chairperson can tell this story.

Chapter **19**

Ten Reasons to Use a Professional Recruiter

Your ability to quickly hire top talent to capitalize on market changes allows for value creation on a startling level — and professional recruiters help to enhance that ability. Professional recruiters spend all day, every day finding the specialized candidates you need. They're attuned to you and your competitors, as well as industry and market trends. These pros focus full-time on your search, employing all the tools at their disposal. They'll also handle all the financial negotiations with the candidates you choose. The end result of these efforts is successful, long-view hires of executives who will set your company apart and help you soar. Still not convinced? Read this chapter for ten more reasons to use a professional recruiter.

Satisfying Stakeholders

There are several stakeholders in any executive search, from internal staff to external candidates. A solid professional recruiter can satisfy all these stakeholders. Internal staff take comfort in knowing that the professional recruiter is doing everything possible to fill their need, and that the resulting candidate will be on target. And candidates will view a search conducted by a top executive recruiter as a credible one, making it much easier for you to select from the best of the best.

Easing Your Burden

Today's internal HR function must contend with an intensely competitive marketplace, a fluid and mobile workforce, an unpredictable global environment, the demands of investors and stakeholders, and the economic fallout when strategy fails. In other words, its hands are full. Fortunately, professional executive recruiters can help lighten the load of HR.

Professional executive recruiters work closely with internal staff to assemble position profiles that fit your business culture and leadership models, while remaining sensitive to changing workplace and workforce issues as well as evolving management styles. They then turn to their corps of library and market researchers, as well as their own leading-edge information services and database resources, for direct sourcing of world-class candidates. Finally, they mount aggressive one-on-one marketing campaigns to deliver your opportunity straight to the targeted executives highlighted by their research. The upshot? HR is freed from these responsibilities.

Reducing Opportunity Cost

A good recruiter can shorten the time to market in several ways. One is by identifying what aspects of your company will appeal to (or repel) candidates, and matching candidates accordingly. Another is by expertly defining your need and identifying what the ideal candidate really looks like. Finally, a good recruiter can warn you when you've set your sights on a *purple squirrel* (the perfect — and nearly impossible to find — candidate) and explain the impact that searching for such a candidate will have on the hiring effort and on the salary you'll need to pay. The bottom line? Recruiters help you market your company and position to attract the best candidates. That saves you time. Opportunity cost is often exponentially more valuable than the cost of the search.

Being Nimble

Back in the dark ages (a few years ago), a talent search was like a two-dimensional board game. The process was so simple and structured, even less-skilled members of the HR staff could handle it. Now, talent searches are more like videogames.

It's zap or get zapped, all in real time. In such a fast-paced environment, you must be able to clearly define your mission — no wasted energy and no blurred vision. That means you need a team of people who think in three dimensions — nothing else will do. A good recruiter can do just that. A good recruiter — someone who's ready to take on a fast-paced, complex world — can help you seize new opportunities as they arise, enabling your organization to move more nimbly and quickly.

Building Trust

A good recruiter excels at establishing trust with your internal clients and stakeholders, often acting as a sounding board. But good recruiters are good at building rapport with potential candidates, too. This helps the recruiter to sell the position, mediate discussions, negotiate, resolve issues or questions, and close the deal. It also helps the recruiter to assess the likelihood that the candidate will accept the position if offered. A recruiter who has built trust with a candidate is much more likely to find out if that candidate is leaning toward rejecting your offer, enabling the search team to address the candidate's concerns before it's too late.

Being Discreet

When you need to keep your search confidential — maybe an individual is about to be let go, but you need to fill his role as soon as he leaves — a professional recruiter is the way to go. Professional recruiters can probe the market, reach out to employees at competing companies, and even guide candidates through the early stages of the hiring process without revealing your company's identity.

Inviting Continuous Improvement

Why stop recruiting after you fill the job? Far better to keep your staff focused on the core business but put a recruiter on the lookout to replace the weakest players on your team. That way, you'll see continuous improvement. When you use a professional recruiter, you don't have to just hire one position at a time. You can be hiring *always*.

Bringing Competitive Intelligence

Because of their deep industry knowledge, search firms can be an excellent source of market knowledge on topics ranging from compensation to organizational structure to talent mapping. No internal HR professional will be able to uncover this type of information!

Increasing Retention

Recruiters are experts at identifying a candidate's intrinsic motivation for considering a new job. They can home in on a candidate's hot buttons and sell to her, improving your chances of hiring the right candidate for the job. And when you hire the right candidate, that candidate is more likely to stick around, increasing your retention rate.

REMEMBER

Odds are, there's only one "best" candidate for your open position. That candidate should be handled by an experienced recruiter — someone who does this 20 times before breakfast.

Getting Your Money's Worth

Professional recruiters employ rigorous techniques to locate, identify, and evaluate top candidates. They'll also work on your search exclusively. In effect, you're paying for this exclusivity. It enables the recruiter to focus on your needs and your needs only, which in turn produces both qualified candidates and quick results. What other professional group guarantees its work — some for up to one year — even though it has little control over the quality of the hiring manager or whether the hired executive likes the company or his direct supervisor? What other professional group is willing to work on a pay-for-performance basis? If you find one, let us know!

Glossary

active candidate: An individual seeking immediate employment. Active candidates are usually unemployed, unhappy with their current employers, or facing unemployment in the near future.

applicant: Anyone who applies for a job. Applicants are considered highly motivated job seekers and active candidates. *See also* active candidate.

behavioral interview: An interview format in which interviewers seek to assess and understand the interviewee's career history and performance. The premise of this type of interview is that past behavior is the best predictor of future conduct.

benchmark candidate: A person who represents the "ideal candidate." The recruiter and search chair interview the benchmark candidate to gauge whether the job description is clear and correct. This interview occurs before the recruiter actively begins the search.

benchmark interview: An interview with the "ideal candidate," which is used to gauge the recruiter's understanding of fit.

boutique recruiting firm: An executive search firm that is operated in a hands-on manner by a small number of experienced partners. Many senior consultants from large firms have jumped ship to set up their own boutique firms. This is a main reason behind the steady decline in market share for larger firms.

candidate: A person being considered for an open position.

candidate report: A report produced by a recruiter after an interview with a candidate. Its purpose is to quantify why the candidate is or is not right for a given role.

candidate road map: A search strategy that details the *who, what, where, when,* and *how* of approaching all qualified prospects in a systematic manner.

candidate universe: The group of candidates who might meet the basic qualifications for an open position and are considered worthy of further investigation. Creating this list of potential candidates is the first step of every search. The candidate universe will vary in size depending on the job type, industry, geography, organization, and hiring manager requirements.

CCB: *See* confidential candidate brief.

confidential candidate brief (CCB): A document used by the recruiter in lieu of a résumé or CV during the qualifying stages of a candidate search. The CCB asks specific questions about a candidate's experience relative to the position that needs to be filled.

contingency recruiting: A form of recruiting in which fees are paid to the recruiter only after a candidate he or she identified is hired. This type of recruiting is usually done only for positions that pay less than $125,000 base per year.

corporate culture: The behaviors and views that shape how a company's employees and managers interact. Corporate culture typically develops over time but may not be expressly defined.

counteroffer: Either an offer given by a candidate's current employer to keep him or her from accepting a job elsewhere or a candidate's request to improve on an offer being made by an employer.

curriculum vitae (CV): A document prepared by a job seeker that describes in detail his or her career history, education, and qualifications. It may also list publications, awards, affiliations, or presentations. CVs have legal standing, meaning there can be consequences if they include false information.

CV: *See* curriculum vitae.

employer brand: An employer's reputation. Employer brands can be positive or negative. Employers with positive brands can more readily attract, high-quality candidates.

employment agreement: A contract between an employee and an employer that defines the rights and responsibilities of each. It typically covers issues like total compensation, job responsibilities, and authority, as well as start date, notice period, and severance. When both the employee and the employer agree to the terms, they sign the employee agreement.

engagement fee: The fee charged by a retained recruiter at the beginning of an executive search. Also called a *front-end retainer.*

executive recruiter: *See* recruiter.

executive search: The process of identifying, assessing, and recruiting high-level candidates for leadership positions.

external candidate: Anyone being considered for a position who does not already work inside the organization.

fee: The price for conducting part or all of an executive search or recruiting project. Fees are usually based on results, time, materials, a percentage of the hired candidate's total compensation, or a combination of these.

fit: The quality of the interaction between a prospective candidate and the executive(s) at the organization where he or she is being recruited.

front-end retainer: *See* engagement fee.

guarantee: A contractual assurance provided by an executive search firm to clients. Guarantees may include promises to replace a candidate who leaves his or her position for any reason within a certain period; to *not* target a client's employees when conducting searches for other clients; or to *not* recruit employees from companies the client has special relationships with.

hands-off agreement: *See* off-limits agreement.

headhunter: A slang term for *executive recruiter.*

informal reference check: The process of confirming a candidate's background and experience through sources other than those provided by the candidate. These sources can include regulatory filings, online information, and (most important) conversations with former colleagues, supervisors, clients, vendors, and competitors. The informal reference check must be conducted delicately and confidentially so as not to jeopardize the candidate's career or standing in the business community.

internal candidate: A person currently working within an organization who is being considered for a different position there.

interview: A meeting between a recruiter, hiring manager, or other company representative and a candidate being considered for a position.

job board: A website designed to connect active job seekers with employers with relevant job openings. Employers often maintain their own job boards in addition to using third-party ones. Job boards can be general or specific to an industry, function, or geographic location.

job description: An official document describing the skills and experience required for an open position.

job order: The formal specifications for an opening, including title, reporting relationships, skills required, education, desired experience, and existing relationships.

leadership pipeline: A subcomponent of a succession plan. A leadership pipeline is used to identify and prepare top-performing employees for leadership roles.

LinkedIn: The world's largest social networking tool for professionals.

long list: A list of candidates created in the early stages of a search engagement. *See also* short list.

noncompete clause: A clause in a contract under which one party (usually an employee) agrees not to enter into or start a company in competition with another party (usually the employer). Also called a *restrictive covenant.*

nonsolicitation clause: A clause in a contract that restricts individuals or organizations from soliciting employees, customers, or business opportunities for a set period of time. Normally found in executive-level employment agreements.

off-limits agreement: An agreement that prevents a recruiter from targeting executives at one client company for employment at another company — in other words, putting them off-limits. The standard off-limits policy, outlined by the Association of Executive Search Consultants, stipulates that a search firm will not approach a company that it has worked for during the previous two years. Also known as a *hands-off agreement*.

onboarding: The process of assimilating a new hire into an organization. For top-level positions, this involves quickly deciphering the corporate culture and actual reporting structure and developing relationships with key people.

passive candidate: A person approached by a recruiter who is *not* looking for a new job.

phantom stock: A compensation plan that gives the holder of the phantom stock the right to receive a cash payment at a specific time or when a specific event occurs (such as the sale of the company) in the future. This payment is linked to the value of the company's real stock.

poaching: A slang term for recruiting high-value employees from another company, often competitors.

position profile: A detailed document that describes the ideal candidate, including key responsibilities and relationships. A marketing tool, the position profile is shared with prospective candidates to sell them on entering the search process.

proposal: A formal contract drawn up by the search firm, usually in the form of a letter agreement. It specifies key issues such as guarantees, timing, fees, exclusivity, confidentiality, and so on.

prospect: Someone the recruiter thinks might be successful in the role he or she is attempting to fill and who has shown some initial interest. *See also* suspect.

psychological testing: The administration of psychological tests to gain an objective overview of a candidate's character, strengths, weaknesses, and working style. Typically used as one component of a wider, integrated evaluation strategy.

recruiter: A person who fills job openings. A recruiter's job includes reviewing each candidate's job experiences, negotiating salaries, and placing candidates in amenable positions. Also known as a *headhunter*.

recruiting firm: A specialized management consulting firm that conducts executive searches.

recruitment advertising: Specialized advertising designed to promote a job opening and entice job seekers to apply.

reference check: A systematic and methodical investigation into a candidate's past job performance based on conversations with people who have worked with him or her. Like an employment interview, reference checking is most effective when it is thoughtfully integrated into the hiring process.

references: People who have worked with a candidate and can verify their personal and professional background, skills, character, and so on.

referred candidate: A person referred for consideration by someone familiar with the hiring organization.

relocation package: Payments made by the employer to a candidate who is being asked to relocate to assume a new position.

replacement guarantee: A promise to replace hired candidates who leave their positions within a certain period — usually between 3 and 12 months.

requirement: A necessary quality or qualification. This might include a particular skill requirement, level of experience, or personal characteristic.

research: In executive search, the investigative process of sourcing people who may become qualified candidates for an open position. Research is an ongoing (and time-consuming) effort for most executive recruiters.

restricted stock: A compensation plan that gives the holder of the restricted stock the right to sell stock only after it has vested.

restrictive covenant: *See* noncompete clause.

résumé: A document prepared by a job seeker to describe his or her background and skills. Résumés are used for a variety of reasons, but most often to secure new employment. Résumés are similar to CVs, but CVs are more detailed.

retainer: A fee paid upfront to the recruiter by the client. Executive search retainers are usually paid in monthly installments over an agreed-upon period.

retained search: A search conducted by a recruiter who receives a retainer upfront. Retained searches are generally used only for positions that pay $150,000 or more. This payment model is similar to those used by other highly skilled professionals, such as architects, accountants, lawyers, and so on.

ruse: An action intended to deceive. Inexperienced recruiters or researchers may use ruses to obtain sensitive information. This practice is highly unethical.

screening interview: A job interview done to determine whether the applicant is qualified for a particular job. This interview is typically the first one in the hiring process. It can be done over the phone or in person.

search committee: A group of people formed for purposes of helping the hiring manager recruit and screen candidates for an executive position.

search committee chair: The person responsible for managing a proactive, timely, fair, and legal search process to find and hire an executive.

search committee interview: An interview in which members of the search committee — either as a group or one-on-one — assess the candidate.

search process: A series of predefined and interrelated processes used in an executive search to locate, evaluate, and attract the best executive for a job.

search research: A systematic search for information about specific industries, organizations, and executives to dispassionately interpret events. It is an essential component to developing an executive search strategy.

short list: The list of candidates created in the final stages of a search engagement, after candidates have been prescreened, interviewed, and vetted before being presented to the client. *See also* long list.

signing bonus: A payment made to a candidate upon his or her joining the organization. This payment, normally in the form of cash or equity, is often used to compensate executives for any cash or equity they might lose by leaving their current employers. It's also used as a gesture of goodwill to thank an executive for agreeing to leave his or her current position for the new one.

situational interviewing: An interview technique in which the interviewer uses the job description to make a list of required skills and responsibilities and then poses questions about hypothetical situations that pertain to those skills and responsibilities. Candidates are assessed by how they would solve problems and exploit opportunities. Questions such as "How would you deal with . . . ?" and "What would you do if . . . ?" are situational interview questions. Most hiring managers consider them very useful for executive candidates.

social recruiting: A type of recruiting that involves the use of social platforms as talent databases or for advertising. Popular social media sites used for recruiting include LinkedIn, Twitter, and Facebook.

sourcing: The act of proactively searching for qualified job candidates for a current or future open position. This stands in contrast to the reactive reviewing of résumés or applications submitted to a company. The point of sourcing is to collect data about qualified candidates, such as names, titles, and job responsibilities. Typically performed by an HR professional, sourcing is used to identify both active and passive job seekers. Sourcing is typically done via phone or Internet.

SOW: *See* statement of work.

staffing firm: A firm that focuses on providing temporary help or contract workers to clients for fixed periods.

statement of work (SOW): A formal agreement that captures the work products and services to be completed. These include (but are not limited to) work activities and deliverables to be supplied under a contract or as part of a project timeline.

stick rate: The percentage of recruited and placed candidates who remain in their positions through the guarantee period.

stock option: An agreement between two parties — in this case, the company and the new hire — that gives the new hire the right (but not the obligation) to purchase stock in the company at an agreed-upon (and perhaps discounted) price within a specific period of time.

stress interviewing: An interview technique designed to see how candidates react under pressure.

succession plan: A plan to address the selection, development, evaluation, and compensation of the executive team. The creation of the succession plan requires major input from the board of directors.

suspect: Someone the recruiter *thinks* is qualified to fill a search assignment, but whose suitability has not yet been confirmed. *See also* prospect.

talent mapping: The process of building an intelligence chart for a given organization or industry. Talent mapping involves identifying the names, titles, responsibilities, and accomplishments of people in companies in the targeted industry who may be qualified for a position, either now or in the future. *See also* candidate universe.

total compensation: The monetary value of the complete compensation package. Total compensation goes beyond base salary to account for all monetary and nonmonetary instruments. These may include a signing bonus; an annual bonus; a long-term incentive plan; profit-sharing; a phantom share, restricted share, or stock option plan; health insurance; life and disability insurance; a pension plan; private school fees for children; accommodations; club memberships; housing allowance or loans; and so on.

vesting: The process by which an employee accrues non-forfeitable rights over employer-provided stock incentives or employer contributions made to the employee's qualified retirement plan account or pension plan.

Index

A

abilities of candidate, 130, 224

abundance mind-set, 149

accomplishments of candidate, asking about, 207, 210–211

accounts payable department, sourcing through, 164

acqui-hire, 107

active candidates, 74, 177–179

Active Hire, 96

activities, in job description, 125

Acton, Brian, 24

Advanced People Search feature, LinkedIn, 166–170

advertising, 72, 74

Aevy, 96

affiliates, scouting, 73

affordability in planning, 44

agenda for search committee, 263

Albert, Carl A., 26

Albright, Jerry, 89

All Star Jobs, 96

Allstate Insurance Company, 225

alumni networks, sourcing through, 172

American Staffing Association, 56

analytical skills, 33

AngelList, 96

Apple, 18, 27

applicant tracking system (ATS), 80

applications, sifting through, 181

apps, mobile recruiting, 95

Art of War, The, 41

Arthur Andersen, 24–25

assessing prospects, 192–196

assessment tools, 35, 87–88

Association of Executive Search and Leadership Consultants, 12

associations

industry association websites, 163

professional, scouting, 73

recruiter, 94–95

ATS (applicant tracking system), 80

attention-grabbing job ads, 133–138

attributes of successful executives

business intelligence, 33–34

character, 31–32

emotional intelligence, 35

evaluating in interview, 198

integrity, 262

intellect, 32–33

leadership, 34

overview, 30–31

peer reference checks, 231

attrition, 10

authority, in job description, 125

autonomy, 16, 18

Autry, James, 38

awards, participation, 21

B

background checks, 83, 225, 226, 229, 262

Bacon, Francis, 30

Bar-On EQ-i Leadership Report, 35, 88

battle scars, 32

benchmark candidates, 184–188

benefits, 241. *See also* compensation

biases, personal, 113, 200

big search firms, 60–61

BlackPlanet, 91

BlueSteps, 96

board of directors

in search committee role, 54

soliciting input on job description, 128

Bock, Laszlo, 36–37

body language, during negotiation, 248

Boolean Black Belt Sourcing and Recruiting, 96

Boolean search strings

general discussion, 164–166

on Google, 170–171

on LinkedIn, 166–170

boring job postings, 81

Boss, Jeff, 106

bosses

of candidates, calling for reference check, 231

job order, including information about, 114–115

supervisors, references from, 231

bottom-line salary, 240

boutique search firms, 60–61, 260

brain drain, 10

brand, building, 173, 179, 260, 261–262

brand maturity, 73

Brazil, Russia, India, China, and South Africa (BRICS), 22

Brin, Sergey, 18

About the Authors

David E. Perry: David is an executive recruiter, job coach, author, and motivational speaker. He not only teaches companies how to hire (and keep) the right people, but also coaches candidates on how to make business decisions that will shape their careers.

David is managing partner at Perry-Martel International, a boutique executive search firm in Ottawa, Canada. In his 30 years as an executive recruiter, he has billed more than 60,000 hours and generated more than $300 million in negotiated salaries. He has a 99.53 percent stick rate and a one-year, 100 percent guarantee. Thanks to his unusual but effective tactics, the *Wall Street Journal* dubbed him the "Rogue Recruiter."

David graduated from McGill University with a double major in economics and industrial relations and has written six books, including *Guerilla Marketing for Job Hunters* and *Hiring Greatness: How to Recruit Your Dream Team and Crush the Competition.* He is a father of four and husband to one, and lives in western Quebec.

Mark J. Haluska: Mark is a 17-year veteran of the executive search profession. He has gained a strong reputation for having a unique way of penetrating even the most highly guarded walls of corporate America in his quest to "obtain access to" the top 10 percent of the continent's executive talent on behalf his clients. Mark earned a degree in accounting with a minor in business administration from Loyola University.

He is contributing co-author of the best-selling series of books *Guerrilla Marketing for Job Hunters,* and co-author of *Hiring Greatness: How to Recruit Your Dream Team and Crush the Competition.* He is also the architect of the Hiring Greatness hiring app, the first ever corporate hiring app of its kind. Mark provides guerrilla corporate outplacement services where he has a job seeker/client "back to work" rate of just over 94 percent.

Mark has completed more than 520 national and international executive searches negotiating salaries ranging from six figures to well in excess of over $4 million for very senior executives. During his 17 years in the profession, he has only had to replace two candidates for clients, representing a 99.6 percent success rate.

Mark resides in the Pittsburgh, Pennsylvania, area. He has two children, Nicole and Mark, Jr.

Dedication

This book is dedicated to Dr. Bruce M. Firestone, who, in the winter of 1988, said to me, rather matter-of-factly, "Fear of success is what's holding you back, David. Just get on with it. You'll figure it out." In those few seconds, he changed my life, and indirectly helped change the lives of thousands of others who have read my books on job hunting and recruiting. Bruce has worked tirelessly behind the scenes with hundreds of entrepreneurs over the past decade, so it's no surprise that just a few days after he told me this, he announced his intention to bring an NHL team to our city. As founder of the Ottawa Senators hockey club and several other successful businesses, Bruce embodies the integrity, vision, passion, and courage every company longs for. Moreover, he's an example of humility seldom seen today. This dedication is my simple way of paying tribute to this outstanding man.

—David Perry

In memoriam to Christian Michael Haluska, July 23, 1971–November 10, 2015.

—Mark Haluska

Authors' Acknowledgments

Back in 1674, the poet John Donne wrote, "No man is an island, entire of itself." The same holds true in 2016. In the case of *Executive Recruiting For Dummies*, it was not one person (David), or two people (David and Mark), or even three people (David, Mark, and their Dummifier, Kate Shoup) who shaped this book. Many other people lent their expertise as well. Without their help, you would not be holding this book in your hands.

First, the editorial team. Thanks to Kate Shoup, Elizabeth Kuball, and Tracy Boggier. Thanks, too, to Stacy Kennedy, who pitched David on writing this book in the first place. And a special note of appreciation for editor at large Fred Perry for encouraging simplicity and clarity.

Second, "Team Martel-Perry." Thanks to Anita Martel, Christa Martel-Perry, Corey Martel-Perry, Mandy Martel-Perry, and Shannon Martel-Perry for keeping the lights on, the noise down, our clients happy, and the coffee flowing! Also on Perry-Haluska second team are Christopher Milne, Vesta Milne, Ethel Luther, and Lyudmila Pupina. Your support and encouragement throughout this endeavor — not to mention putting up with the occasional moodiness — have been priceless.

Third, our executive recruitment advisory team. Thanks to Joe Zinner (special advisor), Peter Leffkowitz, Jim Durbin, Skip Freeman, Adam Kaplan, Rayanne Thorn, and Janette Levey Frisch, Esq., for reviewing chapters as they became available and offering honest critique.

Fourth, our client advisory team. Thanks to Steve Munro, Rudy Richman, Steve O'Hanlon, and Stan Janus for reminding us of what it takes to recognize greatness.

Finally, we'd like to thank the thousands of clients and candidates we have worked with through the years for allowing us to help make their companies and their careers a success. This has enabled us to grow not only professionally, but personally as well, and to enjoy the lifestyles we have worked so hard and so long to achieve.

Publisher's Acknowledgments

Senior Acquisitions Editor: Tracy Boggier

Project Editor: Elizabeth Kuball

Copy Editor: Elizabeth Kuball

Technical Editor: Joe Zinner

Contributor: Kate Shoup

Production Editor: Vasanth Koilraj

Cover Photos: © natalia bulatova/Shutterstock

Made in the USA
Las Vegas, NV
14 December 2022

62757299R00173